Don't Let the Sun Step Over You

Don't Let the Sun Step Over You

A White Mountain Apache Family Life
(1860–1975)

Eva Tulene Watt

with assistance from

Keith H. Basso

The University of Arizona Press   Tucson

The University of Arizona Press
© 2004 The Arizona Board of Regents
All rights reserved
♾ This book is printed on acid-free, archival-quality paper.
Manufactured in the United States of America

09 08 07 06   6 5 4 3 2

Library of Congress Cataloging-in-Publication Data
Watt, Eva Tulene, 1913–
Don't let the sun step over you : a White Mountain Apache family life
(1860–1975) / Eva Tulene Watt with assistance from Keith H. Basso.
p. cm.
Includes bibliographical references and index.
ISBN-13: 978-0-8165-2392-4 (cloth : alk. paper) — ISBN-10: 0-8165-2392-4
ISBN-13: 978-0-8165-2391-7 (pbk. : alk. paper) — ISBN-10: 0-8165-2391-6
1. Watt, Eva Tulene, 1913– 2. White Mountain Apache women—
Biography. 3. White Mountain Apache Indians—Biography. 4. White
Mountain Apache Indians—History. 5. Watt family—History. I. Basso,
Keith H., 1940– II. Title.
E99.A6W369   2004
979.1004′9725—dc22   2004002524

Publication of this book is made possible in part by the
proceeds of a permanent endowment created with the assistance of a Challenge Grant from the National Endowment for
the Humanities, a federal agency.

To the memory of

Ann Beatty Tulene (c. 1880–1968)

and

Etolia Simmons Basso (1906–2002)

Contents

List of Illustrations   ix
Western Apache Pronunciation Guide   xi
Introduction, by Keith H. Basso   xiii

Part One **"We Sure Did Travel All Over"** (1860–1929)
Chapter One   3
Chapter Two   45
Chapter Three   77
Chapter Four   107
Chapter Five   127

Part Two **"A Really Good Place"** (1930–1944)
Chapter Six   149
Chapter Seven   164
Chapter Eight   184
Chapter Nine   200
Chapter Ten   222

Part Three **"Leaving Home Was Hard"** (1945–1975)
Chapter Eleven   251
Chapter Twelve   271

Last Words   289
Acknowledgments   291
Family Genealogy   294
Chronology of Important Events   297

Notes   301
Glossary of Apache Terms and Expressions   321
References Cited   325
Photograph Credits   331
Index   335

Illustrations

Maps

1 Southeastern Arizona   2
2 San Carlos Apache Indian Reservation   148
3 Fort Apache Indian Reservation   250

Photographs

Rose Lupe with her daughter-in-law   5
Woman bringing grass to sell at Fort San Carlos   6
Western Apaches delivering grass   7
Joseph Hoffman   9
William Lupe   17
Members of William Lupe's family   18
John Lupe   19
John Lupe's home at Oak Creek   20
Western Apaches riding the train   22
William Goshoney   27
Government boarding school at San Carlos   34
Western Apaches waiting to collect rations   47
Western Apaches seeking rations   48
Western Apache homes near Fort San Carlos   52
Government boarding school at Rice   54
Western Apache girls with superintendent, Rice   55
Western Apache girls at Rice Indian school   56
Western Apache woman uprooting an agave plant   61

Homes of Western Apache mine workers   67

Western Apache women carrying firewood   69

Roosevelt Dam   79

Western Apache laborers (Eugene Tulene Case)   80

Western Apache homes on shore of Roosevelt Lake   81

Temporary Western Apache home near Roosevelt Dam   82

Western Apache women gambling   85

Western Apache laborers on the Apache Trail   89

Western Apache laborers working with mules   90

Western Apache laborers using mule-drawn sleds   91

Fish Creek Canyon   95

Apache Trail descending to Mormon Flat   98

Mormon Flat Dam   99

John Tulene and Ann Beatty with son Dewey   100

Silas John Edwards with assistants   120

Students at St. Johns Indian School (Jack Tulene Case)   130

Gáán dancers at St. Johns Indian School   131

Western Apache students departing for vacation   139

Ann Beatty and Charley Marley's wickiup   151

D. V. Marley   152

Ann Beatty with unidentified children   154

Western Apache woman grinding corn   159

William Taylee   165

Entrance to the salt cave   172

Western Apache homes on Cibecue Creek   177

Western Apache family at home near Cibecue   178

Blue, Charley Marley's donkey, ridden by Jack Tulene Case   190

David Dale, Western Apache medicine man   211

Eva Tulene Case, about 1930   234

Joe Tulene Case   238

Western Apache cowboys herding cattle   243

Eva Tulene Case and her son Reuben Kessay   253

Eva Tulene Case, 1947 or 1948   261

Eva and William Watt, about 1952   265

Eva Tulene Watt with her children John and Ora Watt   269

Ann Beatty at home in Cibecue   284

Western Apache Pronunciation Guide

The Western Apache language contains four vowels:

a as in "father"
e as in "red"
i as in "police"
o as in "go" (varying toward *u* as in "to")

All four vowels can be pronounced short or long—that is, with greater or lesser duration of sound. Long vowels are indicated typographically with double letters (e.g., *aa*).

Each of the vowels can be nasalized, which is indicated by a sub-script hook under the vowel (e.g., *ą* and *ąą*). In pronouncing a nasalized vowel, air passes through the nasal passage to give the vowel a soft, slightly ringing sound.

The four Western Apache vowels can also be pronounced with high or low tone. High tone is indicated by an accent mark over the vowel (e.g., *á*), showing that the vowel is pronounced with a rising pitch. In certain instances, the consonant *ń* is also spoken with high tone.

Western Apache contains approximately thirty-one consonants and consonant clusters. Fifteen of them are pronounced approximately as in English: *b, d, ch, h, j, k, l, m, n, s, sh, t, w, y, z*.

Another consonant in Western Apache is the *glottal stop*. Indicated by an apostrophe ('), the glottal stop can occur before and after all four vowels and after certain consonants and consonant clusters. Produced by closure of the glottis to momentarily halt air passing through the mouth, the glottal stop resembles the interruption of breath one hears

between the two "ohs" in the English expression "oh-oh." The glottal-
ized consonants and consonant clusters in Western Apache are *k'*, *t'*,
ch', *tł'*, and *ts'*.

Other consonants and consonant clusters are the following:

dl as in the final syllable of "paddling"

dz as in the final sound of "adds"

g as in "get" (never as in "gentle")

gh similar to *g* but pronounced farther back in the mouth; often
sounds like a guttural *w*

hw as in "what"

kw as in "quick"

ł This consonant, sometimes called the "silent *l*," has no coun-
terpart in English. The mouth is shaped for an *l*, but the vocal
cords are not used. The sound is made by expelling air from
both sides of the tongue.

tł as in "Tlingit"

ts as in the final sound of "pots"

zh as in "azure"

Introduction   Keith H. Basso

They kept on keeping going.—Eva Tulene Watt

Perseverance is the greatest heroism.—Alan Light

This is a rare and remarkable book. Composed of dozens of narratives
by Eva Tulene Watt, a White Mountain Apache born in 1913, it brings
to life a vanished time—and some striking men and women who lived
it to the fullest—in a way that recasts history. A work of devotion and
courage, *Don't Let the Sun Step Over You* affords a view of the past that
few have seen before, a wholly Apache view, unsettling yet uplifting,
that weighs upon the mind and educates the heart.

The book grew out of a project that began on June 11, 1997, when
Mrs. Watt, a long-standing acquaintance of mine, suggested out of the
blue that I might like to record on tape "a few family stories from long
years ago." Surprised and curious, I accepted her invitation, and ten
days later, in the kitchen of her home on the Fort Apache Indian Reservation, we held a recording session.[1] It would not be the last. At Mrs.
Watt's behest and with increasing regularity, she continued recording
stories for the next five years, an astonishing turn of events I never
would have predicted. Neither did I foresee that her unstinting work
would eventually result in the largest body of historical accounts yet
set down by a White Mountain Apache person. In August 2002, when
Mrs. Watt announced that her work was largely done, her taped collection of narratives had exceeded two hundred hours; my transcriptions
ran close to seventeen hundred handwritten pages. For me, a field-
working anthropologist, assisting in Mrs. Watt's storytelling project

was a deeply enriching experience. Mrs. Watt, whose humility is complete, said once or twice that for her it was a pleasant one.

In the fall of 1999, when the project was well under way, I asked Mrs. Watt whether she had any interest in publishing some of her stories. "Yes, I think so," she said, fingering a butter knife atop her kitchen table. "But it's not for me I'm doing it—it's not for me myself. It's for those younger generations that come along here in later years. See, they're not gonna know how we used to live. They're not gonna know all the places we went to, or how we got food, or all the things we done. They won't know hardly nothing from long years ago. But it's good for them to know. White people, too. They make up lots of stuff about us Indians that's not true. I don't know why they do that. They should hear our stories first, 'cause then they can make better stories for themselves. It's better that way." I said that I agreed. "OK then," she replied in a bright tone of voice, "let's try and make a book." Moments later, after removing a brindle cat that had jumped into her lap, Mrs. Watt added, "You know, it just could be that maybe some will read it."[2]

Readers will discover that Mrs. Watt's book—a diverse assemblage of recounted events, biographical sketches, and cultural descriptions—is shaped and held together by several pervasive themes. First, Mrs. Watt looks back on stages in her life, a wayfaring one that led from remote Apache communities in central Arizona to Anglo towns and cities hundreds of miles away. Concurrently, she takes stock of people whose lives influenced her own: members of her family and clan, together with persons outside her circle of kinship whose multiple skills and abilities earned them marked respect. Finally, and most widely embracing of all, Mrs. Watt reveals how Western Apache people lived during the early part of the twentieth century, a dark and turbulent period when their treatment as wards of the U.S. government left much to be desired. However one chooses to view the book—as affecting autobiography, atypical family memoir, or telling tribal chronicle— *Don't Let the Sun Step Over You* is a work that stands alone. Distinctive and unorthodox, it is conspicuously unique.

Although Western Apache history has inspired numerous works by non-Indian authors (professional and amateur historians, social anthropologists, archaeologists, journalists, and dozens of novelists have all weighed in on the subject), Apache people themselves have been reluctant to comment publicly or at length on their own arresting past. In breaking with this one-sided pattern, Eva Watt has performed a far-reaching service, for her book offers more than a wealth of observations about a key historical period in which she and her family were active Apache participants. In addition, it displays a view of history itself—an Apache perspective on representing the past and highlighting what was important about it—that differs fundamentally from conventional approaches.

When Mrs. Watt was asked what the word "history" meant to her, she responded unequivocally:

> It's what was going on long years ago that's finished with now. For us, it's mostly stories about our relatives and where they went and all they used to do, and there's other people in there, too. See, long years ago, people were always doing something, always going someplace, so that's what they talked about and put in their stories. There's lots of Apaches in there and all they were doing, so you can see what happened to them and know what they were thinking. It's like their tracks, lots of tracks. Those stories are like those people's tracks.

Mrs. Watt's remarks bear on a useful distinction drawn by Clifford Geertz (1976) between "experience-near" and "experience-distant" accounts of social phenomena. Conventional accounts of Western Apache history, which fall into the latter category, pursue a sweeping tale of colonial expansion encompassing the military conquest of Apache groups, their confinement to reservations in Arizona Territory, and subsequent efforts by government agencies to "civilize" their descendants. Chiefly concerned with the convoluted workings of federal Indian policy, and lately couched in the recondite parlance of "hegemonic systems," "capitalistic forces," and "institutional processes," these accounts advance at a pronounced remove—or experiential distance—from the situated lives of Apache men and women.[3] So great is the distance, in fact, that the people whose lives they were are rendered all but invisible. Persistently described in monolithic terms ("the Indians," "the Apaches," etc.), their personal and social identities are summarily swept aside, and how they actually spent their days is anybody's guess. Compared with the kind of historical narratives favored by Mrs. Watt—those with "lots of Apaches in there and all they were doing"—experience-distant accounts, though informative on other fronts, have almost nothing to say. One searches them in vain for signs of Apache tracks.[4]

These discursive practices create a threadbare picture of the Western Apache past, and some tribal members, including Mrs. Watt, consider the image demeaning. Most troubling to her about works she has read is their wholesale dismissal of Apache human agency: the near or total absence of actual persons, in actual situations, responding to their circumstances with concrete acts and plans. For what this produces in turn, she believes, is the damaging impression that Apaches were disinclined to do much of anything, and therefore that their lives were "really slow and lazy." In Mrs. Watt's opinion, this problem is most acute in treatments of the early postmilitary era (c. 1886–c. 1930), when her people are portrayed as subsisting on reservations in a listless and indolent state often called "peaceful submission." She challenged this portrayal as follows:

> Those books make you think that after the fighting was done, everybody was just lying around doing nothing, just waiting around for rations. That's not true. *Lots* was going on. See, people were busy every day—going here, going there, doing this, doing that. They had to 'cause those rations don't last very long. Those people were *poor*! Anyway, they were looking for jobs, and helping each other out, and going to dances, and looking after their kids. They were busy with all kinds of stuff. I heard stories about it from my grandmother Rose and my mother. I seen it myself with my family. It's not in those books, though. Lots is missing in those books 'cause there's hardly no Indians in there. You can't see hardly nothing in there about how we used to live.

Much is missing indeed. As thinly described in experience-distant accounts, the Apache world Mrs. Watt once knew is really no world at all. Spectral and anonymous, it exists without faces and names, families and family events, local communities and local goings-on. Silent and still, it is lacking in laughter and play, speech and conversation, pleasurable diversions and grueling forms of work. Tepid and bland, it is barren of anger and conflict, tragedy and grief, love and affection. (Children, indicatively, are nowhere to be found.) It is a textual world, in other words, implausibly devoid of purpose or activity, a "slow and lazy" world in which nothing seems to happen and no one seems to care. Thoroughly demoralized and given to heavy drinking, or so one is led to believe, the entire population waits in deep passivity as potent systems and forces threaten to overwhelm it. And there's not a dog in sight ("Not even one!"), which Mrs. Watt, whose sense of humor is as pointed as it is gentle, finds more than a little amusing.

But something more important is missing from the picture. Though plagued by hardship and ravaged by disease, the Western Apache population was *not* completely destroyed, and that stubborn fact raises questions that conventional accounts consistently fail to address. How did some Apaches manage to carry on? How did they meet the challenges they faced? What did they do that enabled them to survive? According to Mrs. Watt, and just as one might expect, different Apache families responded in different ways. But experience-distant studies, which view the historical landscape from such a lofty rise, are prevented from discerning how they went about it or why, in a number of cases, their efforts were successful. During one of our recording sessions, Mrs. Watt surprised me when she likened the situation to gazing at the earth from the cabin of an airplane. "Books about us kind of remind me of that," she remarked. "I mean, you can see a long ways off all right, but you never do know what's happening down there on the ground." The ground, of course, is where most of history unfolds, and without people to observe—and plenty of human agency to give them credibility—the Western Apache past will remain clouded and out of reach. A different view is needed to bring it into focus, a clearer field of vision trained upon the earth, an Apache gaze, experience-near.

This is what Mrs. Watt provides in *Don't Let the Sun Step Over You*.[5] In a voice all her own—spare, factual, unflinchingly direct—she tracks her family's course from a starting point in the late 1800s.[6] With the Apache wars recently at an end and most Western Apache people living in dire poverty on the San Carlos and Fort Apache reservations, it was a harsh and harrowing time. Under the authority of nervous U.S. Indian agents, pitiless government school officials, and menacing mounted police, everyone saw clearly that overt acts of resistance (which were punishable by terms in jail) would be foolish and self-defeating. But families like Mrs. Watt's did not succumb to despair or sink into inactivity. Instead, they accepted the world for what it was, carefully took its measure, and reacted accordingly with the means at their disposal. They resisted, in other words, in the most basic way they could: they resolved to endure. As Mrs. Watt put it, "Some of those families had hardly *nothing*, but they just made up their minds to keep on keeping going."

This is a dominant theme in Part One of Mrs. Watt's book, a theme that finds expression in dozens of storied tracks her relatives left behind. Tracks of arduous travels and troubles along the way. Tracks of trachoma and the scourge of tuberculosis. Tracks of ceremonials that brought an end to drought. Tracks of medicinal plants with which people fought and conquered illness. Tracks of brutal boarding schools, dynamite and crushing rocks, and the hiding of coins in a baking powder can where no one ever found them. Tracks large and small. Tracks that startle and move. Tracks not seen before. Tracks upon the landscape of the Western Apache past.

And what a past it was! In sharp contravention of standard accounts, the world described by Mrs. Watt hummed with life and vitality. The members of her family were always working at something, and whatever it happened to be, no matter how taxing or onerous, they rarely saw fit to complain. On the contrary, except when pressed by severe privation, they accomplished their tasks with cheerful equanimity and unvoiced feelings of gratitude; they were, after all, together and much of a piece. They paced themselves and took time to relax. They joked with each other, poked fun at their own mistakes, and enjoyed the rewards of convivial talk, especially listening to stories. They squabbled now and then, but not for long; it was considered beneath them and derided as childish behavior. Drawing on bodies of practical cultural knowledge and relying when necessary on assistance from kin, they dealt with adversity by finding ways to surmount it. This they did with resourcefulness, forbearance, and seemingly endless patience. Valuable under any conditions, these particular qualities acquired added importance when the family was on the move, and for more than a decade, when Mrs. Watt was still quite young, that was most of the time. "It seems like we were always going someplace," she recalled. "For a while that was our life."

Closing down homes at Cibecue and Oak Creek, secluded communities in the rugged western region of the Fort Apache Reservation, Mrs. Watt's family—Ann Beatty and John Tulene (her parents), Rose Lupe and Tulene (her paternal grandparents), Donna Tulene (her sister), and four or five of her brothers—made ready and set forth. They traveled on foot and horseback, carrying their possessions in bundles fashioned from flour sacks, and gave little thought to the rough terrain that stretched for days before them. They traveled in search of employment and U.S. government rations. They traveled to gather acorns, harvest potatoes and cotton, and trade with roasted agave along the border with Mexico. They traveled to asbestos mines, boarding schools, trading posts, gambling grounds, ceremonial events, and a sacred cave that gave them salt. They camped near springs and seeps, sleeping at night in shelters made out of brush, and seldom had dealings with strangers. "We kept pretty much to ourselves," Mrs. Watt said. "Lots of times we didn't see nobody, but if we met some people we knew already, we went along with them. My father and my brothers still watched out for us. It seems like they were always looking around."

On journeys lasting for weeks and months, the Tulene family went south to Wheatfields and Fort San Carlos, Bisbee and Douglas, Naco and Fort Huachuca. They went north to Snowflake and Holbrook, east to Show Low and Whiteriver, west to Young and Camp Verde. They stayed for a while at Miami, where they survived the influenza pandemic of 1918–19, and a while longer at Roosevelt, where John Tulene and his sons had jobs on Roosevelt Dam. Later they spent several years in labor camps along the Apache Trail, where workers had begun to widen the road that became Arizona State Route 88. But wherever they happened to be, and whenever the time seemed right, they felt free to pack their belongings and return to their homes below the Mogollon Rim. "We always came back to Cibecue and Oak Creek," Mrs. Watt remembered. "My mother and my father done things there they had to do, and then they took off again. Going and coming! Going and coming! It wasn't 'til after my father died that we kind of settled down."

The family's years of continuous travel were scarred by tragic events. Not long after Mrs. Watt was born, her grandfather died near Wheatfields from a gunshot wound in the chest, an accidental killing brought on by curiosity. When Mrs. Watt was four or five, she watched as one of her brothers, a boarding school pupil at Rice, expired after handling pieces of wood charred by a bolt of lightning. A few years later, while the family was en route from Mormon Flat to San Carlos, her father, already ill, hemorrhaged violently and died on the outskirts of Globe. Following this calamity, Mrs. Watt was sent by her mother to St. Johns Indian School and Mission, a Franciscan facility close to Laveen, where she arrived at the age of twelve with barely a word of English. While she was there, her only sister, who was just seventeen, died at San Carlos from a raging case of tonsillitis.

After the death of her daughter, Ann Beatty, a destitute widow afflicted with trachoma, returned to Cibecue and lived for more than a year with her brother and his family. She then remarried and moved to the tiny community of Chediskai, where she and her husband, Charley Marley, built a log cabin, fenced pastures for their horses, and raised abundant crops. Wild game was plentiful, and except for a few commercial items that the couple obtained on visits to Cibecue and a place they called Tsééch'iizhé (Sandstone), their household was self-sufficient. An herbalist and midwife, Mrs. Watt's mother also made trips to Oak Creek and Cibecue in order to care for women who requested her assistance. But as soon as her work was done she hastened back to Chediskai, a home she cherished for its serenity and bounty. The bruising years of travel were finally at an end. For Ann Beatty and her seven remaining children, a new life had begun.

In 1929, at the age of sixteen, Mrs. Watt withdrew from St. Johns Indian School and joined her family at Chediskai. She stayed there for nearly fifteen years, farming with her mother, hunting with her brothers, and wrangling horses with her stepfather on cattle drives to Holbrook. As Mrs. Watt makes clear in Part Two of her book, it was a time she greatly enjoyed. Tucked away on Canyon Creek at the base of Chediskai Mountain, she found herself immersed in the older ways of her people, and these created a kind of order, rigorous yet gratifying, like none she had known before.

> I liked it down there at Chediskai. It's real peaceful 'cause there's hardly any visitors. There was only six families down there, and they were all related, so everybody helped everybody else. You know, those people had respect for everything. Every morn-

ing, they got up early and prayed for everything. They went by the older ways. Those people were strict, too. If they told you to do something, you better do it right away. "Don't say no," they said. "Don't even think about it." They knew what they were talking about 'cause there's hardly no trouble that way. Nobody talked mean or got in fights. Everybody was just friendly all the time.

Those old people were smart. They knew how to do everything. They could farm and hunt real good, so nobody ever did starve. And when somebody got sick, those ladies knew what herbs to get—"We need this one, we need that one," they said—and where to go and find them. It's the same way with the medicine mens, they knew who to get. "We need his prayers," they said, "so let's go and ask him to help us." Those people were busy all the time. They were *busy*—irrigating the fields, pulling out weeds, making woods [firewood], grinding corn, tanning deerskins, all kinds of stuff. They really talked Apache, too. No English. They didn't like that. It's just *perfect* how they used to talk their own language.

I was raised with boys. After my sister Donna died, I was the only girl in the family. So my brothers took me with them lots of times when they went somewhere. "If you want to go with us, come on," they said. So I did. They showed me how to shoot the gun and tame the horses and look for rabbits and squirrels. They didn't want me hurting myself, though. "Be careful," they said. "Watch what you're doing." I was the only girl, so they kind of looked out for me.

My mother showed me the things on the woman's side—you know, different ways to cook and looking after the corn and drying food for wintertime. She showed me how to make baskets and pottery and moccasin shoes. She never did wear any other kind of shoes, only moccasin shoes. That old man, Charley Marley, the one that's my stepfather, he was real kind. He was just like a father to us. He prayed for us every day early in the morning. He told us not to do this, not to do that. "Don't be lazy," he said. "We got work to do." He was a funny old man. He used to say funny things that made us laugh.

It was good down there at Chediskai, real pretty, too. We used to have fun down there. There's always stuff you had to do.

There were also plenty of narrative tracks. Tracks of fish-head soup. Tracks of all-night gambling for valuable horses and saddles. Tracks of bears and mountain lions. Tracks of a double murder at Oak Creek. Tracks of a bearded outlaw. Tracks of a stuttering medicine man whose songs were never flawed. Tracks of another medicine man, short in stature, who shrank the land as he walked. Tracks of a splendid place where every day seemed open and fresh. Tracks of a way of life now lost and gone for good.

The family's years at Chediskai were not without wrenching moments. When Ann Beatty was well past middle age, she was struck by lightning on one of her visits to Cibecue. Badly burned and unable to speak, she was semiconscious for several days. But Mrs. Watt's mother would once again prevail. Following intensive ceremonial treatment by specialists at San Carlos, she regained the ability to walk and talk, resumed most of her normal activities, and despite recurrent seizures went on to lead a spirited life until she was very old. One of her favorite sayings was *Ch'igoná'áí nitis dahsol'ees hela'*—"Don't let the sun step over you!"—an ancient Apache adage with which she awakened her children before the break of day. A powerful metaphor with broad religious overtones, it was a call for stamina, self-discipline, and industriousness, virtues she personified to an extraordinary degree. "My mother never did get lazy," Mrs. Watt reported with evident admiration. "She was making baskets and moccasin shoes right up 'til the end. It seems like in my mother's mind, she never had trouble at all. Lots of trouble came her way, but she just ignored it."

In the spring of 1944, Mrs. Watt, who by then was a mother herself, made a difficult decision: She placed her four-year-old son, Reuben Kessay, in the care of her mother and stepfather and embarked on a series of wage-paying jobs to help support her family. She ventured far from Chediskai, and except for irregular visits to check on Reuben's progress and give her mother money, she was gone from home for more than twenty years. As related by Mrs. Watt in Part Three of this book, it was a period in her life that proceeded by fits and starts, an unpredictable time when much seemed guided by chance. And although it wasn't easy, it was never really unpleasant. (Indeed, as time went on, it produced some lasting rewards.) Like her relatives before her, Mrs. Watt kept moving from place to place, doing at each what had to be done, steadily staying busy in a world of shifting demands. "I was traveling again!" she said with a chuckle. "I was going here, going there. I had *all kinds* of jobs."

Her tracks attest to that. Tracks of burning timber slash on the ridges above Carrizo. Tracks of cooking breakfasts in a bustling Show Low café. Tracks of keeping house for a couple in Phoenix and working for their daughter as a nanny in Spokane. Tracks of a kindly Cherokee, William Watt, father of John and Ora Watt. And tracks at last of returning home, where things were not the same. Tracks of abandoned Chediskai. Tracks of empty Oak Creek. Tracks of the past fading fast before the hand of time.

Mrs. Watt became a widow in 1987. Several years later, she left her home in Cibecue and joined her daughter at Cradleboard, a modern community complex located north of Whiteriver, the administrative headquarters of the White Mountain Apache Tribe. In 2002, she went to live with her son and his wife, Reuben and Beverly Bones Kessay, in their spacious house near Hon-Dah, where a sparkling tribal casino-resort attracts visitors day and night. Treated with fond attention and beloved by handsome grandchildren, Mrs. Watt is comfortable and secure. But thoughts of earlier days, much less well-appointed, sometimes cause her to smile. "Look at all these *things*," she says, gesturing round the living room where she sits and entertains visitors. "I remember when we had hardly nothing. It's not really funny, but in a way it is."

Now and again, Reuben Kessay drives with his mother from Hon-Dah back to Chediskai, a trip of some sixty miles across the Fort Apache reservation. Although the old family home has long been deserted (the structures are gone, the cornfields lie choked with weeds), they spend the day agreeably and sometimes reminisce. Mrs. Watt speaks to her son, as she has spoken to me, as if the years of her youth were surpassingly rich and full. This she does without the slightest trace of bitterness or self-pity, even when pointing out that poverty and misfortune made living far from easy. "Eva," I asked her once, "don't you ever get *sad* thinking about those days? You told me yourself those were pretty hard times." A quizzical expression came over her face. "Why am I gonna be sad? I was with my family and lots was going on. I *like* thinking back to all the places we went to and what we done together." She then turned the question back on me: "Are you sad for when you was young?" I said that I wasn't. "Good," she exclaimed. "Nchǫǫgo natsíńkęęs da!"—Don't think unpleasant thoughts!

According to Mrs. Watt, this ageless piece of wisdom has served her people well. On countless occasions, she explained, Western Apache men and women have found the will to carry on by ridding their minds of unpleasant thoughts. Even in desperate times, prolonged dejection, though certainly understandable, was considered an indulgence that benefited no one and only made matters worse. So persons burdened by depression or anxiety were told to train their minds on things that needed doing, because the very act of doing them, especially in family groups, worked to combat gloom and nourish a measure of hope. More often than not, hope won out. Sooner or later, conditions improved and broken spirits mended. Laughter was heard again. Many Apache families refused to let the sun step over them and resisted thinking unpleasant thoughts. Physically tough and mentally resilient, they kept on keeping going. Which is why, one suspects, Mrs. Watt continues to rise at dawn, drinks a mug of strong coffee, and then gets busy with light household chores. It is, she recommends, a pleasant way to start the day.

On just such a day in the fall of 2002, Mrs. Watt looked up from a typescript of *Don't Let the Sun Step Over You* and patted it with her hand. "What's nice," she said, "is you can go in and out of this. I mean, you can look in there anywhere and find out a little, and then, if you want to, you can quit. Then, if you want to, you can look in there again and find out a little more. That's kind of like how we used to learn our family's stories—not all at once, just one or two at a time, just now and then. After a while, though, those stories start piling up, and that's when they start working on each other. That's when you can see how they go together. It's kind of like those [jig]saw puzzles that's got lots of pieces. When the pieces start coming together, the picture on top gets big."

When I invited Mrs. Watt to expand upon these remarks, she was more than willing to do so. For a very long time, she assured me, a major portion of Western Apache history came in the form of family stories.[7] Yet acquiring these stories, reflecting on their significance, and passing them on to others is no longer common practice. Until fairly recently, family stories were an integral part of Apache family life, a regular feature of growing up that stimulated thought and instilled a sense of personal and group identity. One learned who one *was* from one's relatives, and the stories they told, whether centered on kin or not, helped to define one's place in Apache society. In the process, Mrs. Watt noted, one's "mind got bigger."

Acquiring family stories was a relaxed and unstructured affair. Often told impromptu, completed in just a few minutes, and typically inserted into casual conversations, the stories, though plentiful, were fleeting and intermittent. Learning large numbers of them, Mrs. Watt observed, was mainly a matter of "hanging around home, mostly in the evening." Some family stories were rendered expertly, others with less finesse; some were compelling, others not so much. But whatever their separate merits, and whenever they came one's way, they were almost always informative. And as time went on, acting unbidden and on their own, they began "working on each other" in illuminating ways: connections emerged, commonalities surfaced, consistencies (and inconsistencies) appeared. Like pieces of a jigsaw puzzle, the stories "came together," producing composite images of Apaches in the past, the kinds of lives they led, and how, as times changed, Apache lives changed as well. In this dynamic fashion, the past became part of the present—indeed, a part of the self—and one's deepening awareness of history became a valued possession. "Sometimes," Mrs. Watt said, "it seems like those people from long years ago never did go away. You can see them real *clear*, hear them talking, too. I'm glad I know those family stories. I'm thankful for our family story way."

This family story way, Mrs. Watt suggested, is one that readers may wish to pursue in roughly analogous form. If so, open her book to any page and read one or two stories. (The organization of *Don't Let the Sun Step Over You* is only loosely chronological, so beginning at the beginning, though recommended, is not a requirement.) Then put the book aside and get on with other things. Return to it at some point and read a few more stories. (Each is distinct and self-contained, and topical continuity from one to the next may be faint or nonexistent; this is as it should be, because Apache family stories were neither told nor acquired in any particular sequence.) As the stories accrue, take note of patterns and themes. Look for signs of them elsewhere. Let them develop and deepen. (This results from heightened curiosity and spontaneous interaction among the stories themselves; it is not the product of deliberate or studied analysis.) Proceed as before, bringing to bear on subsequent stories insights gained from previous ones. At junctures along the way, and when all of the reading is done, allow the stories to arrange themselves into overarching constructions—Mrs. Watt's "big pictures"—of former Apache worlds. Dwell on these worlds. Marvel and laugh and shudder at what took place within them. Revisit them from time to time. Dwell on them some more. According to Mrs. Watt, the process never ends.

Finally, dwell on the people who inhabited these worlds, the ones still richly remembered, the ones Mrs. Watt can occasionally see and hear—people like Ann Beatty and John Tulene, Rose Lupe and Charley Marley. Attend carefully to their tracks, because they are the tracks of heroes. Not heroes of the mythic type—not sagacious chiefs, terrifying warriors, or elusive renegades—but those of a less fabled variety that Patricia Nelson Limerick has aptly termed "sustainable." Limerick writes that "sustainability in a hero means, very concretely, providing inspiration that sustains the spirit and the soul. While inconsistency can disqualify a conventional hero, a degree of inconsistency is one of the essential qualifications of a sustainable hero. The fact that these people fell, periodically, off the high ground of heroism but then determinedly climbed back, even if only in order to fall again, is exactly what makes their heroism sustainable. Because it is uneven and broken, this kind of heroism is resilient, credible, possible, reachable. Sustainable heroism comes only in moments and glimpses, but they are moments and glimpses in which the universe lights up" (Limerick 2000:315).

Eva Tulene Watt has fashioned here a narrative universe lit up with sustainable heroes. I am convinced that Mrs. Watt is one of them, although this is an opinion I know she would reject. For she believes that thinking immodest thoughts, like thinking unpleasant ones, accomplishes nothing worthwhile. Western Apache heroes have better things to do. Like Mrs. Watt, they have to keep on going. Fortunately for us all, they hold close to family stories, and now, at last, a sizable body of these will be preserved in written form. So, too, will a view of history that Western Apache people can comfortably call their own, a view that challenges conventional accounts by showing them to be exclusionary, partisan, and seriously incomplete. Unquestionably, and in more ways than one, *Don't Let the Sun Step Over You* is a bold and heroic work.

Part One

"We Sure Did Travel All Over"

(1860–1929)

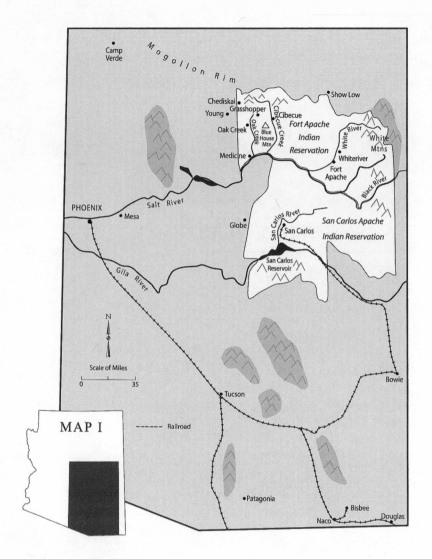

Map 1. Southeastern Arizona.

Chapter One

I don't remember too much from when I was small. It seems like the family was always traveling, though, I remember that. That's how it was in those days—people traveled all the time, looking for something to eat, looking for something to do. People went where they were needed. Wherever we went, it seems like we had relatives that we stayed with. My grandmother Rose used to tell us, me and my brothers, "You have to know who your relatives are. If something happens, they're the ones that will try and help you out." So wherever we went, I guess that's what we did—we got to know our relatives and learned about them.

Rose Lupe—Captured by an Outlaw—The Death of Tulene—A Catholic Priest near Christmas—All Kinds of Medicines—Frank Case, Storyteller—"Grandpa's Drowning!"—William Lupe—John Lupe—Lupa—Blue House Mountain—"He Chewed It Up Like Crackers!"—Hard Candy—William Goshoney—They Sang All Night—"Use the Rain"—How to Get Up Fast—Ann Beatty—Revolt at San Carlos—Carlisle Indian School—Robert Beatty—School at Cibecue—Wild Horses—Emma Tulene and Willie Stevens—John Langley Tulene—"We Sure Did Travel All Over"—"Don't Let the Sun Step Over You"—Nest'án Yolílé (She Brings Home Fruits And Vegetables)

Rose Lupe

My grandmother was Rose Lupe. Her clan is Tséch'ishjiné [Rocks Protruding Out Darkly People]. She was my father's mother. She was from

Oak Creek.[1] She was the one that raised me, her and my mother. She was always taking care of me. She lived with us a lot of the time, even after she went to San Carlos and started having children over there.

My grandmother Rose said it was real hard when she was a girl. She said, "There's no way you could get clothes or nothing. They used to use those baby deerskins, the ones that have spots on them. They used to tan those and use them to make clothes with." She said, "Everything was hard to get. We used to eat snowbirds, those little tiny ones, in the wintertime." She used to talk about it a lot. She used to cry a lot when she talked about it, too. One time, my oldest brother, Eugene, got mad at her. He said, "How come you want to cry? You're not in that time still. Now you're safe. I don't see why you want to cry." My grandmother said, "I think how we suffered in those times, that's what I'm thinking about."

My mother said that my grandmother got married when she was only a little girl yet. Long years ago, they used to give their daughters away to the mens and families that wanted them. I think that's how she got married. She was very young, probably about twelve or eleven. She never did go to school.

My grandmother Rose was a short one. My mother was tall. I wonder why, in those days, all the ladies were tall. The mens were tall, too. But after that, they started getting shorter and shorter. All in my family were tall, all except Joe and me. Maybe it's because of my grandma, she was a little one, too. My grandma was a nervous lady. She was easy to cry. She used to talk about having a hard life all her life, and that made her that way, she said. When she got excited, you could hear her talking a long ways off.

Captured by an Outlaw

My grandmother Rose used to talk about when she was a young girl. She said it was dangerous to show yourself anywhere. See, Geronimo and those other outlaws were out and you had to be hiding all the time—especially young girls, like she was. She was living in Oak Creek and those outlaws used to come over there. They went all over, everywhere. They went all the way to Camp Verde. They were looking for horses, stealing horses.[2]

Rose Lupe (left) with her daughter-in-law, Amelia Case, at
Rice, San Carlos Apache Indian Reservation, about 1940. This
is the sole surviving photograph of Eva Watt's grandmother,
a traditional herbalist whose copious knowledge of medicinal
plants benefited many people.

My grandmother Rose was captured. That happened before my
time. My father told me about it. He was there when it happened.

Up towards Globe there's a little pointed mountain. They were
camping there, close to that pointed mountain. They were camping in a
deep wash, way down where nobody could see them. They were down

Western Apache woman bringing grass to sell at Fort San Carlos, San Carlos Apache Indian Reservation, date unknown. She is carrying a cradleboard on her back.

there—my grandmother and grandfather and my father and two other boys. They were cutting grass. They used to cut grass for the army.[3] They sold it. One bundle cost a quarter. So that's what they were doing, cutting grass to take over there to San Carlos so they could buy themselves something to eat. That's how people made their money.

My grandfather was down there by their camp. It was in a deep place. They couldn't see anything up towards the top 'cause there's lots of mesquite trees up there. My grandfather told my grandmother not to go up there. He said, "There's lots of grass growing right along here. Cut the grass down here. Don't go up there." But she won't listen! She went up. She said, "There's more grass up there. There's lots of grass under those mesquite trees."

So she went up there. My father was with her. He was about twelve or thirteen years old. He was laying down under a mesquite tree, cutting grass, and that's when he seen it! He seen something move! So he just laid low under the tree and started looking. He just quiets down. "Yes," he said, "be quiet." Then he saw that man! My father said he was just *full* of eagle feathers, the soft ones. They were all over him. And he was going real low, stooping down as low as he can. My grandmother

Western Apaches delivering and stacking grass at Fort Apache, Fort Apache Indian Reservation, about 1889. Enormous amounts of wild grass, cut and transported mainly by Apache women, were sold to the garrison at Fort Apache as fodder for horses and mules.

was walking between the trees, going from one tree to another, and that man was getting closer to her, getting closer. My father couldn't do nothing. He started yelling and that's when that man hit my grandmother. He knocked her down. He picked her up and ran with her. And right there, behind some big rocks, he had his horse. He put her on the horse and took off. There's another wash there, close to where they were camping, and they went up that one. I don't know where they went after that.

My father was scared 'cause his mother was taken. He didn't know what to do. He ran down to the camp and told them that she was taken. That's when they all got scared, my grandfather and those three boys. They tried to follow her but they couldn't find her. Then they got the grass they already cut and throwed the bundles in the wagon. They took off to the army camp at San Carlos—it's not very far from where they were at—and they told them what happened. They told those armys [soldiers] that an outlaw captured my grandmother. They went all over everywhere looking for her. They came back. They didn't find her. He was a real tricky man! He took her to that big tall mountain behind Bylas. They went up and up to a rocky place in there. It's hard for horses unless you know what you're doing—the rocks cut their feet—and at that time there's no good trail.

But my grandmother came back. She came back about four days later. She came back to Joseph Hoffman's home. That outlaw man didn't hurt her. All he wanted was his meat cut up in pieces. He killed two deer and he wanted her to make jerkies for him. He said he's not supposed to do it himself. So that's what she did. "Slice it thin and dry it," he told her. "When it's not too dry, pound it on a rock, not too much, just soft enough to roll it." That's what she did and then she packed it all in his bag. She said he's got a big leather bag. She said he's got *everything* in there—material, dishes, even little pots and pans.

She said that he built a fire. Then he put a piece of deer meat on a stick. He just rolled it over the fire. He didn't like his meat well-cooked. It's almost raw, barely warmed up. He tried to give her some of that meat, but she said she didn't want it. He's got little corn cakes—I guess it's cornbread—but they're little tiny ones. He carried those with a string through a hole in the middle. He gave her one. She said that was good. She ate that little corn cake but she wouldn't eat the meat. It wasn't cooked, so she won't eat it.

When she finished making all those jerkies, that man gave her two pieces of material and a blanket out of his bag. This was at night, real early in the morning. He told her, he said, "Go home." Slowly, she went off. She looked back to see if there's anything moving around, and she seen him making a torch out of brush. That's when she really took off! She thought he was gonna come after her again. It scared her so much 'cause that man was *fast*! She ran! She ran all the way down the mountain! She said she got lots of stickers in her feet, but she just didn't care. She left her moccasin shoes behind. I guess he made her take them off so she won't run away.

She ran all the way to Rice, to Joseph Hoffman's home. He was one of my grandpas. She got there just when the sun was coming up. I guess those armys were watching the camp. She hollered at them and two of them came over. They asked her how she got away. She told them.

Joseph Hoffman, medicine man, San Carlos Apache Indian Reservation, about 1940.

Then those armys took her back to where she was. They took her up there. Everything was *gone*! She said that you can't even see that somebody was there! The fire was covered up with dirt. That man throwed gravel on top of it. It looked like a natural place. Those armys told her that she was lying. "There's no fire, no ashes, nothing!" So she took a stick and started digging—and there were the ashes again. They were still a little bit warm.

When they brought my grandmother back to San Carlos, she was really feeling bad. She cried and cried, thinking about it. She said, "I thought I was never gonna see my husband and my son again." That's what she told them. My father told her, "It's your own fault for showing yourself. You're not supposed to cut grass up there."

So they left San Carlos and came back to Oak Creek. They stayed over there with my grandmother's brothers, William and John Lupe. She won't go anyplace for a long time, for over a year. She didn't want to go nowhere. She said, "That man *sneaks around*!" She said, "You think he's gone somewhere far away and he might be sitting there close to you. And you don't even know it! He sneaks around! You can't hear him! He's worse than a cat!"

One thing he did before he let her go was cut her hair. In those days, the ladies parted their hair down the middle and tied it back. Well, he untied it, and then he cut off the front part on both sides and tied it back again. She said he did that to all his captives. He marked them that way. So her hair was chopped off. It looked like he did it with a knife, my father said, 'cause it was all uneven. It wasn't done with a scissors.

The Death of Tulene

My grandmother's first husband was Tulene. That was his name. He was from somewhere around Camp Verde. His clan is Bisząhą [Clay Riverbank People]. He was born at a place called Tú Ńlį́į́' [Water Flowing], so that's why they called him Tulene. He got killed on the road to Roosevelt somewhere near Wheatfields.

My grandfather lost his life for curiosity—for curiosity he lost his life. They were all there in a wickiup. My grandmother said somebody was shooting. Somebody was shooting out there and my grandfather wanted to see why they're fighting. My grandmother told him, she said, "Stay in bed. Leave them alone. Let them go and fight among themselves." She said, "They fight all the time. You don't need to know who they are."

But that man won't listen! He got up and put his boots on and went outside. He was standing right by the wagon and the harness was hanging on the wheel. They were still shooting. A bullet hit him right in the heart. He fell over and that's when they heard the harness fall off the wagon. I guess he was holding onto it and it fell down with him.

My father and Eugene jumped up! They went over there. Eugene said, "My grandpa is killed! Somebody killed him!" Eugene got a gun and my father grabbed a gun. They started shooting real bad. My father said, "I'm gonna kill every one of you *mean* people!" He said, "You *stupid people*! You don't even realize you killed somebody that's not even in your own party." He was *mad*!

There's lots of Mexicans that used to come up there. They were having a party. They were drinking moonshine whiskey. They sold that moonshine or traded it for cooked mescal.[4] That's why they were up there. Our family had lots of that cooked mescal and those Mexicans wanted to trade whiskey for it. But they got drunk and started shooting.

The family was going to Roosevelt but they never made it. They had to turn back. They came back to Cibecue 'cause of my grandpa. My grandmother Rose took it real hard. They got back to where John Lupe's field was, under Blue House Mountain, and she stayed there a while with her brother. She stayed there over a year after her first husband got killed. She just went back and forth between there and Oak Creek.

A Catholic Priest near Christmas

My family was Catholics. My grandmother Rose was the first one. She said that they were camping somewhere along the river [Gila River] down there near Christmas. She was down there, her and her sister, working on somebody's farm. Long years ago, the Apaches used to have fields along that river and that's what she was doing, helping those people out in their fields.

A Catholic priest used to ride there.[5] One day, she said, they were sitting by the roadside when he came. She was sitting there with them. He started talking to those ladies. He wanted to know what they were doing and all that. There was a man with them that understood English, so he interpreted for the priest. Those ladies got interested in it. They just sat there and sat there and listened to it. Finally, the priest left. He said, "I'll come back and see you tomorrow." The next day, they were working in the fields. They were looking for him, waiting for him to come back. And when they seen him coming, they went up to the road to meet him again. Then they were in it—they became his class. After that, he went to the fields and sat under a cottonwood tree, so they went over there and had their meetings with him.

Then, after she married that man from San Carlos [Frank Case], she seen a priest there, too. She knew what they are. She went over to the church, I guess, and that priest gave her some papers to take home with her. Then, every Sunday, that priest came after her. Every Sunday he came over there and took her to the church. And finally she took my father, then my mother, and then all the kids. They followed her up there. So that's how they became Catholics long years ago. My grandmother Rose got interested in it.

All Kinds of Medicines

My grandmother Rose knew all the herbs. She used to gather roots and stuff for *izee* [plant medicines]. She carried all kinds of medicines with her. She cured people. She used to show me which plant is this and which plant is that. She used to give me a leaf. "Go find this one for me," she said. Lots of times she didn't see good 'cause she had only one eye. It's white. She was braiding a basket and they told her to go check on something. She got up to do that. When she got up, I guess one of those frame pieces hit her in the eye, right in the middle. It hurt her real bad. All the water inside her eye drained out. Then that black spot in the middle of her eye turned white. She had only one eye after that. That's the reason she showed me all those things. When she went after medicine plants, I had to go with her to show her where they are. And when I found one for her, while she's digging up that one, I was looking around for another one. I used to help her that way.

There's so many different medicines. She even used old dry bones,

bones that turned white from the sun. They have to be real dry. We used to go out looking for them. All she needs is one piece, one big piece. She cleaned it up. She washed the dust and dirt off. She scrubbed it with a little broom or brush. Then she put it out to dry. When it's dry, she cracks it on a rock, and then she grinds it, makes it into a powder. After that, she mixed it with some kind of root and that was one of her medicines.

She taught me plants and herbs and lots of things to eat, things that grow, teas and medicines and all that stuff. My mother knew all that, too. It's nice to know those things. See, in those days, everything was hard to get. So, if you saw anything like that, you knew it was good, especially in the springtime, 'cause lots of plants come up from the ground—wild spinach and watercress and another one that looks like lettuce. Maybe that's why the people were healthy. They ate all those vegetables from the ground. Berries, too, they ate lots of berries. And yucca—they cooked that and it was just like molasses. It tasted like sorghum syrup.

My grandma showed me how to cook with acorns and piñon nuts and *ch'iłdiiyé* [walnuts]. And mushrooms. They used to find mushrooms on walnut trees. My grandmother cut them off a little ways from where they're stuck to the tree. She brought them home and soaked them in water. Then she boiled them with meat, some dry jerky that she keeps all the time. She cut those mushrooms in little strips. Then she mixed them with acorn powder and a little water and poured them in with the meat. She made a stew that way. It tastes good.

I lived with my grandmother Rose all over, everywhere. She was even at Mormon Flat. She followed us all the way down there and stayed with us for about two months. Then she went back to San Carlos. My grandpa Frank [Case] got his army pension there—I guess he got some kind of a check—so that's why she went back. She was still making baskets. She could see good enough for that, even after she lost her eye. She used to make bowl baskets, the kind you sew over and over again. She sold them in Globe. And sometimes, when the wagon trains went through the reservation, people came by and bought them from her at home. Some of them paid her money and some gave her lots of food. Her baskets came out good! It seemed to me they were perfect.

Frank Case, Storyteller

My grandmother Rose traveled a lot! She went *everywhere*! After my grandfather [Tulene] got killed, she stayed with her brother, John Lupe. She went down there to Tséétęh Na'áá [Rocks Standing In The Water], down there to his fields. Then she started going back and forth to San Carlos to get rations. That's where she got acquainted with that man, Frank Case. I guess she was thinking about him 'cause one time she went down there and never did come back 'til a year later. That man was a scout for the army.[6] They got married. She got caught down there at the army camp! Her brothers were mad at her when she brought that man back home. "You should have brought him back a long time ago," they said. "Why didn't you let us know what's going on down there?"

That man's father was Ha'i'ąha [Mescalero Apache] and his mother was from here [Western Apache]. I think that's the way it was. He was from Mescalero, somewhere down there, and those Mescaleros captured a lot of [Western Apache] women. I think his mother was one of them. He was born over there and became a scout for the army. He moved to San Carlos to the army camp, and that's where my grandmother found him.

He got shot someplace close to Patagonia. I guess they were looking for Mexicans, chasing them back 'cause they're coming into the United States bringing all kinds of stuff. He was riding a horse and they shot at him. It hit him in his hip, right in the middle, and shattered his bone. He couldn't walk good after that. They tried to give him crutches but he never did use them. It looks like he's got a short leg on the side where he got shot. He walked with a cane. He limped. After he got shot, they took him out of the army. They gave him a pension, and he lived on that down there at San Carlos. My grandpa Frank used to love to dance. He stood in one spot, and he had his cane in front of him, and he danced around it. "That's what the ladies like," he said. That was *funny*!

My grandmother Rose started having children with that man. She had six children with him. The first was Lewis, then Clark, then Freeman, Bessie, George, and Raymond—they're all Cases. My grandmother had two children with her first husband, my father and his sister, my aunt Emma. She used to say that all together she had fourteen kids. I guess she lost six. They were just babies when they died. She kept losing them. She said that she lost three at one time to TB.[7]

He [Frank Case] was a real kind man. He used to sit there, and we were sitting all around him, and he told us stories about old times. That's why all the kids liked him, 'cause of his stories. Back then, kids used to *listen!* "Sit and be still!" he said. When the sun went down, when it got dark, he started with the stories. He used to tell us all different stories—Fox, Turkey, Bear, Turtle, Rabbit, all the animals. He's got roasted corn. There's an empty can to put your corn in, and every time he tells a story, after it's finished, you put a corn [a single kernel] in your can. And after all the stories are over with, about four o'clock in the morning, you have to eat those corns—'cause if you don't eat them, you never will remember the stories.

"Grandpa's Drowning!"

You know, my grandpa Frank almost drowned. We were at San Carlos and it rained up high towards Hill Top. It's *real dark* up there all morning, like it's really raining hard. And we went to one of my uncles that day 'cause he told us to come and get some vegetables. He gave us all we wanted—corn, squash, beans, potatoes, everything. When we got ready to go, my uncle took the wagon with the vegetables in it across the river [San Carlos River] for us. He said, "I don't want to take these vegetables off and pile them back on, so I guess you're gonna have to walk across." So we started crossing the river. We got about halfway across, and that's when we seen the driftwood coming down. "Hurry! It's gonna get flooded!" We hurried. We got across.

And my grandpa was behind us. He was talking to somebody back there. Then he started walking across on his cane. He almost got across. He almost got to the edge on the other side of the river, and that's when he tumbled over. The water starts rolling him down. I was screaming my head off! "Grandpa's going! Grandpa's drowning!" And his sons, two of them, jumped in the water and went after him. They pulled him out and put him on the shore. They put him on his stomach and they were pressing on him and lots of water was coming out. After a while, he sat up. "You see, we told you to hurry up. You just sat there

and talked too much. You could talk your life away." That's what they
told him.

William Lupe

My grandmother Rose had two brothers and one sister. William Lupe,
F-1, was the oldest.[8] He was the leader of the people living at Oak Creek
and Chediskai. He had two wives. One of them was a Pima.[9] They had a
fight with the Pimas and captured that girl. I guess she got acquainted
with my grandfather right away, coming back this way, and she just
stayed with him. She was just a young girl. She had more kids than his
other wife. His other wife was Apache. She was from Oak Creek. My
grandpa Bill had a *big* family.[10] He had almost twenty-five kids coming
from those two wives. I think he had fourteen from one and ten from
the other. But lots of them died from TB. From the '20s on back, that
TB was *bad*!

John Lupe

John Lupe was the next one born after F-1. Then my grandmother Rose
was born, and then her sister, Lupa. John Lupe was F-3, that was his
brand. He had a farm below Medicine on the Salt River, way down
there. They call that place Tséétęh Na'áá. Now there's nothing but mesquite trees down there. Back then, there was more water in the river.
My grandfather made a big irrigation ditch way up above his fields, a
big one.

He had lots of people working for him down there. My mother and
father used to live with him down there. They kept up his farm for him
while he had other things to do. He used to plant lots of corn and wheat,
and lots of watermelons, cantaloupes, all those things. And he used to
plant beans, little tiny ones, black ones. And sorghum, he grew that,
too. If people working for him had kids, he cut some of that sorghum
and gave it to them. They're satisfied with that!

They cut the wheat with little sickles. Then they tied it in bundles
and set those out in the sun. Then, when the grains start coming out,
they put the bundles on a big canvas and beat it with sticks. That's how
they took all the grains out. After that, they threw it up in the air

William Lupe (F-1), prominent medicine man and leader of the Western Apache community at Oak Creek, Fort Apache Indian Reservation, 1918. Probably at the photographer's request, he is displaying a shield, a lance, and what Eva Watt described as a "prayer cloth." His cap is furnished with the breast feathers of an eagle.

and let the wind blow all the leaves and stuff away. Then, after that, they put it in sacks. They packed those sacks back to Oak Creek. My grandpa had a lot of mules, and they packed those sacks on the mules. He gave half a sack to his neighbors, half a sack to each family. And if there's lots of children in the family, he gave them a whole sack. He took the rest of the wheat to get ground up into flour.

John Lupe had a farm at Oak Creek and another one close to Blue House Mountain, at Tséé Bika' Naaditin [Trail Goes Across On Top Of Rocks]. And he had big fields down there below Medicine at Tséétęh Na'áá. That was a *good* farming place. Lots of boys went to him 'cause he's always got something to eat. They worked for him for food. And he had a big shade that he made into a home for them. He put cottonwood

Members of the Western Apache community at Oak Creek, Fort Apache Indian
Reservation, about 1930. The four young women standing side by side were
daughters of William Lupe and cousins of Eva Watt. From left to right: Irene
Lupe, Betty Lupe, Jane Lupe, Molly Lupe. The mother of Irene and Molly, a
captured Pima, was one of Lupe's two concurrent wives. His other wife, an
Apache from Oak Creek, was the mother of Betty and Jane. With these two
women Lupe had more than two dozen children.

limbs on top, thick, and all the way around on the sides. They covered
that up with canvas so no rain gets inside. He used that for the boys'
home.

　　My mother used to say, "They were all a happy family together."
My grandpa's wife and one of his daughters cooked for those boys.
My mother said, "When your grandpa found one of those boys, if he's

John Lupe (F-3), prominent member of the Western Apache community at Oak Creek, Fort Apache Indian Reservation, date unknown. The cap he is wearing is adorned with eagle wing feathers.

hungry and standing around, he picked him up and brought him down there. He stayed around the place for a while, for two or three days, and then your grandpa found something for him to do. 'Go ahead and work in the fields,' he said. Or 'Go work on the irrigation ditch.'"[11]

There was a boy down there at Oak Creek that burned his foot. It was all curled in, his foot, his toes. It was just like a ball. And his leg on that side was just *skinny*, just the bone, no meat, and the skin was all scarred up. He used to come around with his cane—it's a homemade cane like a crutch—and he put it under his arm and ran around on one foot. When he got naughty, they took his cane away and throwed it up on top of the shade so he won't go nowhere. He crawled around but he can't get up.

My mother said that they were working, cooking yucca, and they built a fire. It's *hot*! They didn't know he crawled over there. The yucca was in the ground already, and I guess he kept pulling on it—you know, the end that's sticking out—and brought out a lot of fire with it. That's

John Lupe's home at Oak Creek, Fort Apache Indian Reservation, 1918.

how he burned his foot. I don't know how he got close to that fire—it's
hot!

Nobody heard him 'cause they were all working way out on the
hillside. They were getting dry beargrass to put under the fire so the
wood will burn. The fire keeper, a man, was supposed to be watching
the fire. His horse ran off, so he went chasing after it. He brought it
back, but that boy was already burned. He was about three years old
when it happened.

Those boys did everything, even taming wild horses. My grandpa
had lots of horses working for him and he had a lot of plows. Instead of
using a leather harness, they used a rope and made it like a harness for
a wagon. Then they put the horses on the plows. Four boys went around
and around together, plowing with four horses side by side. They got
the plowing done in no time that way!

John Lupe almost got killed when he was a young man. It was before he got married. He was with a bunch of mens and they had a fight
with some white people somewhere around Young. There used to be
a stone house along the wash up there. It was standing when I first
seen it. They say it fell down, but I don't know. Anyway, right there is

where they were fighting. My grandfather almost got shot—almost—but he was fast! The bullet hit a rock in front of his head. He said that somebody got shot in the leg. He said it didn't hurt him very much.

Lupa

There was another one, my grandmother Rose's sister. Those two used to go everywhere together. They were real close. But that lady went to Mexico and never did come back. I guess she fell in love with a Mexican. They got married and she went to live down there at Naco. The Mexicans called her "Lupa."

She found that Mexican man over at Mammoth. That's where she met him. He tried to keep her there but the family said no. They brought her back to San Carlos. She used to sit up there on the hillside, looking around, looking around. My grandmother said, "My sister is lonesome for her boyfriend." She kept looking around, looking around.

And right there where the train stops a bunch of Mexicans was working for a while. And somehow one of them knew about the man she was running with. I guess she used to go down there to talk to that worker. She used to sit by the water tank and wait for him to come. And then, before they knew it, she got on the train and took off! She went to Naco and never did come back!

In those days, the train took people everywhere for free. They didn't chase you off. They let the Indians ride free for thirty years, I think, 'cause the railroad tracks went through the reservation. They could go anywhere they wanted. Then, after thirty years, they had to pay. So nobody rode the train anymore.

They didn't know for two or three years where that lady went. She was just *gone*! And then, finally, one of the Mexicans that worked with my brother on the railroad tracks told him about her. My brother told my grandmother Rose, "Your sister is living in Naco." So she jumped on the train and took off, her and her daughter Bessie. They found her sister down there.

I went with my grandmother two times to visit her. We rode the train. That lady lived in an adobe house and she had three boys. She was happy to see us. She kind of forgot her own language. I used to talk to her boys in Apache. They just laughed at me. My grandmother

Western Apaches riding the train from San Carlos to Bylas, San Carlos Apache Indian Reservation, about 1923.

Lupa said, "They don't hear you. They don't know what you're talking about." She looked just like my grandmother Rose, but she was taller. Like I told you, my grandmother Rose was a short one.

Blue House Mountain

I was born behind Blue House Mountain. You know the road that comes down from Grasshopper now, the one that goes all the way down to the wash? There's a big flat place there and that's where I was born, in 1913.

We lived with my mother's mother and her husband. Calvert Tessay's grandmother and grandfather lived there, too. There were just two families there. And higher up, about two or three miles, there's some more families. In those days, people used to live way out, not just in Cibecue. They were *scattered*—families at Oak Creek, Spring Creek, Grasshopper, White Springs, Chediskai, all over. But then they moved to Cibecue so their kids can go to school. They had to, 'cause if their kids didn't go to school they got throwed in jail or had to pay a fine. Policemen came looking for the kids. Some came all the way from Whiteriver 'cause there was a boarding school over there.[12]

My older brothers remembered a lot about their mother's mother and father, more than I did. I seen them—but not very much—'cause we were traveling then. My brothers used to talk about my grandmother raising those big squash, big ones. She planted corn there, too, all different kinds. There's that black-looking corn, dark red, the one they call *nadą́ cho* [big corn]. Another one was *nadą́ łigai* [white corn], *nadą́ łitsogí* [yellow corn], *nadą́ dotł'izhí* [blue corn], and other kinds, too. And she grew sugar cane and beans, orange-looking beans, old-timer's beans. And those plants they make baskets with—*chigolshahá* [devil's claw] they call it—she grew that one, too. That way she won't have to go looking for it. She had it right there, close to her home. She and my mother made baskets all the time.

When it's time to plant the corn, they got a piece of cedar, a straight cedar branch. They made one end, the thick end, a handle, and they sharpened the other end and made it into a point. Then they put a rock on top and tied it to the handle part with *igáyé* [broadleaf yucca]. They used that to dig holes for the seeds. Without that rock on top it's not heavy enough.

They never did have plows in those times when I was small. I think my grandfather [John Lupe] was the only one that had plows back then. I don't know where he got them. Later, the government gave away a bunch of plows at Cibecue. Everybody came to see if they could get one. Those that didn't get one made their own. They used oak or cedar and they made it—the blade part, the part that goes down in the ground—like the ones from the government. They made it real sharp. I seen one at Spring Creek where my uncle, Robert Beatty, used to live. I don't know what happened to it. Maybe he put it down in the ground where he stored his fruits and vegetables. That plow might still be there.

We lived in a wickiup at Blue House Mountain and there was a shade outside. That wickiup was *warm*! It was warm, even in wintertime. My mother said that my grandmother used to go after a plant that has real red flowers. She brought a big bundle of it home. She chopped it up and put it over the fire to boil and after that it's just like syrup— you know, real sticky. Then she gathered real soft dirt and dug a hole in the ground, and she put the syrup in there with the dirt. Then she chopped up some kind of grass and throwed it in there—not very many, just a few, just enough to hold it together. Then she started churning with a stick. She churns and churns and churns.

After that, when it's all well mixed, she took it with a bucket inside the wickiup and put it on the wall. She put it on, about that far up from the ground [5–6 feet] and about that thick [1–2 inches] all the way around. Then she built a fire in there. The heat dries it real fast. It stays *warm* in there! Even when it's snowing outside, it's still warm inside. When you build a fire in there the smoke goes straight up. I guess that wickiup was about as big as this room [12–14 feet in diameter]. Everybody slept in there.

My grandmother on my mother's side had no teeth. She used to pound her food on a round rock and then suck on it. She took that little rock with her wherever she went. She got a skin and made a sack out of it and kept it in there. That rock was about this big [6–8 inches in diameter] and it's real thin. It's one of those blue rocks from Salt River. She found it down there. She had another rock about this long [4–5 inches] and that was her hammer. Anything she ate, she put it on that flat blue rock and pounded it with her hammer. Then her food was ready to eat and she sucked on it.

"He Chewed It Up Like Crackers!"

I remember I got an infection under my chin. It got real big. It swelled up real bad. We were living below Blue House Mountain and they were working on the corn. It was cold and I guess that made it worse. *Cold!* It was aching so bad! I couldn't sleep at night.

They went after a medicine man that was good for that.[13] He used Na'ishǫ' bibésh [Lizard's knife]. It's an arrowhead, a sharp one. He rubbed *hádndín* [cattail pollen] on it.[14] Then he talked and talked and talked. He was praying for a long time. Then he held that Na'ishǫ' bibésh to all the four ways. After that he lifted it up three times, and the fourth time—*into his mouth!* He chewed it up like crackers! It sounds just like he's chewing crackers! Then that thing turned to water in his mouth. He blew on my infection. He blew that water on it. He told my mother to put something around it, a rag or something, and keep it there. Then he told me, he said, "Now you can go to sleep. I know you're sleepy." I went to sleep. That was in the morning. In the afternoon, I woke up. The aching was gone and that infection was draining out. I don't know how he did it, but that's what he did. I don't know how it's done. After that, I got better fast.

Hard Candy

There was a store at Grasshopper then.[15] A whiteman kept it. It's the stone house that the cowboys use now, that one. Every time I went up there the man that ran the store gave me a piece of hard candy, and I just kept it and kept it. My grandmother found out what I was doing. She said, "I never see you eat your candy. What did you do with it? Did you throw it away?" I kept it wrapped up in a piece of cloth, I don't know why. I never did eat it.

My [maternal] grandmother was grinding corn, parched corn, grinding it into powder. She said, "What did you do with your candy?" She said, "Go get it." I went and got it. I gave it to her. She cracked it on her grinder and ground it up and mixed it with the corn. "Now, eat your candy this way 'cause you won't eat it by itself!"

I don't remember much about my grandmother. She died when I was still small, when we were living at Mormon Flat. We didn't come home for the funeral. It was too far away.

William Goshoney

My mother's mother's brother was William Goshoney, A-2. He was my
mother's uncle. He was born at Cibecue. He married a lady from Cedar
Creek. Then they moved to Whiteriver. We used to go over there and
stay with them.

He was a medicine man. He knew lots, even Lightning, even that
one. They said he got hit by a lightning and nothing happened to him.
You could see the scar—it's like a burn—all the way down on one of
his legs. He was learning that Lightning, and I guess that's why it was
picking on him.[16] He said himself that the person teaching him told him
that it was gonna be that way. He told him, he said, "After you learn
real good—if you learn *real good*—then it won't bother you no more."

After he got hit by that lightning, I guess he was unconscious for
about three or four days. Then he came back. He opened his eyes
and started looking around. "Hey," he said, "I want something to eat."
That's what they were afraid of 'cause he's not supposed to eat. So
some old lady went and brought him some corn, real fine like flour,
and she made soup for him out of that. There's nothing in it—no salt,
no kind of grease—just plain cornmeal and water. He drank that. He
wanted coffee. He wanted this, he wanted that. He can't have it. They
gave him that corn soup for four days.

Then they boiled a little red plant and gave it to him. It cleaned him
out good. Then they gave him some real thin soup with meat. They
boiled the meat, took all the oil out, put some more water in there, and
boiled it again. They boiled the same meat two times. He drank that
soup. He wanted more of it. "I'm still hungry," he said. They gave him
some more.

Then he told them, he said, "I became a lightning myself. I was going from place to place." He said, "When the clouds were about to rain,
I was with them. I went down first, then the water." He said, "That's
what I was dreaming about." He said, "I was singing those songs."

So they picked four old mens and he started singing. He was talking to them, telling them about it, and singing those songs. He said,
"This is a Water song, a Rain song. If you want rain, you sing this song
and it will rain." One of those mens told him to sing it. Goshoney said,
"I remember it. I don't have to think about it. It just comes through my
mind." He sang that song for them.

William Goshoney (A-2), Western Apache medicine man, near his home at Whiteriver, Fort Apache Indian Reservation, about 1940.

He sang for those mens all night 'til morning. They said, "It's time that we rest for a while." They said, "We'll try again tonight." He sang every night for twelve nights, I think. Every night he did that. And the twelfth night, before he finished singing, it started raining *real hard*! Some ladies that were there got up and went inside. But he just sat there. He didn't move. The mens stayed out there with him. He just sat there in the pouring down rain. He was a young man when this happened.

They Sang All Night

You know what happens if you get hit by a lightning and touch a squash? It dries up. And if you touch a corn plant, the same thing happens—it dries up. That's what happens if you get hit by a lightning.

And ladies won't have children, too. They can't have children after that. Some people don't believe in what the older people used to say, but it's true. I tried to tell Victor Beatty, my mother's brother's son. I said to him, "Don't marry that girl, even though you've been with her for a long time." See, that girl got hit by a lightning, her and her sister, and she got it worst. They were in their wickiup and they saw a gun outside with the barrel pointed up. It was leaning against a tree. They went over there and grabbed it, and just about then a lightning hit it right on the end of the barrel. It got her on the hand and on her arm. They tried to tell her family to get A-2 to work on her. "He's good for that," they said. But that lady's father said, "I'll do it myself." He did, but it didn't work for him. It didn't work good. So when those two got married they couldn't have kids. They were married for over twenty years and still they had no kids. She was sick from that, too. It gave her heart trouble.

Lightning goes after anything that's got a sharp point. It goes after those little yuccas, *igáyé ts'osé* [narrow-leaf yucca], and that's why they used to chop them out right away if there's any growing close to the wickiup or house. Lightning always goes after those, so they dug them out and throwed them away. It goes after pine trees, too. One thing it never hits is a sycamore tree. It never goes after sycamore trees.

If somebody got hit by a lightning, my grandpa [William Goshoney] took care of it. He mixed some kind of herbs and boiled them. He gave the one that got hit a bath with it. He washed out their wounds real good. Then he gave them a big dipper full of it to drink. He says, "Drink this four times. Drink four big dippers full." Then he says, "If any of those fumes got into your system, if you inhaled them, this will get them out."

He worked on one lady that way. She got hit by a lightning—well, not exactly hit but it was real close. It hit the tree she was sitting under. She couldn't get up. She was just laying there. So that man, my grandpa, gave her a dipper full of that medicine. She drank it right away, as soon as she knew what was going on. Pretty soon, she started vomiting—yellow, green, orange. The next part was *black*! Then it was yellow again. He said, "If it's yellow the first time, all the colors will come out. If yellow comes out again, that's it, it's finished—you're going to get well." It was early in the morning when this happened.

They invited him to stay and pray for that lady at night. "What do we need?" they said. He told them. So they got all the stuff that he was gonna need. He started singing. He sang all night 'til morning. That lady was awake 'til way past midnight. Then he told her, "Well, I won't be bothering you no more. I'll just be singing for the rest of the night, so if you want to, go ahead and sleep." They fixed a bed for her right there. She went to sleep right away. He was sitting there close to the bed and a bunch of mens was helping him sing. They sang all night.

In the morning, before the sun came up, they woke that lady up. They started praying for her again. They took her out in the four ways and then around and back. He told her, he said, "Don't touch anything. Don't touch any plant that's growing, especially corn and squash." Then he told her, "Don't eat corn." That lady just sat there. He had to sing for her four nights. After that, she was all right.

"Use the Rain!"

One time, Goshoney made it rain. They had no rain for a long time. The people were worried. The rivers were drying up. The springs in the mountains were drying up, too.

So Johnny Lee—he owned one of the stores in Whiteriver—he asked some man from Canyon Day, "How can we make him [William Goshoney] sing for us?[17] He's the one that can do it. He can make it rain." They went over there to his home and asked him. Goshoney said, "Don't make a mistake. Don't ask me what I want you to give me or how much 'cause I don't want to hear about it. If you want to give me anything, it's on your own. Give me what you want." He said, "I don't complain. I don't say, 'It's not enough.' I don't say, 'I want more.'" He said, "That's the way it's supposed to be. That's the way I was *told* it's supposed to be. So I don't complain."[18]

So those traders got together. Johnny Lee and those other traders in Whiteriver went out and got him some groceries. In those days, people were *hungry*, so they gave him a whole bunch of groceries from their stores. They gave him some money, too. He accepted that. Then he said, "Well, we have to get started right away. If we don't, I might change my mind." That old man was stubborn! So they got ready real quick. Those traders brought lots of groceries to where he was gonna sing. They brought them there for the people to see.

Goshoney sang right there where the Baptist church in Whiteriver is at now. He lived down below by the river. Everybody brought their wood up there, whatever wood they could spare. They were camping all around the singing area. Goshoney told them, he said, "Don't come too close." He said, "If you come too close, you make me feel like I'm out of breath. So don't get too close, don't get too crowded." That's what he told them.

He started singing that night. It was *dry*! *Hot*! He sang four songs. Then some people were just *mean* to my grandpa. "I don't think he knows what he's doing," they said. "The way he's going, I don't think it's ever gonna rain." He knew right away what the people were saying about him. So after four songs, he stood up. He told the people, "Nobody must talk against me. Nobody must say, 'He can't do it,' or 'He's not praying right,' or anything like that. I don't want no part of that, not here. You can say it far away, if you want to, but not right here." Then he said, "I'm not doing this for myself. I'm doing it for everything—our land, our horses, our farms, our deer, our birds." He mentioned everything. Then he said, "If you don't believe, go away from here."[19] That's what he said. That's what he told the people.

He started singing again, him and the mens that were helping him. Close to midnight, the wind started blowing. It started blowing this way *real hard*! There's lots and lots of dust! Pretty soon it started blowing backwards the other way. Then the wind stopped blowing and the dust storm went away. He stopped singing. There was lots of clouds now. He started singing again and the fourth song he was singing is when it started dropping water. Then the thunder started, and pretty soon it started raining *hard*! That's when everybody got too excited. They were yelling their heads off! They were dancing in there! They were really *dancing*!

After he finished that fourth song, he told the people, "You people are wearing moccasin shoes, I know, and it's hard to get them wet.[20] But don't take them off! Let them get wet! And don't put a cover on your head or over yourself! Get wet! That's what we want! This is what you asked for! Use it! Use the rain!" So everybody did that. They kept on dancing! Their moccasin shoes were all muddy and wet and dirty, and still they kept on going, dancing and dancing. They kept going like that all night.

It was raining and raining, and it was thunder and lightning, and in the morning they were still dancing. Goshoney said, "Don't cover up! Keep on dancing!" Everybody was just soaking wet and dirty, some of them falling in the mud, all muddy, mud all over their clothes. One man said he lost his moccasin shoes in the mud. "They're in there some-where, but I can't find them. If you see them, give them back to me. They slipped off my feet in the mud."

My grandmother and my mother were in there dancing. They were dancing when it started raining, and when he told the people not to run and not to hide they stayed out there. They kept going! In the morning, my grandmother was marked from up here [chest high] all the way down. She was just *muddy*! I guess she fell down several times.

They had food ready but they can't eat 'til the rain stops. It stopped in the morning, so that's when they ate. Johnny Lee got his groceries and cooked a meal for everybody. He fed all the people after the rain. He was giving out loaves of bread to the people.

It rained all over the reservation. It rained in Whiteriver first and then it spread all over. It was raining for four days, off and on, and the grass and everything started coming back. The rivers got back up, too, and that's when everybody was *real happy*!

How to Get Up Fast

We used to visit that man [William Goshoney] all the time. He got mad if you didn't visit him. He was a funny old man. He got mad all the time. He had a stick, a cane, and he hit the ground when he's talking to you. He hit the ground hard with his old stick. Some of the children sat there and cried when he did that.

He always sat on his leg. He didn't squat. One knee was on the ground and one was up high. He said, "Do you know how to get up *fast?*" He said, "This is the way you're supposed to sit. This way, you're ready to go at any time." He said, "Don't sit on your butt! That way, you'll never get up!" He used to tell us that. That old man got up *fast!* He was sitting on his leg, and then, before you know it, he was standing up!

When he was a baby, that's when they gave him his name: Go-shoné. The Apaches, when they had a little baby—you know, a tiny one—the mother or grandmother sang a song to him. "Shoné, shoné"—that means "stinky one." When they took the baby out of the cradle-board, they sang that "stinky one" song for him. "Shoné, shoné." That's how Goshoney got his name.

Ann Beatty

My mother was Ann Beatty. That was her name. Her clan is T'iiskaadń [Cottonwoods Standing People]. She was born at Cibecue right across from the old day school. She was living close to there when she died. Her camp is still there. The posts got burned but some of them are still sticking out of the ground. She was a real tall old lady. She never did want to wear any kind of shoes. All she wore was moccasin shoes. That's all she ever wore.

My mother went to the government boarding school at San Carlos.[21] She got caught down there. They wouldn't turn her loose, so she stayed there and went to school for a while. I don't know how old she was when she got caught. She was grown, she said. She must have been around seventeen years old. I don't think she went to that school for more than two years.

She told me how she got caught. A bunch of people left from Cibe-cue. They were going after mescal at Nadah Cho Si'áń [A Big Agave

Heart Sits], down there by Patagonia. That's where they went. Coming back, they stopped below the fort at San Carlos. There used to be a lot of fields down there close to the river. Now they're under the lake [San Carlos Lake].

Anyway, that's where my mother got caught. She was walking to a waterhole to get some water. Two policemen followed her and caught her.[22] They asked her if she was going to school. They told her she had to go to school. They asked her what she was doing. She told them that they went after mescal and were going back to Cibecue. They said, "After you get through with that water, after you take it back over there, we're taking you to the school." So that's what they did. She got caught and went into that school. My mother said it had two floors. There were houses and buildings and a big fence all the way around.

My mother said they used to give the girls a handful of beads, all different colors. And they gave them a needle, a beading needle. Then those girls would go and do beadwork when there's nothing they had to do, like on Saturday and Sunday. And some of them would string up the beads and wear them around their neck. That's how it started, I guess. That's how Apaches learned to do beadwork.

Revolt at San Carlos

My mother used to talk about that school. "They used to be stingy with everything," she said. "They didn't give us enough to eat. We were always hungry. And if you want to get a drink, and you're supposed to be busy with something, the matron won't let you do that. She won't let you go to the bathroom, either, she won't let you go. She whipped the girls, too. If they did something wrong, they got punished. She whipped them with her switch."

My mother helped the girls run away. Years later, she said, "It wasn't funny when I did it, but now, when I think about it, it's funny." After she was in there for about a half a year, the matron whipped one of the younger girls. She was about thirteen or fourteen years old. The matron whipped her for something. Those bigger girls were all feeling bad about it, so some of them jumped the matron. It was inside a room. They broke the door down and went in there and jumped on her. I think they whipped her, too.

The government boarding school at San Carlos, San Carlos Apache Indian Reservation, date unknown. As a teenage girl, Ann Beatty was picked up by San Carlos police and placed in this school, where she remained for about two years. During that time she and others attempted to flee after a younger Apache girl was whipped with a barbed-wire switch by the school's Anglo matron. Later in life, Ann Beatty acquired a copy of this photograph and would occasionally show it to her children, saying, "Lots of children suffered here."

So they put all the girls in that room. My mother was in there with them. They were supposed to stay in there. But somebody went and put something sticky—like *jeeh* [pinyon pitch] or a gum—in the back door where it locks. The matron thought she locked the door but it wasn't locked all the way. Then she left and went off somewhere.

So all the girls were in there. Then those bigger girls each took a younger girl and lined up. They knew that the back door was open, so that's where they went. They told the younger ones, "Be quiet, don't cry. We're going home." They sneaked out.

They went across the playground and nobody seen them. My mother said they went to a hole that went under the fence. There was a ditch there, where the water from the kitchen washed out, and they crawled under the fence into the ditch. Those big girls usually carried a blanket and they were standing there, playing with their blankets, in front of that hole. They went under the fence—first a big girl, then the little one she's taking care of. Nobody knew it. Nobody even *knew* it!

They went up and over a wash, my mother said, and then they kind of scattered. They followed the wash as far as they could and settled down against the wall. That wash was deep, she said, and they couldn't see over it. Nobody could see them in there. Those little girls were *good*! They didn't cry or nothing. And about five o'clock, sometime around there, the bell rang for supper. Nobody came! They kept ringing the bell, ringing the bell, ringing the bell. *Nobody came*! They escaped.

But somehow a man that's working at the school was smart enough to look for their tracks. He found out where they went. He chased them down. He seen one of them in the wash. He told them to come out. They got scared. My mother said that they were running around everywhere. Finally, in the evening, they all went back to the school. They had to go back in there. They were gonna put those girls to bed without no supper, but that night the superintendent came over to the school. When he came, they went ahead and fed them. He told them to do that, so they did.

The next day, I think, they had a meeting with the principal. Those girls and their relatives went up there for a meeting. The principal told them, he said, "You're gonna have to ask your children what happened to them. They're stubborn, but go ahead and ask them." So somebody asked them, "Don't you like it here?" Some of the girls said they liked it. But one of the girls said, "Are you supposed to beat us like the matron did?" That's how the principal got in trouble, when she said that. He said, "Who got beat up?" That girl said that she did. She said, "It's not well yet. My back is hurting. I can't lay down no more." So they made her take her blouse off. There's lots of blood where it [the matron's switch] stuck into her and it pulled out some of her skin. My mother said her back was just *raw*! That matron was using a barbed wire switch. That principal lost his job. They kicked him off the reservation. That matron got fired, too.[23]

Carlisle Indian School

Right after that, they picked some girls to go to Carlisle.[24] My mother was one of them. They put them on a train right there at San Carlos. She said that she couldn't sit up on the train. She said that it made her sick, all those things moving outside. She just lay on the floor all the way. They got there. They stayed there. See, they don't let them come home. They just keep them there going to school. She said that she stayed there over one and a half years. Then they let her come home.

She said that it was better at Carlisle than San Carlos. They had enough to eat. And if they did something wrong, they don't whip them. They sent them to a room somewhere, and they had to stay there by themselves. Over there, they don't put two Apaches in the same room. They don't put other tribes together, too. The girls were mixed so they can't talk their own language to each other. They had to talk English. If they don't understand, the others taught them. Even in the dining room and everywhere they went, people talked to them only in English. My mother spoke English 'cause she went to Carlisle. All those that went to Carlisle spoke English real good. One of them didn't come back. She got sick and died over there.

Those girls came home on the train to San Carlos. Their parents were notified ahead of time. There was a place at the school for them to sleep if their parents didn't come and get them right away. They just stayed at the school 'til somebody came and got them. I guess they were all waiting for my mother where the train stops. All of them were waiting for her when she got off the train.

She never did go back to Carlisle. Her relatives were over there at John Lupe's farm on Salt River. They took her over there. See, there's no cars, no roads, nothing. She said that was the best thing in those days—no roads, only trails—and when the police from San Carlos came over there, looking for the children, they don't know which way to go. So they turned around and went back. I think my mother was about twenty years old when she came home from Carlisle.

Robert Beatty

My mother's brother was Robert Beatty. He was older than she was. He lived at Cibecue and Spring Creek. All of his children, except one, died from TB. He lost three boys and three girls. They were *pretty* girls! They died one after the other. I guess they just passed that sickness on to each other 'cause of the dishes they used and the things that they ate. Victor Beatty was the only boy that was saved. After Victor there was another boy, James, but he died when he was about sixteen. People tried everything for that TB. It helped for a little while but then they got sick again. Gussie Dehose had the same kind of sickness in her family. She had two beautiful sisters. But they died, too, one after the other.

My mother told me how they got the name "Beatty."[25] My uncle Robert had a fight with Túnch'íí' [Whiskey]. His English name was Peter Patterson. They got throwed in jail at Cibecue, and instead of taking them to Whiteriver the policeman took them to Globe. They took my uncle to a court. He couldn't write, so he couldn't spell his name. He named himself to the judge. The judge didn't understand it. My uncle said, "It's an Indian name, just write down 'Indian.'" And the judge said, "There's lots of Indians coming in here. I can't write down 'Indian,' it won't be right." So my uncle named himself again. "I can't get the sound," the judge said. "I can't pronounce it, but you have to have a name." Then he asked my uncle, he said, "Well, is it all right if I give you *my* name?" My uncle said, "Yes." So he became "Beatty." I don't know who that Judge Beatty was, but he gave my uncle his name.

School at Cibecue

I went to the school at Cibecue for a little while, maybe one month.[26] Later, when I was older, I went to school at St. Johns. We used to walk to the school at Cibecue from Spring Creek. Me and my brothers lived there with my uncle Robert. We used to walk from there to the school every morning—me and my brothers Joe and Dewey, and Victor and James Beatty. There's five of us, all boys except me.

Sometimes my uncle let us use the horses. We rode double-back and went over there to the school. But mostly we walked. I guess it's about four or five miles, it's not very far. At first it seems far, but after you get used to it, it's not far to walk. In the wintertime, my uncle felt sorry for us, so sometimes he brought the horses for us to ride to school. But it's too cold to ride a horse. Walking was warm, but it's too cold on horseback.

When we got over there to the school, they put us down in the cellar. There used to be a woodstove down there and it's warm. We sat there 'til school starts. They had lots of apples down there and we sat there and ate apples. They gave us lunch. School got out in the afternoon. Then we walked back home to Spring Creek. Sometimes my uncle came for us in his wagon.

It's only a two-room school. There was about twenty of us, not very many, and they split us in half, boys and girls. The teachers were white people, a man and his wife. That man's name was Delano, I think, something like that. He was *mean*! Nobody liked that man.

Wild Horses

My uncle Robert had lots of horses, maybe fifty head of horses. He had some right there at Spring Creek and some close to Spotted Mountain. He turned them loose up there. He had a pasture at Blue House Mountain, too. My brother Albert looked after my uncle's horses. He tamed them himself. My uncle told him, "Take whichever ones you want. I can't use that many, anyway." So my brother got his own horses that way. He gave my mother a horse with a baby with it. After a while, those two horses came to about twenty horses. Some of them were wild. There's still wild horses up there around Chediskai Tower. They're *wild*! You can't get close to them! Their tails are real long. I don't know how many times they tried to gather them all together. They caught some of them but they never caught them all. They're still out there. My mother used to say that some of them were hers. Those horses are very smart.

Emma Tulene and Willie Stevens

My father's sister was Emma Tulene. She was younger than my father. She married Willie Stevens. His father was a Mexican and his mother was Apache. His clan is Nádots'osíń [Slender Peak Standing Up People]. He was working at Fort Apache. The army was mostly gone, but still some mens had to stay there and watch the place. He used to come to Cibecue and Oak Creek on his days off. They had a big dance at Oak Creek—they danced for four nights, I think—and that's where he got acquainted with my aunt Emma. Then he went back to Fort Apache.

Later, my aunt went to Fort Apache with some of her relatives. They were selling bundles of grass to the army, and Willie Stevens was taking care of the horses. He was buying grass for the horses and that's how he met her again. They got married and started having children. They had nine children. First was George. Next was Jesse, Carl, Jimmy, Sam, Henry, Sadie, Virginia, and Sarah. Those are all my first cousins.

They lived at Chino Springs for a while with Willie's father and mother. Then he became a policeman and they moved down to East Fork.

He [Willie Stevens] knew some policemen in Globe that used to work for the army at Fort Apache. They asked him if he could come down there and work with them. So he and my aunt Emma moved to San Carlos and stayed there for a while. He became a policeman at San Carlos and then they asked him to come to Globe. So they moved to Globe. He was a county policeman in Globe 'til he retired. He worked in the courthouse there.

John Langley Tulene

My father was John Langley Tulene. His clan is Tséch'ishjiné. His father was Tulene. His father was from around Camp Verde, from some place they call Tú Ńlįį'. That's why they called him Tulene. He's the one that got killed by Mexicans on the road to Roosevelt.

My father was born somewhere on the trail to Payson, coming this way to Cibecue, probably close to Young. See, in those days, people were always traveling, so they had their babies wherever they were. And they didn't stay there after the baby was born—they moved on again. A lot of people were not born on the reservation, they were born outside. Like my brother Augustine, he was born at Mormon Flat. But he says he's from here 'cause his parents were from here.

My mother and father were raised close together. They used to travel with my grandmother-to-be, my grandmother Rose. They knew each other but they're not relatives. They got acquainted 'cause they traveled together. My mother said they got married when she was about nineteen or twenty. That was after she came back from Carlisle. Before she got married, my mother's uncle, Goshoney, was strict with her. He used to say, he said, "No one—no one!—will even come close to her." He used to make fun of her. "You better keep your britches on!" he said.

My mother and father had eleven children. They were all born about two years apart. The first was Eugene. My mother said he was born just before it was 1900. The next was Paul. He died when he was going to the boarding school at Rice. Next was Albert and then Jack. Then Donna, my sister, but she died when she was still young. Next was Joe, and next was me, Eva. Then Dewey. A girl died after him. She was just two days old. And another girl died after that one, too. She was stillborn. The last one was Augustine. All that's living now is Augustine and me.

I was the only girl in the family. I had one sister, Donna, but she died when she was seventeen. I had seven brothers and I guess I was treated more like a boy than a girl. I always wonder, "Why ever did my sister Donna die?" She was my only sister.

"We Sure Did Travel All Over"

My mother and father never did stay in one place very long. We sure did travel all over, it seemed like to me. Sometimes we stayed with John Lupe's family 'cause he needed help harvesting his wheat and taking care of his horses. Sometimes we stayed with my uncle, Robert Beatty, across from the old school at Cibecue or up at his fields at Spring Creek. We went to Camp Verde, too, and Fort Apache and Whiteriver and San Carlos. All over! My parents went wherever they're needed. They stayed with their relatives.

We were always traveling when I was small. One time, we were down there by Salt Banks. I remember going down to the river [Salt River]. They were cooking meat down there. We ate. Then they went inside the cave and brought out a sack full of salt and put it on a horse. We went across the river and up on top of the canyon [Salt River Canyon] to some asbestos mine. We stayed there for a while. I guess my father knew somebody that was working there. They were cracking rocks. They brought them out and dumped them on the ground. Then they cracked them and got all the asbestos out and filled up their sacks. I remember that.

My grandmother Rose went everywhere with us. It seemed to me like she was with us all the time. Even though she's married to that man [Frank Case], she left him at San Carlos and came with us. I guess he didn't mind it 'cause he never said anything about it. He had a bunch of boys and they were all at home. And my aunt Bessie, his daughter, she was home to cook for him.

One time, we went all the way to Camp Verde. My grandmother Rose and my mother knew all the acorn trees on that side. We went over there for acorns and my father got a job with a rancher. So while he was working, we stayed there and picked and picked and picked. I guess that man paid my father some money and took him somewhere to a store. He brought a whole bunch of groceries home. I remember that real good.

My father kept working for that man. I guess he was fixing fence, repairing fence. When he got through, we started back home. That man that he was working for loaned us a wagon 'cause we had too many acorns to carry on the horses. He had three wagons, little ones with two wheels, and he loaned us one of them. We put all those acorn sacks in there. Then we came back home to Oak Creek. I don't know what happened to that wagon. Somebody probably took it back.

My father had relatives at Camp Verde, and another time, when I was real small, we went over there. I don't remember very much, only a little bit. I know we were somewhere where there was lots of manzanita brush, lots of it, and when we went to get water I got lost in the manzanita. I thought they were real big trees, I guess, but they were just small. I got scared and started screaming. My mother found me. She told me to be quiet. "There's nothing wrong with you," she said. "Be quiet!"

"Don't Let the Sun Step Over You"

In those days, people were strict to their children. We used to get up early, real early before the sun was up. They told us, "Ch'igoná'áí nitis dahsol'ees hela'" [Don't let the sun step over you!]. And they always remind us of why. Some people were going somewhere. They were sitting under a walnut tree. They were cracking nuts, eating them. One of those people said, "Come on, let's go." So they all left except for one boy. One boy stayed behind. "Wait," he said. "I want to crack one more nut." He was going to crack one more nut but enemies were behind him. They got him, hit him on the head. He got cracked himself! So that's the reason they told you that story—you're not supposed to say no, 'cause if you say no something like that might happen to you. That's why they always told that old story.

They wanted their children to be strong. They made us go swimming early in the morning, even in wintertime. They throwed a big rock to break the ice. "Jump in! Jump in! Don't go putting your feet in first!" They got after you, if you tried to feel the water first. "You have to jump in," they said. "You have to jump in there!"

And when we came back, if we got cold from the water, they won't let us sit next to the fire. "Get warm outside," they said. "Go run! Go play! Run! That way you're gonna warm up fast, not sitting here by the fire." So we ran around and played tag out there. We ran around and chased each other. It works! It makes you warm real fast! After we got warm, we ate something, a little cornbread or something. Then the grown people went out to work. They ate mainly at night, in the evening. Nowadays, these people don't treat their children like they treated them back then. They just let them stay in bed, sleep a lot, do whatever they want. Nowadays, the kids are just running over them.

They used to make young girls grind corn. "Grind corn! Grind! Grind lots of corn and that will make you strong." And they made them go get wood early in the morning. They told them, they said, "Don't pick up dead wood that's on the ground! Find those dry sticks that's still on the trees! If you have to, use both hands to break them off. Jump up and break them off. If you break one off that's too long, put one end on a big stone. Then pick up another big stone and hit it right in the middle—then you'll have two pieces." That's the way they taught us to chop wood. I was about six or five when I started grinding corn and going out to get sticks for the fire. Sometimes I went with Joe, sometimes with Donna. I didn't go by myself. They told you not to do that.

They told you about the Bat, Ch'ábaané. It's way up there on a cliff and it comes down with a burden basket. It goes from side to side, sticking on the wall of the cliff. It goes down to the bottom. Then it starts looking for kids. If it sees one, a stray, it throws him in the basket and goes up the cliff. That's why you're not supposed to be by yourself. You're supposed to be with somebody at all times. Otherwise, they say, that Bat will come and get you. My grandmother Rose used to tell us that.

And my grandpa Frank used to sing that song, the one that Bat is singing when she's coming down the cliff. The Bat says:

I never fall,
I stick to the rocks.

Wherever I jump,
I stick to the rocks,
My feet are sticky.
I jump and I stick to the rocks.

In those days, people could go a long ways without anything to eat.
They didn't mind it. In a way, they're like the animals. You know how
the animals are—sometimes they don't get much to eat and not all the
time. But then they get food and eat what they need, and then they start
going again. It was like that with Indian people. They were strong, too.
They used to run a long ways, walk a long ways, miles and miles. But
they never seem to get tired. That's why the parents were strict. No
matter what happened, they wanted their kids to be strong.

Ndaa means "enemy," you know. When they said "Ndee ndaaye',"
it means "A human enemy is coming!" That's what they used to say in
those days. When we were small, they won't let us cry real loud. They
said, "Ndee ndaaye'! You have to cut it out!" They made us shut up
right away. They know what it leads to 'cause they always told the story
about what happened around Superior. Indians were going through
there and got attacked.[27] A bunch of mens was shooting at those Indians, killing them, so they were throwing their babies off the cliff.
That's what they told the children and they just quieted down right
away. Nowadays, these people don't know. Nowadays, children don't
listen.

When we were small, my mother used to go and help harvest corn
or wheat. Lots of times she did that. She put a little canvas down. She
told us, she said, "Stay right here! Don't move! Don't go anywhere. Stay
here. Here's water, here's some bread." She said, "Don't take too much
for yourself. Make it be enough for everybody, so all of you can have
some." So we stayed there and stayed there 'til she came back. If we
got sleepy, we slept right there on the canvas. We never did move.

Nest'áń Yoliłé (She Brings Home Fruits And Vegetables)

They started calling me Nest'áń Yoliłé. It means "She Brings Home
Fruits And Vegetables," something like that. Nobody knows it now
'cause all those that used to know it are gone. One of my grandmas gave
me that name. Her name was the same, Nest'áń Yoliłé. She gave me her

name. Her clan was the same as my grandmother Rose, Tséch'ishjiné, and they called each other *shik'isn* [my sister].

I don't know where that lady was from but I seen her first at Camp Verde. She carried everything in her blanket—her clothes, what she's going to eat, her cooking stuff, even a little ax—all tied up in a big bundle. She puts it over her back and starts walking. She walks from Camp Verde all the way to Oak Creek. And when she's ready to go back, she gathers whatever she's got and packs it in her blanket and starts walking again. She won't get a ride. They tried to give her a ride and she won't do it. She used to slap her legs. "This is gonna do the walking! This is what I'm supposed to use!" She used to walk from Camp Verde all the way to Roosevelt, and then to San Carlos and then down to Bylas. There's some people that lived close to Safford and she walked over there to visit with them. Then she walked back to Camp Verde. She won't ride nothing—not a horse, not a car, not a wagon. Her name was Nest'áń Yolilé. She was the one that gave me her name.

Chapter Two

Lots was going on, especially at San Carlos. We went down there after rations, and that's when my brothers—Eugene and Paul and Albert—got captured by the children catcher. He took them to the boarding school at Rice. My brother Paul died. Eugene ran off. Then we went to Miami. We stayed there a long time. My father worked in the mine there. That's when that bad flu came around. Lots of people died, *lots* of them, but we didn't lose nobody. My mother fixed that medicine, *izee libaahí* [dull-color plant medicine], and that's what saved us. That's the only thing that saved us.

*Rations at San Carlos—Badger's Eyes—Smith, the Children Catcher—"We Almost Got Stolen!"—Boarding School at Rice—He Never Had a Chance—Nadah Cho Si'áń (A Big Agave Heart Sits)—Somebody Was Teaching Him—An Awl for Ann Beatty—A Wagon for John Tulene—Silver Balls in the Water—Miami—"She Used to Hide Me All the Time"—A Sunrise Dance—*Izee libaahí *(Dull-Color Plant Medicine)—"We Got Out of There"*

Rations at San Carlos

They used to give rations away at San Carlos.[1] They did that before the winter. Everybody knew about it, so whoever's ready to go went down there together. They went from Cibecue, Oak Creek, Grasshopper, White Springs—they all went down there to get their rations.[2]

It took about six days, horseback. The trail went from Blue House Mountain to Cibecue, down to Salt Banks, across the river [Salt River], and up to that big mountain there, the one they call He Can't Remember His Song [Sįh Doo Yinaldíh Dah]. Then they went to Seven-Mile Wash and down that way to San Carlos. They didn't go to Globe, they went straight. They went to San Carlos where the armys used to stay. Where the people live now—what they call San Carlos now—that was Rice. Old San Carlos is under the lake now [San Carlos Lake].[3]

I went down there two times with my grandmother Rose. She took all the *béshnałtsoos* [metal paper]. It was a tin, kind of square, with a number on it. She got them and stringed them up and put them around her neck. Down there at San Carlos, when they're giving out rations, they took one family at a time. "How many are in this family?" They asked all kinds of questions. "Whose children are these?" But then again, it's written on that béshnałtsoos, that number tag. They used to go by that one.

We stayed at Rice and from there we went to get the rations in my grandfather's wagon. His name was Joseph Hoffman. He used to have a little house made of mesquite wood. I don't know how he built it. It's like a log cabin only it's made out of mesquite wood. It was on the side of the road there. My grandfather's wagon came from Mexico. I heard he traded a horse for it. It was a two-horse wagon, four wheels. The nurse down there had one like that. They called her "Castor Oil." They said, "Here comes Castor Oil, we better run!" I guess she gave people castor oil all the time.

My grandmother Rose went from Rice to San Carlos real early in the morning. Even so, she had to sit there and wait. When the people lined up to get their rations, it's like they're going to put cattle on a truck. There's a fence on both sides—what do you call that, a chute?—and there's just enough room for one person to go through. And those younger girls and mens, they're pushing each other and pushing each other back, giggling and laughing, going on, going on. They played too much, and I think that's the reason they put that fence up. My grandmother used to put me over on the side. She put a blanket down for me. "You stay right here," she said. "Don't move! Stay here! If I take you over there, they're gonna squash you!" Those people were pushing and shoving, pushing and shoving, 'cause they all want to get in there first.

They gave out lots of things. They gave out clothes for the mens,

Western Apaches waiting to collect rations at the commissary at Fort San Carlos, San Carlos Apache Indian Reservation, date unknown. The hourglass-shaped hair ornaments worn by two of the women (one seated, the other standing in line) indicate that they are unmarried. The two women in the foreground have raised their blouses over their heads for protection from the sun.

pants and shirts, and material for the ladies, twenty yards each. And they gave out canvas, twenty yards to each family. They gave out plates, spoons, knives and forks, and tin cups. And tin skillets and coffee pots, they gave those out, too.

They gave out government shoes for the boys and mens, and I guess they gave out shoes for the girls and ladies. They were kind of like tennis shoes 'cause that's what my grandmother gave me when we were over there. She said, "Put these on your feet 'cause we're gonna walk back to the wagon pretty soon." There was lots of stickers over there, those little tiny ones, those stickers that spread out on the

Western Apaches seeking rations at Fort San Carlos, San Carlos Apache Indian Reservation, about 1920. The man with a pole, probably an Apache policeman, permitted only a few people to move forward at a time. They proceeded down a wooden chute (visible at left), had their identities checked, and collected rations according to family size.

ground. She said, "Those things might get on your feet." I put them on. They were like tennis shoes. I never wore shoes before.

And they gave out "side-combs," that's what they called them. Those were for the girls to wear. It's a comb with little sparkling things on it, like tiny pieces of glass. It's pretty! Some of those girls painted their faces red with *chíh* [hematite]. They used to grind it up real fine and mix it with oil and put it on. During the summer, it keeps away the sunburn.

They gave out green coffee, too, and sugar and salt. You know, in those days, lots of people don't know what coffee is. They thought it was beans. So they were boiling it, boiling it, and it never got soft. "These beans are no good," they said. "These beans don't cook!" So they just throwed them away. The same way with tea—they don't know what it is. I guess they thought it was some kind of medicine.

The priests showed my grandmother how to cook coffee, so she knew what it was. She told the people, she said, "You're not supposed to boil it. You're supposed to burn it first 'til it gets real dark." She showed them how to do that. Then she showed them how to boil it 'til the water gets dark. "Just drink the water," she said. "Throw the rest away."

We used to bring two burros when we went down there after rations. They belonged to my grandfather, John Lupe. We packed the rations on those donkeys when we started back home. Those little things were real strong, stronger than the horses. We never had any trouble with them. They understood Apache. It takes longer going home than going the other way. Going home it's mainly uphill, and then again those rations were heavy. I think it took about seven or eight days to get back to Cibecue. But it's cool, so walking up the mountains was easy. And that was rations for one whole year. The following year, they did it again. That's the way they used to do.

Badger's Eyes

One time, the whole family went to San Carlos after rations. We went down there from Cibecue. We stayed at Rice with my grandmother Rose and her family. My mother and my father went and got the rations. We were getting ready to go back home, and that's when my uncle Pete —he's related to us on my father's side—came and asked my mother to help cut his wheat. He had *big* fields down there by the river [San Carlos River]. So my mother did that. They usually got all women to cut the wheat. If the mens did that, they scattered the seeds all over, so they don't want them working in there. Mens can do it faster but they're sloppy with it.

So we were down there at San Carlos and that's when I learned about black-eyed peas. My uncle brought a whole sack of those beans to my mother. He gave it to her. "You can have this," he said. "You can cook some for your kids. Some people don't like it, though." My mother started cooking those beans. She had some pork meat, and she cut it up and put it in there with the black-eyed peas. She made tortillas, too, and boiled meat with vegetables. When the workers came off the fields to eat lunch, she thought they were gonna go for the boiled meat. But everybody went and got those black-eyed peas. They really liked them. I asked my mother, I said, "What are those beans?" She said, "Ma' nteelé bidáá'" [badger's eye]. I said, "Why do they call it that?" She said, "'Cause it's got a real small black spot in the middle and the rest is all white. That's why they call it that, Ma' nteelé bidáá'."

Smith, the Children Catcher

When people from Cibecue and Oak Creek went to San Carlos after rations, those Indian police went around looking for children. Like Smith. Somebody named Smith was the main one that used to ride around looking for kids. He went all over, everywhere, looking for kids. And if he found one that's not in school, he took them to the government school at Rice. He captured them and marched them over there. That's what happened to my brother Paul. He went with my mother to the store, and I guess that man was watching them. He waited 'til they came out. He came and asked my mother, he said, "Is this boy going to school?" She didn't say nothing. Then he said, "This boy is supposed to be going to school, so I'm taking him with me." He marched my brother to the school. He put him in there. He stayed there. They won't turn him loose.

Then that man caught Eugene and Albert. He caught them swimming in the river [San Carlos River]. My mother told them not to go there in the daytime. She said, "After five o'clock, after everybody goes home from work, that's when you can go swimming." But they won't listen. It gets real hot at San Carlos, and I guess that's why they went to the river.

That man rode along the river all the time. The kids used to go there to swim and wash and just lay in the cool water. I guess my brothers were jumping around in the water and making noise and all that stuff that they do. That policeman came over there on his horse. My brothers said he sat there for a while. Then he went off. My brother Eugene said, "Who was that watching us?" And Albert said, "That's the policeman, the children catcher. That's the one we're supposed to be hiding from. Let's go!" So they put their clothes back on and just when they were getting ready to go—here he comes again! I guess he was watching them from somewhere where they can't see him. He marched them to the school.

That night my brothers didn't come home, so my mother and grandmother Rose got worried. They sent a man over to the school to see if they're in there. They're in there, but that man they sent couldn't get them out. "I tried," he said. "I tried to tell them you need those boys. They said they can't let them out."

My grandmother Rose got mad. She went over there. She went in there. She told my brothers, she said, "Go on! Get out of here! That's the door right there! Go on!" That man [Smith] tried to stop them. She told him, she said, "This is none of your business! Those are not your kids! You go tell your own kids what to do!" She said, "Those are my own kids, my grandchildren." Then she got after the principal. She told him, she said, "In the summertime you're supposed to let them out! You're just keeping them here 'til school starts again! There's no school going on now!" She said, "I'm gonna report you to the superintendent." I guess that principal got scared. My grandmother was *mad*, answering back, answering back. Finally he said, "If you want them, you can have them back. You can have them for one month. That's when school starts again."

My brothers came home for a little while. Then they went back to that school. They had to stay in there. They got government shoes and clothes, all the clothes they needed. My mother and my father wanted to be close to the boys, so we didn't go back to Cibecue. We stayed down there. And then again, there was nothing at Cibecue, no jobs at all. My father got a job working on the railroad tracks, replacing the broken woods [railroad ties].[4] We lived with my grandmother Rose and her family at Rice.

"We Almost Got Stolen!"

There were two wickiups at my grandma's home—one was hers and one was ours. I used to stay with my grandmother Rose over there where she was living. The boys were mean to me at home, picking on me and pulling my hair. And if I was eating something, they tried to get it away from me. My mother didn't like that, so she told me to stay with Rose. Weeks and months I was with her. The boys stayed away 'cause they know she'll get after them if they start picking on me. And then again she's got no small children, so she likes to have me there.

Western Apache homes and horses near Fort San Carlos, San Carlos Indian Reservation, date unknown.

The railroad tracks went by there, and there's a water tank close to where we lived. Wagon trains used to go over there and fill up their barrels. They're fifty gallon barrels, a hundred gallons on one side, a hundred gallons on the other side. Six or seven wagons used to come in together and park right there by the water tank. But I guess they took too much water, 'cause they [reservation authorities] told them not to park there anymore. They told them the water was just for the trains.

So my brothers built a well close to where we lived. It was summertime and they were home from school. They dug that well at night— lights, lamps—and they worked at that for a long time. Finally, they got water. We started getting our water there. There's lots of mesquite trees down there by the well and there's a space behind those trees. A Mexican and his wife used to live there. He took care of that water tank by the railroad tracks, and when the wagon trains came in—they came mainly from the west, from Globe—he told them not to bother the water. He locked the faucet on the water tank when he seen them coming. Before, there was no lock on the water tank and we used to get our water there. But now we can't do that, so my brothers built that well. That Mexican man found out about it. He came over and asked my brother Eugene, he said, "Can I get my water from here?" My brother said, "Yes, go ahead." That man got some water. He said, "This water tastes better than the water from the tank. The other one tastes like it's got oil in it."

Two of those wagons came by and one of them was wanting water. I guess they heard about that well we had 'cause they came over with the wagon. It's *big*! Eight mules were pulling it, eight on each side. It's hauling groceries, I think, 'cause there's lots of food in sacks on there. Those people came over and filled up their barrels. And they left us two big slabs of bacon, and a big sack of flour, and fifty pounds of potatoes, lard, and I don't know what else we got. They gave us all that food for letting them get the water.

They're a nice family, a man and his wife and two kids. Their wagon is *tall*. It's got two decks. There's a deck on the bottom—that's where they kept all their blankets and stuff—and there's another one on top. The one on top is where they piled the sacks of food. Well, me and my brother Dewey went over there. We were standing there, looking at the wagon. Then we started playing with that lady's kids. Pretty soon, we were playing inside the wagon where they keep their beds. After a while, they started off. We didn't even know it! We were having fun playing inside and we didn't even know it! They were going towards Globe.

My mother found out that we're not around. She told my grandmother Rose. I guess they got scared. My grandmother said, "They were playing with those two little kids. They might be in the wagon. They're going somewhere—*away*!" They told my brother Eugene. He got on a horse and took off. He caught us close to Cutter. All of us kids inside the wagon were asleep. They found us in there. We got out. That lady said, "I'm sorry, I'm sorry, we didn't look in there." She gave us some apples. We rode back home with my brother. We almost got stolen! I guess *anything* can happen to a little child.

Boarding School at Rice

There's a fence around that government school at Rice.[5] My mother used to go over there and try to give my brothers food. The boys were

The U.S. government boarding school at Rice, San Carlos Apache Indian Reservation, 1905. For more than three decades (1906–1940), the primary purpose of this school was to prepare Apache children for assimilation into Anglo society by teaching them manual skills and "civilized" forms of behavior. For many pupils at Rice, including three of Eva Watt's brothers, it was a terrible experience marked by malnourishment, sickness, and physical abuse at the hands of school authorities.

on one side of the fence and she was on the other side. They didn't give those kids enough food. My brothers were always asking for something. I don't know what kind of food they gave those children to eat, mostly beans, I think, and cornbread.

Sewing, mostly, is what they taught the girls. They used to make their own dresses to go to school in and shirts for the boys. They mended stuff that was torn up, too. They got punished for talking their own language. If they caught them talking their own language, they put chili in their mouth—you know, that cayenne chili powder—and then they taped their mouth shut.

They used to make the boys chop wood and work in the fields. They did lots of things, lots of work, and *real dirty* jobs, too. Back then, they didn't have a flushing bathroom. They didn't have that kind of

Western Apache girls with superintendent, Rice Indian School, 1905. For reasons unknown, the girls are building miniature wickiups.

toilet. They had an outside toilet, and they put a pot under there and used it like that. The boys had to go in there and clean those things out. They had to empty those pots and scrub them and clean them out. That's what they used to do. And those boys were whipped. If they did something wrong, they had a hose that they whipped them with. It was terrible the way they went to school back then. I don't think anybody knows how bad those children were treated.

The boys used to tame wild horses, too. They tamed them first, and then they put them to work in the fields. Eugene almost broke his arm doing that. It's dislocated, it looks like he's got two elbows. It was so swelled up! He couldn't use his hand but they made him take care of the horses anyway. He sneaked off from school. He left the horses in a corral by the river and came home. He ran off to his mother.

It was a good thing, 'cause my mother was already cooking. She

Western Apache girls at Rice Indian School, 1905.

was waiting for the family to come in and eat. My brother ate and ate. When my father came in, he asked him what was wrong with his arm. He took the wrapping off and it looks like he's got two elbows. So my father got hold of his arm and twisted it around. It made that popping noise, it went back into place. After that, they put that rag on again. Then my brother said, "I won't tell them that I came home. I'll tell them that one of the horses ran off from me and I had to catch it." So he went back. He got the horses that were in the corral and took them back. He didn't want to be late.

He Never Had a Chance

My brother Paul never had a chance. They had fields of vegetables and corn over there [at the boarding school at Rice] and him and three other boys were hoeing. It started raining hard, so they ran inside and stayed there 'til it quit. There's a wickiup close to the fields—nobody was living in it, I guess they moved away—and a lightning hit it. It burned and burned. The fire went out but those logs were *still smoking*! That man, that Smith, came over there and told those boys to tear that wickiup down. He told them to pull it apart and drag the logs to a ditch.

But it's *still smoking*! One of the boys tried to tell him that it's too fresh to be working on. But he [Smith] said, "Pull it apart. It's gonna start a fire in the field." He made them tear that wickiup down. They dragged the pieces way out there and throwed them in the ditch.

That's when those young boys inhaled that smoke, the fumes. All of them—all *four* of them—got sick and died within a month. The first boy that died went inside the wickiup and was cutting the yucca that holds the pieces together. He's the first one that died 'cause he was inside. The others were pulling it apart from the outside. They all died. They all had trouble with their stomach. They can't eat. Everything they eat comes up! And if they drink water, it comes up smelling just like gunpowder. That *terrible smell*, gunpowder!

They kept my brother Paul in the infirmary at the school. They wouldn't turn him loose, they wouldn't let us take care of him. So my mother sent for Willie Stevens. He was a policeman at Globe. He came and my mother asked him, she said, "I heard my son is very sick but they won't let me see him. I haven't seen him for two weeks now. Would you go over there and ask about him for me?" So he [Willie Stevens] went over there. He finally got my brother out but he was *just nothing*! So skinny! He had nothing to him! His skin was just dry and cracking. They had to take a wagon to get him. They brought him back home in the wagon. He stayed just four or five days with the family—then he was gone. A *young boy* like that!

They said he didn't eat at the school and when he came home it's the same way. We tried to give him things he really likes. He won't eat. My grandmother Rose tried everything for him. She tried to give him herbs, medicine. It helped him but his stomach just got blocked up. His skin turned kind of yellow. And when they talked to him, he didn't understand them. "What are you talking about?" he said. He was afraid of clouds. "There's too many clouds over my head, they're coming too close to me," he said. After he inhaled those fumes, he started talking that way. And he won't let his mother out of his sight. He wanted to be with her all the time. But when his father or his brothers came inside the wickiup, he told them, "Go outside! Go stay outside!" I remember this 'cause my brother Dewey and me were with my mother there. When my mother went inside, we tried to follow her. My brother had a switch. "Go on, get away from me," he said. "Go on outside." Dewey was still breast-feeding. He cried and cried. My brother wouldn't let Dewey inside, so my mother had to come out to feed him. Boy, that was awful. I had no idea what was going on.

Some people went and talked to that man [Smith]. They were relatives of those boys that died. They got after him. They told him, they said, "Do you understand that you murdered those four boys? You killed them by making them inhale that stuff! You should have done that yourself. *You* should have pulled that wickiup apart yourself, not those boys." He said, "It's not the lightning that made them sick. You know it's not the lightning." They told him, "It's bad for people to breathe those fumes, especially young kids. They don't know what they're doing. You're afraid of it yourself and that's why you made those boys do it. Now they're gone!" They almost got that man. Somebody took a shot at him. He was riding around on his horse. He didn't ride horses after that! He quit his job. He took off somewhere and never did come back. He should have respected the customs of the Indians.

After my brother died, Eugene ran away from that school. He didn't like it there. He went down to Roosevelt and got a job there. My mother and my father knew where he went but they didn't tell nobody. They didn't want him back in that school again. The police looked all over for him, even at Roosevelt. They went over there but they couldn't find him. He was working around the lake [Roosevelt Lake] picking up rocks. The police just looked where the dam is at and went on. My brother was way across the lake, way on the other side, so they couldn't find him. He stayed with his job at Roosevelt for a long time.

My brother Albert was still at the school. He told my mother he didn't like it. He said, "The people are too mean in there, the teachers and all of them." They whipped him for some reason, I don't know why. He wouldn't say nothing about it but you could see that big old mark on his back. That's when my mother got him out of that school. She went to the Catholic priest and they went over to the superintendent. She told him, she said, "I'm taking my son whether you want me to or not. From now on, my kids are gonna go to school at St. Johns."[6]

They were taking kids to St. Johns the following week. Albert and Jack went first. Then my sister Donna and Joe went down there. Dewey and me stayed home with my mother and father. Augustine wasn't born yet.

All of us kids went to St. Johns except for Eugene and Paul. Jack went the longest, about eight or seven years, I think. Joe stayed seven or six. Albert went for about three years. Then he went to work for A-2 [William Goshoney]. A-2 asked him, "Come home with me and take care of the horses." So he did that. My sister Donna went to school down there but then she got sick. She had to come home. My brothers used to come back for vacation in the summer. Wherever the family was at—Miami, Roosevelt, Mormon Flat—the priests brought them back for the summer. We were glad to see them! After my father died, me and Dewey went to school down there. That was 1924. Augustine was the last one to go to St. Johns.

Nadah Cho Si'áń (A Big Agave Heart Sits)

We used to go after mescal at Nadah Cho Si'áń.[7] It's down there close to Patagonia. I was about five or four when I went down there. I went with my grandmother Rose. There were about six families with all the strong boys they could find. The boys helped the mens dig the pit for cooking the mescal. It's hard work 'cause that pit has to be deep and big around.

They didn't go on a wagon in that direction 'cause sometimes they fought with the Mexicans down there. They said those Mexicans might try and steal the wagon. That's why the mens took only horses, horses and donkeys. And they didn't make fires at night except when they cooked the mescal. They cooked it at night 'cause then, in the morning, all the wood was burned and there's no smoke that somebody can see. They were careful with their smoke.

The mens and boys took the horses ahead of the ladies. The ladies and girls went down there on the train. We rode on the train to Bowie and Busy Bee [Bisbee] and Douglas. The mens were waiting at Douglas with the horses. We got off there. Then everybody got together and went to Nadah Cho Si'áń. That mescal was *big*! *Tall*! Now it's almost all gone.

They cooked lots of mescal down there. They packed it on the horses and donkeys. Everybody walked back to San Carlos, mens and ladies both. Nobody rode on the train. It takes about a week to get there, maybe more. We didn't walk on roads—there's not many roads in those days—but there's a trail and we used that one. There's two or three mens that stayed behind the rest. After everybody's passed, they swept the trail, the tracks, so people won't know where we went.

When they got back home, they traded with that mescal. My grandmother Rose gave my mother a lot of it and she went and took it to the store. The storekeeper was friends with my mother. That lady told her, "Bring it over." So she took it over there. That lady said, "We'll cut it with the meat saw." They cut it up. Then they wrapped it up in paper and put it in the showcase inside. And when those Indians came around, as soon as they seen it, they bought it. I think that lady sold it all in three days. Then my mother got what she needed from the store.

I think it was the last part of August when they used to go to Nadah Cho Si'án. It's hills down there, bare hills, and you could see lots of *nadah* [agave] on top. It used to be like a *forest*, but now there's not many left. They probably got them all.

What you do is sharpen a big pole, something that's hard and long, about six or seven feet long. They used mesquite for that pole. Then you have to have a big rock to hit it with. The pole goes under there, under the nadah, and it keeps going 'til it gets close to the middle. Then they push on it, up and up and up, and finally that nadah comes out of the ground. It's hard work! Then you cut the leaves off, the thorn parts, and what's left is the middle part. That's the one they're gonna barbecue. It's heavy! You have to carry only one at a time to where they're digging the pit.

Then you have to gather wood. It's not very scarce 'cause there's lots of dry mesquite around. Then you cut up those yucca stalks 'cause you use that for kindling in the bottom of the pit. Then you chop your woods and put them on top of that. You have to split the woods 'cause it burns better that way. And after you think the woods is enough, you put the nadah in there. Then you put more woods on top of the nadah. Then you put rocks on top of that, real careful, 'til you can't see no more woods. The rocks are piled way up high on top of the pit, like a hill. Then you put those leaves, the thorn ones, on top of the rocks. You put them on top of the rocks so the dirt won't get in there. And then you put the dirt on, lots of dirt, with buckets or *táts'aa'* [burden baskets].

Then you light it in four places. You light the first one and then you run to the next one and light it there, and then you run to the next

Western Apache woman uprooting an agave plant, 1906. A prized Apache food-stuff, hearts of agave were roasted in underground pits, pounded into trans-portable cakes, and frequently used as trade goods.

one and light it, and there's one more after that. There's four places. You start with east and run all the way round. The person that does that is the one that looks the healthiest. "So it [the roasted mescal] will have lots of juice in it," that's what they used to say. I did that one time. "You," they said, "light the fire." I ran around and lit it. The next morning I went down to the stream. I was standing there under a little waterfall taking a bath. Then I ran back. "Where did you go?" they said. "Down to the stream. I washed myself over there." They said, "Good, that's what you're supposed to do." They sat there for a long time. They had a big bucket full of tea. They were sitting there, drink-ing tea. Then they said, "We have to go and look at it to see if there's any steam coming out." So we went down there to check it.

The mescal stays in the ground for two nights. With barbecue corn, you put it in the ground in the evening and take it out early the next morning. But with this one, nadah, you have to leave it in there for two nights. Then you dig it out. They have to be real careful 'cause the dirt might go in there when they're digging it out. They take the dirt a long way from the pit before they throw it away.

Sometimes they went down around Fort Huachuca to get mescal. Some Mexicans used to trade for it. One time, my mother got two donkeys. Those Mexicans used to bring wood. "After it's cooked, let's trade," they said. In those days, people got lots of stuff from Mexico—buckets, galvanized cans, axes, and pottery. And those little two-wheel wagons, they got those from down there, too. They exchanged that cooked mescal for what they wanted.

Somebody Was Teaching Him

My grandfather, Joseph Hoffman, was the only one with that name. All the Hoffmans are descended from him. He was from Cibecue but he lived at San Carlos 'cause he married a lady from down there. He had a lot of boys but most of them died. A lightning hit a pine tree when they were bunched around it. That's how he lost his boys. It happened up at Ash Creek. They were with the cattle up there doing the cowboy's job. When the raining and thunder started they got under that pine tree—and that was it! My grandpa [Frank Case] said that a whole bunch of them got hit, not only those Hoffman boys. There were other mens with them. There were about twelve of them under that tree.

Joseph Hoffman saved one of his boys. He sang for him. Those other boys died, not all of them at once but two or three weeks apart. The songs he sang were given to him in a dream. That's how he became a medicine man. He dreamed his songs. When he was just starting out, they said, he sang for four nights. He sat there and sang all night long for four nights. His wife tried to tell him, "Aren't you sleepy? Why don't you go to bed? Why don't you eat something?" He won't listen. He just kept on singing. He sat there by himself for four nights.

I guess some other mens were listening to him. They said it sounds like somebody was teaching him. The first song he sang, he stopped in the middle. He just sat there. Then he started all over again. He did like that 'til he got to the end of the song. Then he waited for a while and sang the same song again. He sang thirty-two songs like that. Four nights he sang all night long. He was singing those songs over and over again. He usually stopped in between songs, but the last night, the fourth night, he kept singing all the way through. In the morning, he was just sitting there. Finally, he went to sleep.[8]

After he woke up, he told the people, "I'm sharing what was given to me." He said, "If you fall in a flood, or if you get hurt from the rain, I can cure you. And if you get hit by a lightning, I can cure you." Then he told the people, he said, "Don't bring me gifts like you bring to other people. You always bring them moccasin shoes or a saddle or a horse. Don't give me those things. I can't accept nothing that's been alive, like a deerskin or a cowskin. I can't accept nothing like that."[9]

He used to eat lots of manzanita berries. One time, a lady brought him a whole sack. She told him that her granddaughter was in a wickiup and a lightning hit it and it started burning. Her granddaughter ran outside. That lady said, "She's all right but she's *down*, you know. I think she inhaled some of the smoke from that lightning."

So he fixed something for that girl. They call it *i'dii ch'il* [thunder bush]. He boiled that and gave it to her. He prayed for her and told her to drink it all, the whole cup. I guess it made her real loose 'cause she was going and going. He said, "Give her some more. Give it to her four times, four cups, until you don't smell that awful smell in there." So that's what she did. That medicine just cleaned her stomach out and she was all right. She's still living down there at San Carlos, I think. She's real old now.

When Joseph Hoffman was young, there was a big dance at Canyon Day. He came up there and they picked him to serve. They picked four boys and four girls. They were dancing together for a whole week! He was the leader on the boys' side and his wife-to-be was the leader on the girls' side. They were always together. He went home. He couldn't stay down there! He came running back to Canyon Day! That's how he married his wife.

She went with him down to San Carlos. She went with him to where he lived. You know, a man used to stay away from his wife's mother. He hides from her and that shows great respect. They don't talk and they don't see each other. She can cook for him but somebody has to take the meal to him. And if he kills a deer or gets meat of some kind, he gives some of that to her. That's the way it used to be. They had great respect. They don't do that no more. Nowadays, some ladies even dance with their son-in-law. My mother seen it happen down there at San Carlos. She said, "They're turning into a fox. Now they're all foxy."

An Awl for Ann Beatty

Those wagon trains I told you about used to camp for the night close to Globe. There's a big wash over there and they dumped some trash in the wash and tried to cover it with sand and dirt. My mother was looking for roots of mesquite trees. Those roots are long, like a string, and she used them for her baskets. She was looking for those roots when she seen that trash hanging out from under the sand. She was wondering what it was, so she started poking around in there. That's when that little pointed thing, that awl, fell out. She picked it up. She was *so happy* that she found it! She dug out all that stuff they buried but it's nothing but trash and cans that they opened. She burned all the paper and she put the cans back in there and covered them again. From that time on, she had that awl. She had it 'til she died. She used it all the time, especially for making baskets and moccasin shoes. It's a little one with a bone handle. My mother just *treasured* that little awl.

A Wagon for John Tulene

My father was given a wagon. It was around Christmas, I think, and the government had a bunch of wagons. I don't know where they made them but they brought them to the army camp at San Carlos on the train. They gave them out to mens with big families. My grandpa Frank heard about it. He asked my father, he said, "Do you want a wagon? They're giving them out to the big families. I got one already." So my father went over there and got himself a wagon. He got the harness, too. He borrowed some horses and then he drove the wagon back to Rice.

My grandpa Frank, when he was in the army, learned how to take care of a wagon. So when my father got home, he told him to go to the store and see if there's any axle grease. He told him, "Go buy some *ik'ah*" [fat; grease]. My father went over there and got the one for cooking. He brought it back. "Not *that* kind!" my grandpa said. "You're sup-

posed to say, "Tsịnagháí bi ik'ahí bijád" [grease for the wagon's legs].
If you say it that way, they'll give it to you." He showed my father how
to put it on. "It walks easier that way," he said.

My father got mules for the wagon. When he got the wagon, they
wrote his name down. They brought the mules on the train to San
Carlos. My grandpa and father went over there. They stayed there for
two days. They got there two days ahead of time. They got themselves
the mules. My grandpa knew more about mules, too, so he showed my
father what to do with them. My father had that wagon for a long, long
time.

My father and my mother used that wagon when they were making
woods [firewood]. They used to make about four loads every day. They
got mostly mesquite wood 'cause it makes lots of heat. My mother sold
those woods in Globe. She parked up there where the courthouse is
now, up on that hill. She parked the wagon up there and the people that
had stores came over there and got it. Those stores used to need lots of
wood. There was a Chinese—he had kind of like a café—and he bought
wood from my mother every time she brought it.

Silver Balls in the Water

Before we went to Miami, we were living on this side of Globe. There
used to be some kind of mine there. That's where they were working,
about seven or eight Indian families. We stayed down there about two
or three months in the summertime. It was *hot*! They were digging in
the ground. They were using pick and shovel.

There was a big hill and a wash below it, and right there, underneath that hill in the wash, there was a wet. My mother thought it was
water, so she started digging that place out and it *was* water. It was all
muddy. She kept digging it out, throwing that muddy water off to the
side. It was getting clearer and clearer. She cleaned it all out and the
water was coming out real clear after a while.

That's when I saw those two things, something like balls. They
were floating in the water. They were silver—I mean, they looked like
silver—and I thought they were marbles or something. I tried to get
them but I couldn't. They're too soft. Well, my mother went home and
me and my brother Joe were still playing down there. My mother left

a dipper there. My brother dipped them out, those silver balls, and he took them back home. He put them in a cup.[10]

We were fussing over those things, me and Joe. My mother wanted to know what we were fighting about. "That's my ball! No, that's my ball! That's my float!" My mother took the cup away from us. She wanted to know what's in there. I said, "I don't know. There's lots of them in the water down there." So she went back down there and looked in the water and there was more of them. She went up to the mine and got the man that's running it. She took him down there. He said, "You can't drink that water." He said, "It's mixed with something." I don't know what he told her but he won't let us drink that water. He told her, he said, "Get your water from the tank up there that we're using. Just come up there and fill your jugs. Don't drink water from down here."

Sometimes my father and mother went to town with that man to get groceries. He had a flat wagon and he always told them, "Don't bring your kids, will you? Come, if you want to, but leave your kids at home." See, that wagon was just flat—it had no sides—and he was afraid that the kids might fall off. Another family's daughter fell off and cracked her head on a rock.

Miami

There was lots of mens working in the mines at Miami. They came from everywhere—San Carlos, Cibecue, Camp Verde, Bylas, Winkelman. The Indians used to live at the far end of town where the road goes off to the right [Arizona State Route 287]. There's a wash there and the Indians lived along the wash. They built their wickiups there.[11]

My father worked at the Bluejay Mine—I think that's what they called it—carrying tools to the workers. They had a little wagon, a cart, that runs on tracks way up there on top of those big white clay mountains [mine tailings]. That's where my father worked. His main job was to fix the tools. He put handles on the ones with broken handles—pickaxes, shovels, things like that. He used to sharpen them, too. He used to heat them up and pound on them and sharpen them again. The workers throwed the tools close to the tracks. My father picked them up and put them in the cart. Then he came back and fixed them. And then,

Homes of Western Apache mine workers near Miami, Arizona, 1931. About a decade before this photograph was taken, Eva Watt may have lived here with members of her family.
During that time, she was hidden repeatedly from mounted Apache police searching for
children to enroll in the boarding school at Rice. In 1918–19, when influenza broke out, Mrs.
Watt's family was one of the few in her encampment that suffered no losses.

when they're fixed, he put them in the cart and took them back to the
workers.

That was dangerous work 'cause sometimes the cart used to slip
off the track and roll all the way down to the bottom of the mountain.
My father didn't like that, so when he had a chance he got another job.
He went to where they're taking the white clay out. He was always talking about it. He said, "I have to dig the clay out. It gets thick in front of
the door." Those mountains of white clay are big now. They have blue
streaks. I guess that comes from the copper.

Sometimes they brought big rocks out of the mine with a wheelbarrow or a cart. They brought them out in the open and the mens used
to bust them with hammers. My father did that, too. See, the Indians
won't go in the hole that goes into the mine. They won't do that. And
then again, they were told that they were just in the way 'cause they
don't know what to do in there. So they told them to bust those boul-

ders. Then they took the pieces to where they separate the copper from the rock.

I guess they burned some kind of ore or something up there. You could see it at night. There's a machine that comes out of the mine and spills it over the side. And you could see all that red fire coming down, coming down, coming down. Red fire! It came down from that burning machine on the side of that big clay mountain.

I think those mens, the Indians, got paid about thirty dollars a month. But in those days a dollar is *a lot of money*! My father made enough money to feed the whole family. It seems like he never did spend it, though. My father and my mother were really taking care of their money. "We're saving it for a hard time later." That's what they used to say. My mother had a baking powder can, a big one. It was just *full* of coins and stuff. And at night, when everybody went to sleep, she dug a hole somewhere and put it in there. I found that out later when she told me herself. She put that can in the hole, way down in the ground, close to where we lived. She said she put a big rock on top. If the rock was moved, she knew that somebody must have been watching her. "It never was moved," she said.

"She Used to Hide Me All the Time"

My grandmother Rose wouldn't let me go to school. She used to hide me all the time, me and Dewey both, when we were living at Miami. See, those police from San Carlos went all over looking for children. They had the names of the parents in a book, so they know how many kids are in the family. And if they found them—you know, school-age children—they took them to that school at Rice. They kept them in there.

We lived in Miami on the far end, below the Catholic church where the road goes to Superior. There's a sand hill there—there's houses on it now—and the Indians used to dig out places on the hill to make their homes. Then a big rain almost washed them out, so they moved up higher, across the wash on the other side. That's where we lived, and that's where those police from San Carlos came looking for us, the children. My grandmother Rose *always* knew when they're coming. I don't know how she knew but she *always* found out. I guess she was always looking.

Western Apache women carrying loads of firewood, location and date unknown.

So she hid me when those police came around. They came at any
time, not just on certain days. We used to go up the wash early in the
morning. We sat there for a long time. The next day, if we went up there
again, it's not to the same hiding spot. We kept going up, going up, way
up high. We were sitting up there by the time they got to our camp.
Sometimes they hollered for us from down there. My grandmother
said, "Stay down! Stay down!" After a while, they went away.

One time my grandmother said, "Hurry up! Put your moccasin
shoes on!" I thought we were gonna go get wood 'cause just about all
we did was go get wood. I put my moccasin shoes on and we went
in the wash all the way to the top. "Go over the top," she said, "just
on the other side." She said, "Watch me and don't move. I'm gonna
be chopping wood right here. If anybody comes to see me, watch me.
If somebody comes to talk to me, watch me. If that happens, go hide
somewhere else." So I went up there. She was chopping wood but I
was sitting there watching her. I stayed up there for a long, long time.

Lots of times, my aunt Bessie was the only one at home when they [policemen from San Carlos] came. They asked her, they said, "Where's your mother? What's she doing?" She always told them, "Oh, she went after wood in the mountains. She left here early in the morning." They tried to follow us one time but there's too many rocks. They couldn't find no tracks. They knew we're up there, I guess, but they never did find us.

We were sitting up there in that brush—*ch'il nteelé* [shrub live oak], they call it—and it just spreads out. It's not very high but the leaves are long. Nobody can see your head sticking up or nothing. My grandmother fixed a little place in there and that's where we were hiding. We crawled in there and it covered us. They can't see us in there. We had water and we had lunch. My grandmother was sewing—I think it was moccasin shoes—and every time she ran out of thread I had to thread the needle for her.

Then, about midnight, we started down towards the camp. Those two policemen were still sitting there! My grandmother seen them but they didn't see her. She was in front of me. She came running back up! I was running to her. "Be quiet, they're still there!" she said. "We have to go back up for a little while. We can go back down when they leave." So we stayed up there. Then they got back on their horses. You could hear the horses going. When we couldn't hear the horses no more, we walked back down. My grandpa Frank said, "They just left." He told us, he said, "You two better go somewhere. Go to some neighbor's house and sleep. They might come back here."

One time, Joe got caught. He got caught in Miami. He was home for summer vacation. He was walking on the road below those big clay mountains and that's where he got caught. He told the policeman to take him to the Catholic church. That priest knew Joe and all the family. He told the policeman, he said, "This boy belongs to St. Johns. He's supposed to go to school there. He's already on the list to go back." So they let him go.

I never went to school 'til I went to St. Johns. I was around eleven or twelve years old. That's why the police from San Carlos were after me. I could have went to school, I guess, but my grandmother Rose didn't want it. She didn't want me in there. "I don't want them to hurt her," she said. She got that idea in her head and she was a scary person [a person easily scared] in the first place. So she hid me all the time. Finally, I followed my sister and brothers and went to school at St. Johns.

A Sunrise Dance

They had a sunrise dance close to where we were living.[12] In those days, they never did have a big sunrise dance. It's small. There's no big crowd and they don't give away lots of stuff like they do nowadays. We went over there and slept with those people that were putting on the dance. In the morning, I seen that sunrise girl. She was up. She was putting on her moccasin shoes. Her godmother was already dressed. She looked real nice.

The girl had to make a fire—that's how they start—but she didn't have the woods already setting there. She had to go and get them. They told her, they said, "Go up the mountain and break the dry branches off of a tree." They told her, "Don't use just one hand. Use two hands together. Pull down evenly and when it breaks off put it aside. When you think you have enough, tie it in a bundle with *igáyé* [broadleaf yucca]. Carry it on your back and come back down. Then make a fire." Her godmother did the same thing, 'cause she has to get wood for her own fire. They got two big bundles of cedar wood.

Then that lady showed the girl how to make the fire. After she made it, she picked up her *tús* [water jug] and rushed to the water. She filled up her tús and brought it back. She put it down. Then she ran to the east and came back and ran around the fire. "Sit down," they told her. She sat down.

They had a big bowl of corn, soft corn, and they put that close to her. She starts grinding. She grinds it all the way through 'til the bowl is empty. Her godmother was watching her. She's grinding corn, too, showing her how to grind, telling her not to put too much on the grinding stone, only a handful. She said, "Don't put two handfuls on there 'cause it's gonna fall off." So the girl did that. She kept it up.

After the girl got done with her grinding, she stood up. "Go get your pot," her godmother said. She got her pot and put water in it. She put it on the fire for the water to boil. They gave her a spoon to put salt in the water, just a little bit, and she did that. Then she starts putting her corn in there, stirring it and stirring it. That lady that's teaching her was doing the same thing, 'cause they have to do everything together.

Then the girl made cornbreads, little ones about that big [3 inches in diameter]. Her godmother was showing her how to do that and the girl was really watching. After she got done with making the cornbreads, she put a few berry leaves in a pot of water. They're leaves of *ch'ink'ózhé* [skunkbush] and she put them in there. She boiled that for about ten minutes. Her godmother did that, too. Then that lady gave the girl her first bite of corn. She fed her. Then the girl fed her godmother. They did the same with that berry tea. The girl drinks first, not much, and then that lady drinks it. After that, they're done.

They don't eat the food that's left over. The girl put the rest out for the people, for her own family and her godmother's family. Everybody just got one bite, that's all. You just got one bite. That's how they exchanged food in those days. But now, just *look* at it!

The godmother didn't go away. She stayed with the girl for four days, teaching her all different things. She told her not to smile too much or she'll be deformed around her mouth. They didn't want that. "If you keep smiling, you'll be smiling forever," they said. That's what they used to say long years ago.

Izee łibaahí (Dull-Color Plant Medicine)

That flu came around in 1919 or 1920, I think.[13] It was *bad*! Lots of people died. At first, people didn't try to take care of it. They thought it was just a cold and you could get rid of it easy. But it's not, it's different. That flu was hard to get rid of.

We were living in Miami then. We were all in a bunch on that sand hill along the wash. When the flu came around everybody got out of there and moved to different places. We moved way down the wash almost to the end. A policeman from Globe came down there and told the people what to do. He brought a whole bunch of sheets, old white sheets. He said, "If you need help, hang this outside your door." Some of them didn't do it. They won't hang anything up. And then, later, when he went to check on them, he found out that the whole family was wiped out. Those that had the white cloth hanging outside, the ones that want help, he gave them some kind of shot. It didn't help. It made some of them worse.

One of my aunt's cousins had a family there. They lived across the wash from us, her and her husband and a girl and four boys. They all got sick. They were supposed to hang up that white cloth outside their door. I guess they were all very sick and nobody knew it. The police went around checking on people—you know, knocking on doors to see if they need something—and that's how they found out that nobody was alive in there. They said it looked like that lady was making bread when she died. The tin she made tortillas on was over the fire and the dough in the pan was still there. She still had a tortilla in her hand. She just fell over.

A lot of people died on that side of the wash. I think four families on that side were just wiped out. On the other side, down below where we were living, a few died, about one in each family. Except for us, we didn't lose anybody. Lots of white people died, too. You couldn't see nobody in town. A priest used to come and check on us. Sometimes he brought a pot of soup for us. They're running around everywhere, those priests. They went around and checked on everybody.

My mother knew lots of herbs and that's what saved us. She got the flu but not real bad. My father got sick right away but not too bad. My brother Albert got sick and we almost lost my sister Donna. But my mother used that herb—*izee libaahí* [dull-color plant medicine], they call it—and that's what saved us. We drank *buckets* full of that medicine!

That herb smells kind of like sage. My mother boiled it in a big pot. She just took a pinch and put it in there. She gave it to us in the morning and then, at lunchtime, she gave it to us again. And then, in the evening before we went to bed, she gave it to us again. If we're feeling bad at night, she gave us the same thing. Izee libaahí is what saved us. That medicine is *strong*!

My mother kept it warm by the fire. When my brother Albert got sick, she used part of it for drinking and part of it to wash him off. And then, if his head was aching or hurting, she soaked a towel in that medicine and put it on his head. She always took a big cupful herself. She said, "I can't get sick. I have to take care of you." She prayed for that medicine. When everybody got sick, my mother was the only one that's still running around.

My sister Donna got very sick. She couldn't hardly breathe. So my mother made a wickiup for her, a little one. It's got just enough room for her to sit inside. My mother covered it with a canvas, and there's a little opening in the side where she can stick her hand in. My sister went in there and my mother put a bowl of that medicine inside. Then she built a fire right close to the wickiup. She had a lot of blue rocks, small ones, and they're turning white 'cause they been in the fire so long. She picked them up with a split piece of oak wood and put them in the bowl of medicine inside. Then she closed the opening. She told my sister, "Let me know if the steam is too hot for you." My sister stayed in there and stayed in there. She started coughing and coughing. You could hear her coughing and it sounds like that junk in her lungs was coming out. She stopped coughing. That steam cleared her lungs.

Then my sister came out. My mother told her to use her blanket. She said, "Wrap it around you, especially your head 'cause I know your hair is wet from the steam. Don't let the air get to you." My mother put her back to bed and covered her up. She slept for about two hours. Everybody was sitting there real quiet. When she woke up, she said that she was feeling better. She got very sick. She got over it, though.

The medicine men tried to help when that flu came around. It didn't do no good. There was lots of them singing, especially around San Carlos. They got choked up in their throat—*sore*! My grandfather Joseph Hoffman got that way. He was singing at night, night after night. He had no voice left. He said it hurt real bad 'cause he's been singing so much.

So my mother got some of that medicine, izee łibaahí, and told him to drink it. He drank it. Then she put it on his throat with a rag. Then she put some cotton in that medicine and put it in his ears. It's real hot when she does that. She kept doing that for him. He was talking again after two or three days. My mother told him, "I think you're getting over it now." She said, "Are you hurting?" He said, "No, not much, only just a little." Then she mixed flour and water and cooked it on the fire. She put salt in there, just a little bit of salt, and mixed it up. She made him drink that. After that, his voice came back to life.

My mother got lots of that medicine for us. She got it for other people, too. They used to come with their cups or a little bucket. They got enough for their family to drink. White people were dying all the time. The policeman that came around said they died every day. Some of them heard about that medicine my mother was making. She was a Catholic and the Catholic priest knew about it. I guess he told the white people, the ones that went to that church. So they started coming over. My mother gave them that medicine. They came to her for izee łibaahí. They paid her for that.

George Button came with his grandmother to where we were living. He was friends with my brothers. He was all that lady had left. The rest of his family was gone from the flu. He got sick himself but he stayed with us and got better. His grandmother was so *happy*! She said, "I lost all I had at home. I'm glad you saved one for me."

Later, when we were at Roosevelt, they came over there, that lady and her grandson. My brothers were getting ready to go back to St. Johns. They were up at the store, and I guess that boy went looking for them. His grandmother asked my mother, she said, "Where did my grandson go?" My mother said, "He's over there with the boys." That lady said, "Where are your boys going?" My mother said, "They're going away to school. They're going to school at St. Johns. They'll be back in the springtime." And that old lady said, "My grandson said that he's going, too, but I don't know. I don't have nobody left but him."

That boy came back with my brothers. He found his grandma sitting there. She said, "Where are you going?" He said, "I'm going with those boys to learn something. I can't go home with you. I have to learn to do something for myself and for you." He said, "If I don't know how to talk English I won't be able to do very much. Everybody's going to school."

Then that old lady started crying. She was *crying*! My mother talked to her. She said, "Why don't you let him go and try. If he gets too lonesome, one of the priests will bring him back." I guess she liked that 'cause she stopped crying. She let her grandson go to school.

While that lady was with us there, my aunt Bessie went to her home and took all her grandson's clothes away. She hid them from her 'cause if she sees them she's gonna feel real bad. When that lady got back home, she was looking all over for her grandson's clothes.

"We Got Out of There"

We stayed there in Miami 'til everybody got well enough to travel. Then we got out of there. We went to Wheatfields and stayed there for a while. Then we went back to Cibecue. Then we went down to Oak

Creek. My grandpa John [John Lupe] was over there, so we stayed with him for a while. Then we came back to Cibecue. We stayed with my grandmother, my mother's mother. She was living by herself. Her wickiup was just about falling apart, so we helped her fix it up. And then, pretty soon, we went down to Roosevelt.

Chapter Three

When I look at that place now—when I go with somebody down to Mormon Flat—it looks awful to me. It's way out in the desert! I wonder, "How in the world did we live there? How did we go on that long Apache Trail and live at Mormon Flat?"

From Oak Creek to Roosevelt—Roosevelt Dam—"Dewey's Loose!"—Chinese Farmers—Dahnagolk'id (Terraced Hills)—A Model T—Outrunning a Racer—Apache Trail—"It Was Raining Rocks!"—Tortillas and Deer Meat Stew—Crowdings of Snakes at Fish Creek—Ikaz (Century Plant Stalks)—Mormon Flat—Seeds from Cibecue—Baskets and Moccasin Shoes—"Go Drink Some More!"—Nellie, the Monkey—Big Dumplings—Wild Dogs—"They Stole Our Name"

From Oak Creek to Roosevelt

Like I told you, my oldest brother, Eugene, ran away from the boarding school at Rice. He went to Roosevelt and stayed there with his job. He sent somebody to tell my father to bring the family down there. "There's jobs over here," he told that man to tell my father. We went to John Lupe's home at Oak Creek. My father told him that we're going down to Roosevelt. My grandpa said, "Well, I guess I won't need you this year." We usually helped him harvest his crops. He said, "You can go down there. It's a long time before we harvest yet. If anything happens, let me know, so I can come and bring you back."

We went from Oak Creek to Roosevelt on horses. We had no wagon. We went down Cherry Creek and down along the river [Salt River] and then over to where the bridge is now. Then over that mountain by the bridge and down again, going towards Globe. We camped there for the night. The next day, my father and brother went off in the morning. We stayed there 'til way late in the afternoon. They brought deer meat back with them and we ate some of that.

We started off again. We went about as far as halfway to Roosevelt. Then it got dark so we had to camp along the trail there. Then, the next morning, we started down again. That night we were still going. We camped when it got dark. You could see the lake [Roosevelt Lake] from there. It was *big*! The lake wasn't very far, so the next morning we went over there and washed. That's when we saw a wagon coming towards us on the road. It's my grandmother Rose! She said, "Pile everything you have and put it on the wagon. Put the kids up there, too. Everybody else, just ride your horses." We did that.

We got to Roosevelt before lunchtime. My aunt Bessie was already cooking. She was cooking for some of the workers. When we stopped there, she said, "Move into that wickiup over there. Somebody used to have it but they went back to San Carlos. Nobody's in there now. I already cleaned it out for you. I already fixed it up."

My brother Eugene came home for lunch. He was really happy we were all there. He gave us a piece of paper. He said, "If you need any groceries, take the paper to the store up there and give it to the man. He knows my name, so just give it to him and he'll let you get what you want." So after we ate, all of us went up to the store. And my mother and father told us, "Sit down." There was a tree there. They said, "Sit under the tree. Sit down on the ground and stay there. Wait 'til we come out." There was a string they used to carry in their pocket all the time. They gave it to us to play with. We made all kinds of designs with it. We sat there and played with that string. When they came out of the store, they said, "Come on, let's go." We went back over there to our new home.

Roosevelt Dam

At Roosevelt, we used to stay on the side of the road that goes to Globe. The families that came from Cibecue and Oak Creek all lived together there. The San Carlos people lived across the road on the other side.

Roosevelt Dam, date unknown.

We stayed there about three or two months. The dam [Roosevelt Dam] was already there. The lake [Roosevelt Lake] was already big. Some of the workers were still doing something on the dam. Others were fixing the road, making it wider. That road used to be real narrow, so they were blasting the rocks and making it wider.[1]

My father carried rocks. He carried them one at a time down the mountain there. But then he got some of those boxes—"powder boxes," they call them, 'cause dynamites come in them—and he wired them together and built up the sides a little bit. Then he put a long stick across, and he wired it down, and then he tied a rope to the ends. He put that rope over his head and down around his shoulders and he packed that thing on his back. He put the rocks in there, three or four at a time, and he carried them down to where they're building the road. Pretty soon, other mens were doing that, making those box things, but my father was the one that started it.

My brothers carried water to the workers—Joe, Jack, and Albert,

Western Apache laborers at Roosevelt Dam. Eugene Tulene Case, Eva Watt's oldest brother, is second from left.

three of them. They did that until they went back to school at St. Johns. They got paid. They got paid pretty good 'cause it's *hot*—it's *real hot*— and they have to walk all the time. They have to go to the top of the dam to get the water. They carried it with buckets or with canteens—you know, those long canvas bags—and they went around to the workers and gave them a drink. But they didn't go down to the bottom of the dam. They stayed on top where they're fixing the road. They said, "You kids, don't go down there 'cause it's real steep and you might fall." So they stayed on top, walking back and forth all day. They were walking all the time. Some of those boys were still small, about eleven or ten, I think.

My mother was always going across [Roosevelt Lake] to get wood. There's lots of driftwood over there, lots of dry mesquite. There was a man at the boat dock and my mother got to know him. She used to ask him if she could borrow the boat to go across. He always got somebody to take her across, her and my grandmother Rose. They brought back *lots* of wood. One time Joe told them, "Don't fill up the boat like that. If you do, it's gonna sink with you."

My grandmother Rose stayed with us at Roosevelt for a while. She

Western Apache homes on the shore of Roosevelt Lake, date unknown.

stayed 'til we started following that Apache Trail. Then she went back
to San Carlos. My grandmother Rose was *always* gambling down there.
She couldn't stay away from it! She used to play cards—all different
games with those Mexican cards—and each lady that plays had to put
a quarter in. My grandmother collected those quarters—she *wins!*—
so she had a little money in her pocket all the time.

"Dewey's Loose!"

One time, my brother Dewey and me were tied up in the lake [Roose-
velt Lake]. They tied up rags and made a string. Then they put it around
us, under our arms, and they tied us to a bush close to the edge. We
were playing in the water and somehow Dewey got loose. He started
floating away. Joe and my sister Donna and their friends were playing

A temporary Western Apache home near Roosevelt Dam, Roosevelt, Arizona, date unknown.

tag in the deeper water. They thought we were safe. Then they seen Dewey! He had long hair down to his shoulders and his hair was spread out in the water. "Dewey's loose! Dewey's loose!" They were just *yelling*! Then somebody went over there and got him out. He was OK. I remember that one. We were tied up to a bush.

Chinese Farmers

We were doing fine. I liked it 'cause it don't snow. We used to go from Roosevelt down to Wheatfields. My grandmother Rose and my mother used to take a whole bunch of ladies down there to cut cabbage for

those Chinese farmers.[2] And if there's any boys along, they dug potatoes for them. It's hard work! It's *hot* down there. Those Chinese gave
us tomatoes—there's lots of tomatoes in the fields—and they told us,
they said, "Go ahead and eat these, go ahead and eat them. There's lots
of water in there." I never ate tomatoes before. And they had something like a watermelon. It looked like some kind of squash to me. "If
you want a drink, cut it open," they said. They grew lots of crops down
there—cantaloupe, watermelon, cabbage, potatoes, corn, other things,
too. That corn wasn't very high, about like this [3–4 feet tall]. The ears
are small. They're real small and the corns taste like popcorn. It tastes
good! After we stopped working, those Chinese paid us with vegetables
and we took them back home to Roosevelt.

  Those Chinese didn't live right at Wheatfields. They lived about a
mile or two from there. They used to come running up, though, looking for people that want to work. Their language is something like
Apache, but not very much. Mostly, they just used hand motions and
a few words in English. They had their own store, a little one, but anybody could use it. They used to help us a lot. If you need something—
flour, sugar, coffee, anything—you could get it right there. They had
a storage place for the food, and all those Chinese got their food right
there.

  One time, two of those Chinese stopped us on the road. We were
coming from Globe. They wanted us to work for them for a while, digging potatoes. My mother said, "We got lots of boys that can go to
work." My brothers went to work for them. They gathered all the potatoes. Those Chinese used to have a wooden cart—it's kind of like a
wagon—and they throwed all the potatoes in there. There's holes in
the cart, lots of round holes, and the little potatoes go through them
and fall on the ground. There's *lots* of those little potatoes and those
Chinese just left them. "If you want them, you can have them," they
said. My mother put them in a gunny sack and took it with her. She
boiled them. Those little potatoes were real good.

  Those Chinese worked all year round—digging, planting, cutting,
cleaning—but it's mainly when they're picking vegetables and digging
potatoes that they need lots of help. They had *big* fields. In the wintertime, they dug the ground and raked all the brush and weeds off. They
didn't burn it in the fields, though. They took it and burned it far away.
I don't know why they did that.

Lots of Apache people lived right at Wheatfields. There was a holy ground and a sweatbath there. That's where they had their ceremonies. They worked for those Chinese two or three days at a time. Then they took off. It never was a permanent job for them. They used to come and go. Those Chinese paid them with food, not money. The Indians lived on that—and cottontails, quails, and other kinds of birds. The mens hunted deer. There used to be lots of big deer down there. The mens were gone for four or five days, sometimes longer than that. They don't come back 'til everybody got something. And whoever got the first one, the first deer, he shares it with the others. Then, after everybody got one, he gets his meat back. That's how they used to do. They used to get those rams [bighorn sheep], too. I wonder where they went to. They just disappeared.

Dahnagolk'id (Terraced Hills)

There was a big camp of people up there at Dahnagolk'id [Terraced Hills]. They're mostly Mojaves and Apaches from Camp Verde. Lots of mens from there were working at Roosevelt. People went up there to gamble all the time, mens and ladies both. The ladies played a stick game that's kind of like dice. They used to play for clothes, material, moccasin shoes, money, blankets, pots and pans, whatever they had. One time, my mother won moccasin shoes right away. Then she won a blanket. My father kept telling her, "Go ahead! Play! You're lucky! Go ahead and play!" So she did. She won a lot of stuff.

The mens had another game. They call it *na'izhǫǫsh* [hoop and pole game]; they used a wheel for that and two long sticks. One time, my mother took us over there to watch 'cause my father was playing. The ladies had to stand at a certain place. Off to the side, right at the middle of where they're playing, there's a big rock. You have to stand right there. You can't go this way, you can't go that way. If you want to watch, you have to stand close to that rock. That's where I was standing with my mother. When she was ready to go, she turned around once and walked backwards for a long ways. Then she could walk facing front again. That game was dangerous for ladies. Children, too. It was a man's game.[3]

That lady that gave me her name, Nest'áń Yolilé, came to see my father at Roosevelt. She stayed with us for about two or three weeks. I

Western Apache women gambling near San Carlos, San Carlos Apache Indian
Reservation, date unknown.

used to follow her around all the time. Wherever she went, I followed
her. My mother got mad at me when I did that. "She's gonna leave you
somewhere behind and you won't be able to come back," she said. But
that lady, if she's got something to eat, she always broke it in half and
gave it to me. I guess that's why I followed her around.

That gambling place was about five or six miles from Roosevelt.
They called it Dahnagolk'id and that lady used to walk up there. I didn't
know she was going that way. I followed her across the bridge [Roose-
velt Dam]. She didn't see me. I went about as far as the middle of the
bridge and then some mens in a truck took me the rest of the way.

When I got across to the other side, that lady was *way* far ahead. I
still followed her. Then, about halfway to that gambling camp, she sat
down to rest. That's when she seen me. She hollered at me. I tried to
hide from her 'cause I thought she was mad. She was hollering at me.
She said, "You better hurry up and come over here. I'm leaving again
pretty soon." I went up there. She said, "What did you follow me for?
I didn't tell you to come with me 'cause I know it's too far for you. But
you're here now and you've got to walk the rest of the way."

We got over there to Dahnagolk'id, and that same day, in the eve-

ning, we went over to a big shade those people had made. There was
lots of them under there, mens and ladies both, and they had oil lamps
all the way around. That lady started to gamble. I was sitting right behind her. She turned around. She said, "Go to sleep. I told you to go to
bed." I couldn't go to sleep. She was throwing dice and every time she
threw them she hollered, "Yahaaa!" Then she grabbed all the money.
She won! What she won was high—lots of coins and green papers, too.
She kept on and on. Some people were saying, "How did she get all our
money? How's she getting it?" She had a bag that closes when you pull
the string on top. She put her money in there. That bag was just *stuffed*!

About two or three in the morning we went back and went to sleep.
She was up again before sunrise! I asked the lady we were staying
with, "Where's my grandma?" She said, "She's over there under the
shade." I went over there and she was already gambling. She said, "Did
you eat?" I said no. There's some ladies selling food over there, so she
bought me something to eat. We sat there and ate for a little while, and
then she went back to gambling. She said, "Don't run off. Don't go too
far." She said, "Some kids will be going to the river [Tonto Creek], but
don't you go over there with them. Stay here." She said, "There's a big
fish over there that might swallow you." I didn't know what she was
talking about.

So I went off, not very far, and sat down. I was just sitting there.
Then I went over to where she was to see if she quit. She's still at it!
"Yahaaa!" That's when I seen my mother and my father. My mother
said, "We're gonna be here for about two days. Come with me." She
came up there to gather that black eagleclaw that they use to make
baskets. There used to be lots of that on the side of the river. She got
about fourteen big bundles before we went back to Roosevelt.

My father was wanting to gamble. He asked that lady [Nest'áń
Yoliłé], he said, "Can you loan me some money so I can gamble too?"
She didn't care. She had that big bag full of money, and when my father
asked her, she just grabbed it and throwed it at him. She said, "Here!
Get what you need."

A Model T

Roosevelt is where I seen a car up close for the first time. It belonged
to a man named Jimmy. He was my brother's friend. He came from

Phoenix. His car was a Model T. I didn't know what to think about it! I thought that thing was driving itself!

He was running that thing around in a circle and everybody came up there to watch. Some mens started yelling. They said, "It just walked in! Come and look at it!" All the ladies went up there, kids and all, they all went. They were standing around that car, all the way around it, just *looking* at it. Then it started going again. Every time it turns, people start running away. They were having lots of fun. Then, after a while, they told my father to get in there. They got him in there and he was riding around and riding around. After it stopped, they got him off and some more got in and they were riding around. Everybody was laughing and yelling. That man was giving everybody a ride. Some of them got scared. One old lady was yelling her head off, riding around and around.

That man asked my mother if she wanted a ride. She said, "No, I don't." She was talking to that man. She talked English real good 'cause she went to Carlisle. She said, "Where do you come from?" He said, "Phoenix." She said, "How much did you have to pay for that thing?" He told her, "Six months' pay."

Cars didn't go fast in those days, only about thirty-five miles an hour. The roads were *rough*! They were narrow, too, so you had to go slow all the time. If the car ran off the road it turned over, but nobody got hurt bad 'cause it's not going fast. They used to call it *béshnagháí* [metal wagon]. Now they call it *nałbiil* [car; truck].

Outrunning a Racer

One time, my grandmother Rose and my mother went to make woods [firewood]. They took me with them. They dropped a blanket and told me, "Stay right here." I stayed there under a mesquite tree. I was sitting there. They went on up the wash. I heard them chopping.

Then I seen my grandmother running down the wash. I was wondering, "What is she running from?" And then I seen my mother running down the other side. I could only see part of her head. "Something is happening!" I stood up to look over there and see what they were running from. They were going *way out*! Then they went under a big mesquite tree. It was thick. I couldn't see them no more after that.

Finally, they came back to where I was sitting. I was screaming

my head off. "Be quiet! Nothing happened to you. What are you crying about?" I guess a rock cut my grandmother's foot 'cause she was
putting something on it. They were running 'cause one of those racer
snakes was chasing them. They said that snake went *fast*! We went back
home after they got their woods.

My mother and my grandmother told my father and brothers about
it. They were talking about it while they were eating. My father said,
"Did it catch you?" My grandmother said, "No, we outran it. That snake
didn't even get close. But why will it chase us like that?" My father said,
"It has little ones about this time of year. It was chasing you 'cause you
got too close to its home." Then my grandmother Rose said, "Well, we
outran it. It's fast but we outran it." Then my father said, "Well, we can
enter you two in the race on the Fourth of July." He was laughing at
them.

Apache Trail

My father and my brother Eugene stayed with their jobs at Roosevelt.
That's why they asked them to go and work on that road, Apache Trail.
My brother was mad 'cause some mens he wanted to work with were
all going back. "That road goes a long ways," they said. "It's gonna take
us too far from home." My brother told them, he said, "You're gonna
starve in no time. There's no jobs where you're going. There's nothing
over there you can do." He said, "I'm making money. That's why me
and my family are gonna follow the road."

See, there's hardly no jobs around Cibecue at that time. It was only
the cowboys that had good jobs, and that was mostly in Cherry Creek.
They used to go over there and work for the white people that had
cattle, rounding them up and branding them. They always had plenty
to eat, those people living at Cibecue and Oak Creek, 'cause they can
grow crops. But when they're way out, like working on Apache Trail,
they can't plant 'cause they're always moving. So it's hard for them,
especially if they had a big family. Sometimes they don't have much to
eat, even while they're making money.

We followed that road, Apache Trail, for about two years. It goes
all the way from Roosevelt to Apache Junction. The road was real narrow—it's real rough, too—so they were making it bigger and smooth.

Western Apache laborers on the Apache Trail, 1906.

It's hard work! It's not by machine, just pick and shovel, that's all they used to make that road. And dynamite, too, they used lots of dynamite. When the workers made the road as far as one mile, we moved camp and went to the next one. One mile, then we moved, one mile, move again, one mile, move again. That's how we used to do.

The morning when we started a man came by. He said, "We're gonna leave pretty soon. Get your stuff ready. Haul it up to the side of the road so we can pick it up." We did that. They had a big wagon. It's flat, no sides, so you have to tie everything on it. My mother put a big canvas on there. Those Chinese farmers gave it to her. It's a real big one. She put it on top of the wagon and put all our stuff up there. Then she wrapped it up and tied it with a wire. That day, everybody else started doing that, too, wrapping their stuff so it won't fall off. One lady lost all her cooking pots. I don't know if she got them back 'cause we went in front of the wagon. We walked. Everybody walked in front of the wagon. That Apache Trail was a slow one.

My father made a straight line of rocks on the side of the road.

Western Apache laborers working with mules on the Apache Trail, Arizona, 1906.

He measured from there to there—he's got a string or rope or some-thing—so he knows to put the rocks so far apart. He was measuring how wide they want the road to be. And he cleared the loose rocks and throwed them off the trail. They followed behind him with that shovel-looking thing [a Fresno scraper] that they drag with a horse. Some-times he walked behind it in case big rocks fall back. He picked those up and put them on the side of the road. It's a hard job, in a way.

They used big horses to clear the rocks. They had big feet, big ones, and there's long hair on its foot. I don't know what kind of horses those are. They pulled those big shovels. It looks like a shovel but it has holes on both sides. There's wires that go to the sides and some-how they tie those wires to the harness. They pushed it down to pick up dirt and rocks when the horse was pulling it. One time, they put me on one of those big horses, *way up there*! I was screaming my head off!

There's no stores on Apache Trail, but the person that's boss had a Model T. He used to go to town on that, either to Roosevelt or Globe,

Western Apache laborers using mule-drawn sleds to move heavy rocks on the
Apache Trail, date unknown.

and come back with groceries that people ordered. He wrote down
their names and then he went and got their groceries. He was real good,
that man. He used to bring more groceries than you need for yourself.
The people paid him when it's payday. He got his money back then.

My mother got beans and coffee from the store, that's about all.
Mostly, she went out and gathered things to eat. Like mesquite beans.
She pounds them 'til they're soft and then she makes mush from them.
That mush tastes good 'cause it's sweet by itself. Manzanita berries
are the same way, natural sweet. They just mashed them up and mixed
them with water, they didn't put nothing in it. My mother went with
other ladies and got mescal, that *nadah*. They cooked it in the ground.
And they went after *hosh nteelé* [prickly pear] and that tall cactus [sa-
guaro], too. They carried a long stick with a hook tied to the end.
It's easy to pull the fruits off with that one. And my father and brothers went hunting—deer, rabbits, quails. They always came back with

something. I was cooking all the time, carrying water and bringing in sticks of wood. That's how we lived on Apache Trail.

Some of the workers had no shoes, clothes all torn up, nothing much to eat. They're hungry lots of the time. In the wintertime there's hardly nothing to eat. So they ate those little potatoes, *isdzáni binii'* [woman's face] they call it. They're like potatoes, only they're real tiny. They have to dig them out. Then they boiled them and ate them. There's lots of other plants they used to eat, like *ko' dahosh* [thistle]. It's got lots of stickers on it. You have to peel them off. The inside tastes just like asparagus. It tastes good.

And if you had any parched corn, you looked for a plant with little bumps on the stalk. There's seeds in there, little speckled gray seeds. They cooked it and got the hulls off. Then they put the seeds in a frying pan and put charcoal in there, burning charcoal. They throw it up in the air when the seeds start popping. When they quit popping, they take all the ashes out and clean the seeds off. You can eat it that way and that's what the grown people did. They ate it without water. But the children ate it mixed with corn and water, a mush, so they won't inhale those tiny speckled seeds. That's the way we used to eat it. It's good.

It seems like nobody in the family got sick, except maybe for headaches, colds, and things like that. My grandmother Rose always left lots of roots with my mother. She said, "If the kids need it, use this one and this one and this one." She showed my mother how to use them. If there's one that she needed, a plant that grows way up on a mountain somewhere, my father went and got it.

I remember only one lady that got sick. She needed a laxative. My mother gave her a medicine that's good for that. It was at night. All that lady's family was there in her wickiup. My mother told us to go back home and go to sleep. They don't allow children, you know, not right there. So we went back home. My mother worked on that lady with that medicine. She got well fast. My mother cured her.

"It Was Raining Rocks!"

They were blasting where the road goes up a mountain. The people were camping below there, off to the side of the road. They hollered from way up there before they started blasting—you could hear them. That's when everybody took their children and started walking. There's a big boulder sitting way over there and they went behind it. They stayed there, real quiet, close to that boulder. Then the dynamite went off! It was *raining rocks*! Rocks were coming down on top of the camp! I was *scared*! One man got hit in the mouth. All his teeth fell out. I think it broke his jaw. When they knew it was over, the people went back to their camps. Everything was all smashed up. Their tents and wickiups were all torn up. After that, they start calling that place Gochǫ' Ha'itin [Bad Place Where The Road Goes Up].

The next day, they found another place for the people to camp. They moved them back away from the road. But there's too many rattlesnakes over there 'cause it's close to those big rocks where they live. Those snakes didn't like it. They were crawling around, crawling around at night, so everybody's scared to go outside. And a big bear came by. Its footprint was *big*! See, the water was down that way. There's a well with a bucket and a water trough. They filled up the trough at night and left it for the horses to come and get a drink. That big bear went down there to get a drink of water. A lot of people didn't want to live there. Some of them moved to another place where there's not so many rocks and some of them quit and went home. They got their paycheck—and then they're *gone*!

It took a long time to finish that road that goes up the mountain. It's steep and there's lots of curves. Finally, they moved up on top. There's nothing but rock up there with only a little dirt on top of it. There's rainwater in those rocks—rainwater in holes in the rocks—and there's one big pool. Everybody used to go there and wash. The mens had their sweatbath over at one end. The ladies used to go to the other end and wash their clothes. They had no soap. They used to get yucca and pound it up real good and put it in the water with their clothes. Then they walked all over their clothes. When they got them out they're real clean.

Tortillas and Deer Meat Stew

On Saturday and Sunday, the people didn't work. They used to go under those cottonwood trees down by the stream [Tonto Creek] and play cards all day. One time, my father came up from there. He said, "What are you making?" She [Ann Beatty] said, "I'm boiling a stew." See, the boss gave my brother Eugene half a deer and she was cooking that deer meat with potatoes. And my father said, "Bring it down there to that gambling place. I bet you could make lots of money selling that food." She said, "I don't have enough tortillas." He said, "Make some more." So she did that.

We took the food down there where they were playing. They were playing that stick game and they were playing Mexican cards. When we came, my father said, "If you people are hungry, my children over here are selling something to eat." Everybody got up and got themselves a bowl of stew and tortillas. We were selling it for a quarter or fifty cents. We sold all of it. My mother made quite a bit of money.

The following week, they told my mother to come back. She boiled some beans and made deer meat stew again. We went down there. They cleaned her out again, beans and all. She did that four or five times. My mother was laughing at the money she made from selling the food. "What am I gonna do with this money I got? There's no stores, there's no place where I can buy something." She was laughing about that.

So my father told my mother, "If you want to go get groceries, you can. I'll ask that man and see if he's going to the store. If he's going, he can take you." So my father went up there. He came running back down. "Get ready to go," he said. "He's gonna come pick you up pretty soon." So she went down there to Roosevelt and got lots of groceries. They came back in just a little while 'cause the road was good behind. Forward was still rough.

Crowdings of Snakes at Fish Creek

One time, it rained real hard. After it quit raining and the sun came out, they told us, "It's time to move!" We moved to Fish Creek. It's about halfway to Roosevelt and halfway to Apache Junction. It's right there in the middle, the middle of both ways. There's a long hill that goes way up, and up there on top is where we camped. There's a stream down below, a little river [Tonto Creek]. We camped there for about a month.

My mother came up there. She was carrying a heavy load from where we camped before. I think it was about two miles. She carried

Fish Creek Canyon, Arizona, date unknown. The families of Western Apache laborers building the Apache Trail were surprised by "crowdings" of garter snakes while camping nearby.

our stuff all the way—a heavy load!—and she was *tired*. Everybody else put their stuff on that flatback wagon but my mother said it was just too crowded. So she had to carry our stuff all the way up that long hill.

She was tired when we got there, so we stayed up there by the road where they kept their horses and shovels and tools. There was a big old mesquite tree. It was on a little flat. She made a shelter there. The man that dragged the shovel around brought her some boards. She put them up and covered them with a canvas. There was a big pile of brush there and she used that for wood. She cooked our supper outside. Then she fixed the beds. We went to bed.

All those other people camped down by the river. There's lots of cottonwood trees down there and it's grassy green. They thought they had a good place to spend the night. My father and my brother Eugene were still sitting outside when those people started *screaming their heads off*! "Here comes another one! There's one out there! One's in your clothes! It's going in your blanket!" I woke up. I didn't know what was going on. They were howling their heads off!

Pretty soon my aunt Bessie came running up there, holding her dress up. She said, "There's lots of snakes down there! Garter snakes! There's lots of them and they're crawling all over everything!" She got scared 'cause one of them wrapped around her leg. "There's lots of them down there! They're everywhere!" My father said, "So build a fire." She said, "That's worse! When you build a fire, they keep on coming. They come right to it!"

So my father and my brother went down there to help. They shook out all the blankets and brought them up for those people. My father told them, he said, "Leave your pots and pans. Let the snakes cook their own supper." Then those people came up there and spent the night. They were all laying around alongside the tools. They slept there all night.

The next morning, when the sun was about to come up, they went back down there to see if their stuff was still there. They brought all their pots and pans back up. And they told my mother, they said, "You were right. We felt sorry for you 'cause you were way up here. We were cool down there in the shade of the trees. But you were right to stay up here." Some of them were afraid to go back down there.

You know, you won't see them during the day. When the sun is out you won't see those garter snakes. But when the sun goes down, when it's way late in the evening, you see *lots* of them, just *crowdings* of them, down there along the stream.

Ikaz (Century Plant Stalks)

We moved to another camping place and my mother made a wickiup. She got those dry *ikaz* [century plant stalks], long ones, and used them for the frame part. She put canvas on it. It was kind of square, like a room.

And a horse got wild. It got scared of something. It was inside a big tent where they kept all the tools. It started fighting and fighting and knocked down the tent, the whole tent, tore it in half. Finally, they got that horse out of there. They found out there's a rattlesnake in there.

So they wanted to build a new tent. A man came over and asked my mother, he said, "I want to see how you made your home." He looked at that wickiup my mother built. The back part had canvas on it, but not very much, so he gave her those torn-up pieces from the tent. He said, "If you can use it, go ahead and take it. But I need your help. I'll pay you for what you're gonna do for me." She said, "OK."

So they went out together and got lots of ikaz. They got all the dry ones and tied them together in a bundle. They used one of those big horses to pull them in. They got about four loads, I think. Then my mother put those ikaz together. She stood them up in the ground and tied them with *igáyé*, just like she done with that wickiup she made. Then that man cut them off so they're all the same height. Then he went and put a canvas on top. He covered the whole thing. There was a large space in there. He and my mother made that place with ikaz so the tools won't get rusty. She showed him how to do it.

Mormon Flat

We followed Apache Trail all the way to Mormon Flat. We stayed there 'cause they were making another dam [Mormon Flat Dam]. They picked my father and my brother Eugene to work there. See, they stayed with their jobs. They never said, "I got to go home." That's why the boss over there don't trust some of the Indians—they worked for

Apache Trail descending to Mormon Flat, Arizona, date unknown.

one paycheck and that's it. "I got to go home," they said. My youngest brother, Augustine, was born at Mormon Flat in 1923. My father got sick there. Before he got sick, he was doing different kinds of work— chopping the weeds, clearing the brush, digging up big rocks.

When I look at that place now, when I go with somebody down there to Mormon Flat, it looks awful to me. It's way out in the desert. I wonder, "How in the world did we live there? How did we go through there and live?"

It was mixed down there at Mormon Flat. There's people from up here [White Mountain Apaches] and from San Carlos, and there are Mojaves and Tontos [Tonto Apaches]. Close to the mountain, close to where the road is, there's a little grocery store, and the Indians used to live around there. On the other side of the road, close to the dam, there's Mexicans and Chinese. But there's nothing but mens living over there, just mens. That was a men's camp.

Mormon Flat Dam, 1935.

There's always lots of gambling going on. They played with those Mexican cards. They played poker games, too. And that stick game, na'izhǫǫsh. The mens used to go down by the river and play that one. They don't play for money. They play for different things—shoes, leather, jackets, hats, a blanket, anything they can find. My father got lucky three times in one day. He won three blankets. He brought them home. The ladies gambled, too. A Mojave woman had a lot of cards and poker chips. Those chips were different colors—red, blue, white, yellow—and every time somebody won a game they put another chip in there 'til there's a big pile of chips in the middle. They said that game is played like rummy. I don't know what rummy is.

My father made friends with one of those Mojaves. His name was Charley Dickens. They hung around together and helped each other a lot. My father made friends with that man through gambling. He used to come over and play cards with my father all night long. Another man used to come over there. We called him "Bundle On Top Of His Head." He had a big old bundle of hair on his head all the time. He was a Navajo

John Tulene and Ann Beatty with their son Dewey at Mormon Flat, Arizona, about 1921–22. This is the only known photograph of John Tulene, one of very few Western Apaches who helped construct the Mormon Flat Dam.

and he talked Navajo. He got acquainted with my father. He stayed with us for a while.

Seeds from Cibecue

There's fields at Mormon Flat. I don't know who those fields belonged to. The fences were down but my father fixed them up again. And there's water a little ways from there, outside the fence, in some kind of well. It filled up—not all the time, just once in a while—and the water went into the field.

The man that brought us in the wagon found a plow, a handmade plow. He loaned us his team and my father plowed the field. My mother had seeds that she brought from Cibecue. My father said, "Go get the seeds. We'll plant them. If anybody says anything, we'll say that we're just using the field for a little while." So they planted corn there and squash and sugarcane and sorghum. Everything came up real good. It was growing good all over.

We used to go down there every day. Some Mexicans lived across from where we lived, and those little Mexican boys and girls went in the field and tried to take the corn and squash and everything. We didn't know about it 'til somebody told us. A man saw the kids in there. He came and talked to my father. My father went down there. I guess he chased those kids away. That's why we went over there and watched the field.

There's a gray-looking squash—I don't know what you call it— and that's the kind we kept for ourselves, that and the corn. That gray squash is real sweet, real good. We cut those up and dried them and stored them all away. My mother was selling the other kind she grew, that crooked-neck squash. Everybody wanted those, so she was selling them. She told me, she said, "Don't let them taste the gray ones. Once they taste it, they're gonna want some. I want those gray ones for us."

Baskets and Moccasin Shoes

My mother made baskets and moccasin shoes at Mormon Flat. She made necklaces and pins, too. She sold those things in Mesa. There used to be an Indian store in Mesa. Some of the workers came from there. They had cars and used to go back and forth. So they came around and said, "Does anybody want a ride to Mesa?" They took my mother over there sometimes, her and other ladies that had things they wanted to sell. They had cabins for them. They got their cabin first and then they went to the store. Then they went back to the cabin and spent the night. They came home in the morning. My mother made money that way.

"Go Drink Some More!"

People didn't drink very much in those days, but sometimes the mens wanted whiskey. They went across to the mens camp and got whiskey over there, moonshine. They used to be ashamed of it, though. In those days, if you seen somebody like that—drunk—you're ashamed for them. And the person that did it, he won't show his face for a long time. "I wonder what I said, I wonder what I did?"—it's going through his mind.

There was one man that stayed with us at Mormon Flat for a long time. He came from Cibecue. He was related to my father, so he stayed with us. He slept outside under the shade. His name was Martin Lupe.

One time he went off with some man, and I guess he got too much of it. He didn't know how to drink moonshine. So he got drunk over there at the men's camp and made a fool of himself. When they brought him back he's got no shirt on. They put him where his blanket was under the shade. My father told them, "Put him there. Put him to bed." He was asleep.

Then he woke up. He sat up and started singing. He was sitting there, singing and singing and singing—just *going* on! My mother and father got tired of him singing, so we went down to the river [Cottonwood Creek]. We sat in the water for a while. Then we came back up. That man was out from under the shade. It looked like he tried to cook something. I guess he was hungry. My mother left some soup for him but he didn't take it. He didn't see it, I guess. He was just laying there. Late in the evening, when we were eating supper, my brother tried to feed him. He didn't wake up, so my brother left him alone.

The next morning everybody got up to go to work. My brother asked that man if he's going to work. "No, I can't," he said. "I'm pretty sick right now." So he stayed there. My father came back at lunchtime. He asked my mother, he said, "Is he still singing those songs?" She said, "No, he's quiet." "Who?" the drunk man said. "You!" my father said. "You sang all day yesterday! You were a medicine man!" He was making fun of him, laughing at him for what he done.

That man got so embarrassed he didn't know what to do. He said, "That man told me to go with him to the dam [Mormon Flat Dam]. Instead, we went to the men's camp. Those people told us to eat, so we ate. Then they invited us to play poker." I guess that's when he started drinking. He got drunk over there. Then they brought him home. One of the mens that brought him back said that poker was against the law or something, so they have to be real quiet when they're playing. He said that man started singing and making lots of noise. That's the reason they brought him home.

They were making fun of him for a long time. They said, "Go drink some more! Go drink some more!" He didn't like that, but that's what they used to do for drinking too much. He didn't touch moonshine after that. Then something happened at Cibecue and somebody came for him. He went back to Cibecue.

Nellie, the Monkey

We were supposed to boil beans and we didn't have any. So my mother went to the store to get some beans. She told me to stay outside but I sneaked in behind her. Two boys and their father were keeping that store. The boys' names were David and Jack. They had a pet monkey in there. It's not in a cage, it runs around loose. That monkey's name was Nellie.

David was there by himself. My mother got the beans. We were going back outside and David called me. He said, "Come back and get some popcorn." My mother was already outside when I went back to get the popcorn. He gave it to me. I started to go outside. I was still looking back at David, and that's when that monkey grabbed me by my dress. She tore it off! Her fingers were strong! She tore off part of my dress.

I started hollering and David said, "What happened? What happened? Are you hurt?" He came running to me. Nellie was still hanging onto me. He told her, he said, "Get away from her! Go on!" Nellie let go of me and just sat there. She sat there with her arms up over her eyes. She was *so ashamed*. I went outside. My mother came and picked me up. She said, "See, I told you to stay outside. That monkey's gonna get you the next time."

Big Dumplings

The priests and Sisters from St. Johns used to bring all the Apache kids from Cibecue and Whiteriver down there to Mormon Flat. They brought them for weekends so they can be with their families. My sister Donna and my brothers—Albert, Jack, and Joe—used to come with them.

The people with kids at St. Johns gathered at my mother's camp. She went down to the field and got corn. My aunt Bessie was there and she scraped the corns off. Then they ground it and made green cornbread. They were making it when the priests came. They had a dishpan full already. They kept on making it. That cornbread was *good*!

And somebody killed a ram [bighorn sheep]. They made stew out of it with lots of vegetables. The man that owned the store came over and showed them how to make that stew. His name was Jack. He brought lots of vegetables from there. He always did that. When nobody bought the vegetables he brought them over and gave them to the people—potatoes, onions, celery, peppers, and squash. We had a lot of squash but he brought us more.

He made that ram stew. He said, "I'll show you how to make it." He coated the meat with flour and then he put grease in the pan. He browned the meat for a while and put the pieces in a big pot. Then he put about half water and half tomato juice in there and covered it up. When those people started coming, he put dumplings on top and covered it again. They said, "The top of that pot is about to jump away. That thing is about to jump off!" Those dumplings were *big*! Everybody was laughing.

We had tables. We lined them all up under the shade. When the children came with the priests, we told them to eat. They all got together and started eating. Everybody got enough of that stew and there's still a lot left over. We made a big dinner for the children from St. Johns.

One of the priests was a jolly old man. He was trying to get a little boy that was climbing up a tree. He was standing on a branch that's sticking out over the water [Cottonwood Creek]. My father told him, he said, "That branch is gonna break. That tree breaks easy, so be careful. Don't go too far, it's gonna break." That priest was trying to catch that little boy. He couldn't do it. He kept backing out, backing out, holding on to a little branch. *Whoa*! He went down in the water!

Wild Dogs

A Mojave lady asked me to go to the store at Roosevelt with her. She had one little boy but that child was afraid of riding in the wagon. So she left him home at Mormon Flat. We went off in the wagon. We got to the place where there's lots of snakes [the road construction camp at Fish Creek] and we sat there for a while under the cottonwood trees. It's too hot! We got going again and that's when a lot of dogs start following us. I said, "Look! There's some dogs coming after us. They're behind us, a whole bunch of them." That lady said, "There's no dogs around here." I said, "But look! There's lots of dogs! They're coming closer!"

That lady stopped the wagon. One of those dogs tried to get on. Then that lady got scared! She made the horses go again. She made them go faster and faster. She had a long whip and she was whipping the dogs away 'cause they're trying to get at the horses. The horses got scared and started running *real fast*! I was thinking that wagon might fall apart.

That man that brings the groceries was coming from Roosevelt. He seen the dogs trying to get the horses. He was shooting at them. They all got away from there. He stopped next to the wagon. He told us, he said, "Don't go by yourself next time. Get somebody with a gun to go with you. If you don't have a gun, borrow one at the store." He said, "Those are wild dogs. They're hungry. They might jump on you."

We went on. That lady got what she wanted from the store. Then we left to go back. I said, "What are we gonna do when we get to the dogs again?" She said, "Don't talk about it. I hope they're gone." We went past that place and I seen just one of them. I said, "There's one standing way over there." She said, "Here, take this whip. If they come to us, you can whip them while I drive." So she put a rope around me and tied me to the wagon. I sat there with the whip. We went on. That dog I seen left us alone. We got back to Mormon Flat in the evening.

"They Stole Our Name"

In 1923, I think it was, they were making a census at San Carlos. We were at Mormon Flat. We couldn't come back 'cause we didn't have no wagon.

They changed our name on that census. Willie Stevens was the one that did that. He was a policeman, a county policeman. He was married to my aunt Emma, my father's sister. And I guess she told him, "Go ahead, do it for them [enter them in the census]. They can't come back, they're too far away. We can't even get a message to them." He did that but he put the wrong name on the census. He put "Case" instead of "Tulene."[4]

My mother tried to fix it when she got back to San Carlos. She told them, she said, "Our name is not Case." She said, "It's Tulene. That's our real name." She said, "We been going by Tulene for a long time." She told them that. That's when my aunt got mad at my mother. She said, "Why don't you just go ahead and leave it that way. That man [Tulene] is gone, anyway. Our grandfather is gone. It might just as well be 'Case.'" My mother said, "My kids don't want to be 'Case.'" But they left it that way. They never did change it.

My brother Albert was the only one who wouldn't use that name. He fought it and fought it. "I'm not gonna go by that name! I don't care who's trying to put it on me! I know my name! I know!" So he made "Albert" his last name. His Christian name was Joseph. He made "Joseph Albert" his name and that's why all his children are Alberts.

Before I married my husband, Bill Watt, people used to call me Eva Case. I didn't mind it too much 'cause lots of people know that's not my real name. But I wish they had our name on that census 'cause now there's no more Tulenes. There's Cases and Alberts and Watts, and there's my oldest son, Reuben Kessay. All my brothers' kids should be Tulenes. But they stole our name and never did give it back. That's the reason there's no more Tulenes.

Chapter Four

My father got sick while he was gambling at Dahnagolk'id. He came back to Mormon Flat. He got worse. He wanted to go back home. He didn't make it. He died at my aunt Emma's house in Globe. That was in 1924. We went back to Rice and stayed there for a little while. Then we went to Safford and Solomon. We worked over there picking cotton. After that, we came back to Rice. My brother Eugene got a job on the railroad tracks. Him and his wife were helping Silas John. My mother got blind from trachoma, so we went to trachoma camp at San Carlos. She got better. She could still see. Then Augustine got sick, sick, sick. We almost lost him two or three times. Then my sister Donna died. My mother was having a real hard time, but she never did complain. She just kept on going.

The Death of John Tulene — Safford and Solomon — Trachoma Camp — A Little Brown Pill — Silas John Edwards — "When Is My Sister Coming Back from Heaven?"

The Death of John Tulene

We were at Mormon Flat when my father got sick. That was in 1924. The mens quit working for a little while and my father went back to Roosevelt with two of his friends. They wanted to gamble, I guess, 'cause they went to Dahnagolk'id.

They were playing that stick game, *na'izhǫǫsh*. They won. The next day, they played some more and won again. They won three games in a row, and I guess the mens over there got mad at them. "Let's play Mexican cards," they said. They were trying to change their luck, so they started playing cards. My father kept on winning.

He said it was *cold*! They were playing outside, in the open, with just lamps and candles. They played like that all night. The next day it never did get warm. They started back to Mormon Flat, and by the time they got to Gochǫ' Ha'itin my father was getting sick. They got back to Mormon Flat in the afternoon. My father said, "I don't feel good. I'm catching a cold or something. My heart really hurts." So my mother made hot pads with medicine for him. She kept it up. She kept it up for a whole week. By that time he was sick with pneumonia. They said it was pneumonia, but I don't know what it was.

My father was getting worse, so he sent for his mother to bring the wagon from San Carlos. He wanted to take the family back there. He expected her to bring just herself and my grandpa Frank. Instead, she brought my grandpa and a whole bunch of ladies and their kids. There's my aunt Bessie and her children, and a daughter-in-law and her children, too. All their clothing and stuff was piled up on the wagon. It's a *big load*. My father didn't like it. He got mad at my grandmother Rose. He told her, he said, "I'm sick and want to go home! I told you to come by yourselves! I wanted the wagon for my family! You weren't supposed to bring all these people! You should have left them at home!" He was mad. He said, "How are we gonna travel? Where am I gonna put my stuff? Where are my kids supposed to sit? If I put my stuff on the wagon, they're gonna have to walk home and that's a long ways." He was *mad*. He said, "Go home! If you want to, it's fine! Go take these people home! Somehow, I'll find a way."

Then that man, Charley Dickens, came to see my father.[1] He talked to him. I don't know what he said. My father wouldn't tell nobody. His mother asked him about it. He said, "You have no right to know what that man is doing!" He was mad at her. He told her, "Go home!"

They waited for my father to load up the wagon. He didn't do it. He just wandered off down along the river for a while. He came back. His mother was still there. He said, "I thought you were gone. That's why I came back here." He said, "I'm tired. I can't move around no more." Then he laid down under the shade. They asked my mother, "What does he need to take? Are you gonna put anything in the wagon?" My father heard them. "I told you, *no*! Take your women and *go*!" Then he said, "But take her." He was pointing at me. "Take her home for me. She's the only girl in the family, so take her home with you." That's when they got scared. "We'll go in the morning," they said.

Then my father told me, "You go home with my mother. You can go with her and watch the stuff we put on the wagon. Make them put all our things together and tell them not to go digging in them." I said, "OK." He didn't trust those ladies that came over there with my grand-mother Rose.

So the next day we left. I was the only one that went with them. My father and my mother and Dewey and Augustine stayed at Mormon Flat. We went off towards Apache Junction. We went up. We spent the night at Apache Junction.

There used to be a little store there. It's just a little old wood shack but it's long. The store was on one side, and on the other side that man kept his hay and some kind of grain for the horses. I guess he sold mostly water and hay 'cause there's so many wagons and wagon trains going by to Phoenix. They used to stop there all the time.

We went over there to get some water. The water was a *quarter a bucket* and there's no way you can get water anywhere but there. We didn't have no money, so that man just gave it to us. "Go ahead," he said, "fill up your canteens." We asked him if it's all right to spend the night. He said, "Where are you parked?" We told him, "Way over there." He said, "Come over here. Spend the night right here with me." He said, "I'm by myself." So we came closer.

He let us use the water trough for the horses to drink. "Water your horses there," he said. He wanted us to put them in a little shed, a little barn, but we told him, "No, they won't stay in there." We just tied them outside. When we were halfway back to the wagon, he hollered at us. That man sold hay and there's lots of leaves from it, almost like dust, like somebody's been walking on it. He gave that to us for the horses. "Sweep it up and take it to your horses," he said. My aunt Bessie went back to our camp and got a big piece of canvas. We put all those hay leaves on it and took it over there for the horses to eat. That man was wanting to throw it away. "You might as well give it to your horses," he said.

The next morning, real early in the morning, we got ready to go—

but there he was! I guess he saw us get up, running around the wagon, and he knew that we're leaving. He came over. He had a big pot of coffee. He brought the coffee and some crackers and cheese. We were sitting there, all of us, drinking coffee and eating crackers and cheese.

We got back on the road before the sun was up. We got to Superior in the afternoon, maybe around four o'clock—it's all downhill, you know. We had relatives that lived there. We went over to visit with them. They were working in the mine there. They asked us to stay for the night. So that's what we did, 'cause we couldn't go up the mountain in the wagon—it's too high and the horses were tired and we had lots of stuff. One of our relatives asked a Mexican man if we could use his wagon and team to take some of our stuff up the mountain. He said, "Go ahead." So they packed that Mexican's wagon and got it ready.

The next morning, that Mexican and one of my cousins went up the mountain with us. My cousin said, "We'll take your stuff up to the acorn camp." We got going in the morning, real early in the morning before the sun was up. The other wagon, the Mexican's wagon, went first. We were going up, and where the road goes through the mountain there, where the tunnel is now [Queen Creek Tunnel, Arizona Route 60], we stopped for water. There's a spring up there on the side of the cliff. That water has been there a long, long time. My aunt Bessie and her sister-in-law went up there. They got all the canteens and filled them up. They brought them back down. It was so *hot*!

We were just about ready to go again—and here comes a car! It stopped right beside us. Charley Dickens was driving and inside is my mother and father and Augustine and Dewey. My father was hemorrhaging real bad. He was tearing up a blanket and putting the pieces to his mouth. He wanted water. I guess that man [Charley Dickens] knew about that spring 'cause he started going up there. Then my grandmother told him, "We got water already, it's right here." So they gave my father one whole canteen. He was rinsing his mouth and spitting the water out. Boy, that was awful!

My father told us to hurry up. "Just keep going," he said. "I'll probably wait for you in Globe." His sister Emma lived there. Then he called me over. But that man [Charley Dickens] told him, "Don't call her too close to you. You don't even know what you have. It might be dangerous for children." My father said, "I just want to talk to her a little bit."

But that man told me, he said, "Stay right there!" I was standing a little ways from my father and he was talking to me. Then he reached in his pocket and picked out something. He tried to give it to me but that man grabbed it and gave it to my grandmother Rose. He said, "Here, take it and tie it onto her dress." Then they went on. When they left, my grandmother picked up my dress and tied it on the inside with a string. I thought it was a dime. Later, I looked at it. It was a five-dollar gold piece!

So my mother and father went in the car. We kept going behind them. That road is steep! The ladies were walking and us kids were walking. We walked for a while, then got on the wagon, walked again, got on again. That's how we got all the way to the acorn camp. We went all the way to the top.

There were some apple trees up there and that's where we stopped. There were people there. A man and his wife came to us. That lady said, "They just left! They drove through here a little while ago. They didn't stop. He's very sick and he's going home." They told my grandmother to stop and rest. "Come over," they said. "Rest your horses. Look at them! They're tired. They're hungry and thirsty. Give them a rest!" They told a boy to go bring the wagon over there for us. He brought it. He unhitched the horses and took them to a water trough. He brought them back. Then he put some hay down for them. Those people fed us. They were already eating.

After we ate, my grandmother Rose was sitting there talking. A bunch of women were gambling right beside her. They were playing cards for acorns. If you won twice in a row, you got one of those twenty-five pound sacks. I guess they knew that my grandmother's a gambler. "Come on, play," they said. She can't say no! She turned around and started playing! And you know what? She won *seven* of those twenty-five-pound sacks of acorns. Then she said, "Well, we have to keep going."

We were just about to go again when a policeman stopped there. Willie Stevens stopped there in his car. He said, "Is that Case lady here?" My aunt Bessie went over to him. "Yes," she said. Then she came running over and told my grandmother Rose, she said, "He wants you right away. He said they need you right away at Emma's house in Globe. That's where they took my brother." So they got on the police car, my aunt Bessie and my grandmother Rose, and they took off with Willie Stevens. And me and the other ladies and my grandpa, we went down to the wagon with all the acorn sacks. We put them on the wagon. Then we took off.

We went on. The horses were *wet*, soaking wet from being tired. Going down was a little better, a little faster. We went all the way to Claypool and on a hill right there, passing the graveyard going towards Globe, Willie Stevens came for us again. He said, "Can you hurry?" So we hurried and hurried. We were getting closer to Globe. Then Willie Stevens came back for us again. He said, "They need the old man [Frank Case] right away. I brought two men to bring the wagon in, so the old man can go. You don't have to worry about the wagon." So my grandpa got off the wagon and was walking towards the car. Then he turned around and told me, he said, "Come on, come on! You're going with me." So I got off the wagon and got on the car with him. It was right close to Globe. We took off.

There used to be an old long school building on that side of Globe. In those days, that was out of town. We went by the school. Where the courthouse is now, right across from there, there were two adobe houses. My father's sister, my aunt Emma, lived in one of them. She was married to Willie Stevens. So they took us over there and we got off of the car. My grandpa went straight inside. Pretty soon, I heard him praying in there. I guess that's what they wanted him for.

I stayed outside with the kids. They were all sleeping, lined up against the wall of the house. My sister and brothers were there. They came back from St. Johns. I guess Willie Stevens called down there from the police station in Globe. Somebody was already coming to San Carlos from St. Johns, so they caught a ride as far as to Globe. One of my brothers told me, he said, "You can't go in the house. You might as well lay down by those kids and go to sleep." I tried but I kept sitting up, sitting up. My father kept calling my name in there, calling my name, calling my name. But Willie Stevens told him, "You can't have young ones in here. You're a very sick man and those young children can't take it. You can't have any little ones in here."

I heard them talking in there and just towards midnight I heard my father talking real loud. He was talking about stuff he left over there at Mormon Flat. He was asking my mother, "Did you bring that? Did you pack that? Did you pack this?" He said, "I should have told you to bring my beads." He said, "I left them over there. I should have told you to pack them for me. I was going to give them to somebody." See, mens used to string those big glass beads and tie their tweezers on it—that's what he wanted to make. He was talking about that. Then he told my mother, "You know, I don't think I'll be going back there anymore." He said, "I think this is my last trip this way." I could hear him. I was right there by the door.

After that, I went to sleep. Towards morning, real early in the morning, everybody was crying in there. They cried for a long time. Finally, my brother Jack came out. I was sitting up. He said, "Aren't you sleepy?" He said, "Go back to sleep." I said, "I can't. Why are they crying in there?" He said, "Your father's gone." And I said, "Where did he go? Where did he go?" I didn't understand. My brother just got a hold of me and hugged me. "I'll tell you later on," he said. "I've got to go. I've got to go and get some tortillas from a lady down below." He left. When he came back, he had a big pan of tortillas. Everybody came out of the house. They left the door wide open. They opened all the windows, too. Everybody ate. Then Willie Stevens left, I guess to tell his boss at the courthouse that he had to go to San Carlos. He came back. He brought a car back and I think he brought a coffin. I know they took a box in there.

Then they told us to go to the lady that made the tortillas. "Stay over there until we come back," they said. So me and Dewey and my sister went down there. We stayed there for a while. Then we came back to my aunt Emma's house. There's nobody there. They were already gone. That lady came running after us. She said, "What are you doing over here? You're supposed to stay down there with me." We told her, "We want to see our mother." She said, "Your mother is gone. She went with them to San Carlos. You have to stay down there with me." We told her, "We can wait up here." She said, "No, there's nobody here." See, in those days, people had respect for their children and they kept them away from funerals. They're not supposed to be there. So we stayed in Globe. My sister was sixteen years old but still she stayed there. She wanted to go but they told her, "No, you stay here."

So we stayed down there with that lady. Her husband came home with a little wagon. It was a homemade wagon and he took all of us for a ride in it. He took us to where they slaughter beef. When we came back, we told that lady, "We're going back to the house." She said, "There's nobody there. Nobody's home yet. Wait here 'til they come and get you." So we stayed there. I don't know what my mind was. Everybody went to bed and I was sitting up. I was sitting up for a long, long time. I guess that lady's husband noticed me. He told his wife something. She came and told me, she said, "Why don't you go to sleep. When they come back, somebody will come and get you. Don't worry, they'll be back. Go to bed." I lay down but I couldn't get to sleep at all. I just lay there awake. I had a hard time trying to sleep.

When they got through over there at San Carlos, they came back. Finally, they came back. They came back after three days. My grandmother Rose was with them in the wagon. "It took them two days to make the grave," my mother said. "They blasted the rocks where he's buried. They blasted the rocks with dynamite." She said, "They were digging it out for two days. It's got big slabs of rock on top of it now."

You know, long years ago, when somebody died like that, they used to take everything they owned and destroy it. That's what they did with all our stuff. But before they did that, my aunt and Willie Stevens took us down to the courthouse in Globe. The Red Cross was in there and they were giving stuff away. Everybody got something for themselves—clothes, blankets, pots and pans—and my mother got some kind of check. They told her to buy groceries with it. We got the groceries and brought them back to my aunt Emma's house. Then they packed all our old stuff in the wagon, and my mother and my grandmother and my grandpa took it down toward San Carlos. When they came back, they told us to take our clothes off and put the new ones on. We did that. Except for my sister Donna, she didn't want to wear that kind of dress. She wanted to wear a regular Indian dress, a long one. So my aunt Emma gave her one of those and she put it on.

When we started back to San Carlos, there was a fire going way off towards the mountains where the road turns off to Tucson [Arizona State Route 77]. It's way back that way and the smoke was just *coming* out. I guess my brother Jack wasn't supposed to tell us, but he said, "That's where all our stuff is burning, all those things they took in the wagon. It's all over there, it's all burning, everything."

So we went on to San Carlos. We stayed at the Catholic church for a while. Then we went back to Rice. Where the train stopped at Rice, on the other side of the tracks close against the mountain, that's where my father was buried. They blasted the rocks up there. My mother said that some people tried to tell them to take the body across to the regular graveyard. She told them, she said, "It's already been blasted, so we can't do that." See, they believe that if you dig a place for a grave, and then leave that one and go to another place and dig another grave, you're gonna lose somebody for the first one. They didn't want that to happen, so they buried my father up there on that hillside close against the mountain.

Safford and Solomon

They burned up our wickiup and everything. You could see all the ashes there. We stayed there with my grandmother for about a week. Then we went to Safford. My grandmother Rose took us up there, just to get away from that place. The whole family went. There's my grandma and grandpa Frank, Eugene and his wife, my mother and Augustine and Dewey and me. Albert and Jack and Joe and Donna went back to school at St. Johns.

The farmer came around in a truck and we packed our stuff in there. We went with him to Safford, upper Safford towards Solomon.[2] It was just a little town then, maybe nine or eight houses. There's lots of cottonwood trees close to where the train stops at the water tank there. That's where all the Indians lived. They got their water from that water tank. There was a faucet there.

We picked cotton for that farmer. My grandmother Rose and grandpa Frank picked with us for a little while. Then something happened at home, back at San Carlos, so somebody came after them. They went back on the train. They said they were gonna come back for us. They never did, so we just kept on picking cotton. That farmer grew vegetables, too, and my mother got after us for picking watermelons and eating them. But that man just laughed. He said, "It's all right. Go in there and get them anytime you want." So we did. But my mother still got after us. "Don't take too many," she said. "He might change his mind."

Then a farmer from Solomon came and talked with my brother Eugene. My brother told us, he said, "That man wants us to work for him in his cornfields. Do you want to go or stay here? My wife and I are going with him. He's gonna bring us back when we get through. Do you want to go up there with us? If you want to go, get ready." My mother said, "We might as well all go up there. If we stay here, you and your wife will be alone." So we went up there to Solomon.

We stayed up there. There was a cabin at the end of one of the fields. There was nothing inside but dust and dirt. That man told us to clean it out and live there. He said, "Clean it out. You can use the back part for your bedroom or put your food in there." We did that, we cleaned it out. But there's too many snakes around that cabin, rattlesnakes. We told him about it and he sprayed it with something. He sprayed inside and under the floor and outside around it. I guess all the snakes took off, 'cause there's no more after that.

That corn farmer used to come there and get us on a big flat wagon. He took us across to the other side of the river [Gila River]. We stayed there all day. Then he brought us back across at night. And when it rained—boy, that river was high! It's hard to get across. The wagon got stuck in the sand and started sinking down, so we had to get out and walk across. The water was high! They pulled the wagon out with mules, six or eight mules.

They were cutting corn over there at Solomon. They left the corn on the corn plants and piled them together in bundles. Then they put the bundles on the wagon and took them off somewhere. Some of the corn used to fall off the wagon in the field. They just left it there. So my mother asked that man, she said, "Can I have some of these?" He said, "Go ahead, pick them up. Here's some sacks." He gave her a bunch of gunny sacks, and lots of times we went home at night with a big sack of corn. My mother dug a hole in the ground, not too deep, and put the corn in there. She made *dijíízhi* [roasted corn]. The next day, she spread it out in the sun.

Trachoma Camp

When we got done with chopping corn, we went back on the train to Rice. We stayed with my grandmother Rose and her family. My mother had trachoma.[3] She was infected real bad. She can't stand to see the light. She had a blanket over her head all the time. If she wanted something, you put it under the blanket and gave it to her that way. Her eyes were just *bloodshot*! It hurt her real bad.

"It's getting worse," she said. Finally, one of my brothers went and told the doctor about it. They took her across to the hospital. They washed her eyes out and cleaned them real good. Then they put some kind of salve inside her eyes and covered them up. She came home with her eyes covered. She just sat there like that. The next morning, a field nurse came over and changed her bandage. She cleaned out her eyes and put some more of that salve in there. They kept that up for a long time.

The whole reservation was infected by trachoma. They found out that more and more people were having trouble with their eyes. My whole family had trachoma. My mother and Augustine had it real bad. I had it and Dewey had it, and Joe and my sister Donna had it. It was all over the reservation, so they gathered the people at San Carlos. Lots of people went down there.

The government put up a whole bunch of tents. They called it "trachoma camp." We lived there in a tent, a wall tent, and my grandmother Rose and her family got one of those, too. We had another tent for our groceries. There's lots of people living in tents—it's over eighty tents, I think. The clinic was up on a hill and every morning we walked up there. They washed out our eyes and then they put that salve medicine in there. Some people didn't go to the clinic. They just stayed in their tents. A policeman went around and got them. He told them, he said, "You have to go to the clinic."

They gave us lots of stuff. Each one of us got a tin plate and a fork and a knife and a spoon and a tin cup. They gave my mother a coffee pot, a frying pan, a dishpan and pans, and a big spoon to cook with. She got all of those. And they gave us army blankets. They were kind of tan-looking with brown trim on the end. They gave each of us two blankets. They told us not to drink out of the same cup and not to use the same spoon. And they told us to use lots of soap in our dishwashing water. "Wash everything," they said. "Wash everything real good."

Everybody that was treated got a card. It's got your name on it and other stuff. My mother kept all our cards. Every time you go to the clinic, they punch a hole in the card, a tiny little hole, and they give you seventy-five cents. See, a lot of people don't want to go to that clinic. So they told them, "You get seventy-five cents each time you see the doctor. Your children, too." And they said, "If your child has bad eyes, and if you leave it like that and don't treat it, they're gonna go blind. There's gonna be blind people all over." So I guess the people got scared. A lot of them signed up for that trachoma camp at San Carlos.

We stayed there for about two months, I think. All we did was just sit there. I used to go to the river [San Carlos River] and play in the water. Then I came back and waited for the clinic again. We went in the morning, we went at lunchtime, and then we went in the evening. When we needed something, they [trachoma camp workers] went to the store and brought it right to the tent. Or you could go to the store yourself. Sometimes my mother didn't need anything, so she saved the money we got. One time, she said, she had over fifty dollars. But you could only go to one store. It's down there where the army camp used to be. You could get groceries there and whatever else you need. My mother showed them all our cards and got what she needed.

Us kids got cured right away. We didn't have too much trouble. But my mother had it real bad. She can't go out in the sun. It hurt her to see the light. She covered her head with a blanket when she went outside the tent. We stayed there 'til she was getting better. Then we went home to Rice with my grandmother Rose and her kids. They gave us some medicine. When it's all gone you're supposed to come back and get some more.

My mother usually made baskets to sell. She sold them in Globe. But now she couldn't do that 'cause of her eyes. The doctor told her not to do nothing like that. She got credit for groceries at one of the stores at Rice. She was friends with the wife of the man that kept the store. I guess that lady felt sorry for my mother 'cause she always gave her credit. My mother got better. She could still see. But then, later on, after she went back to Cibecue and married my stepfather, it started up all over again. She got blind again from trachoma. I was going to school at St. Johns. I had to come home and look after my mother. After that I never did go back to school.

A Little Brown Pill

Augustine was sick all the time. He was sick all the time. He wouldn't eat hardly anything. We almost lost him two or three times.

The Catholic priest found out that he was very sick. He came and baptized him. After that he said, "I have a doctor in Globe that I go to see. I'll ask him to see if he can help you." So the next time that priest went to Globe—it was about two days later, I think—my mother and Augustine went with him over there. The doctor saw the priest first, and then my mother took my brother in there. The doctor told her, "Your son's got a sensitive stomach. It's hard for him to digest his food." Then he gave my mother some kind of pills, little ones, that look like chocolate candy.

So Augustine was eating those things and that really brought him out of it. He started eating again. The doctor told my mother, "Start with oatmeal. Put water and a little milk in there and mash it up real good." So my mother started making that watery oatmeal for him. He kept eating it, eating it, and pretty soon he was crying for tortillas. So she gave him tortillas. He got over his sickness. That little brown pill— I don't know what it was—really helped him out. He never did get sick after that. And look at him now—he's seventy-seven, seventy-eight. That's a long time, isn't it?

Silas John Edwards

My brother Eugene worked at Mormon Flat 'til 1924. Then he got married and came back to San Carlos. His wife was from there. He started working on the railroad tracks. He worked between Bylas and Cutter. They used to have that square-looking little cart and he used to run around on that thing. My mother asked him, she said, "What do you do when the train comes and your cart is still on the track?" He said, "It's easy, you push some kind of button and it flips over. It lifts up on one side and goes over on the other." I guess my mother was worried that he might get hurt.

My brother Eugene and his wife worked with Silas John [Edwards].[4] In the springtime, the people that followed that man used to go to the holy ground. They had their dances there. There's four posts that mark it out and each one, each direction, is a different color. They have different designs on them, too. The mens that helped him [Silas John] lined up all the people and made them take their shoes off. "Put them in front of you," they said. Then they blessed their shoes with *hádndín* [cattail pollen], and they blessed around their legs and feet.

Religious leader Silas John Edwards (third from left) with assistants near Rice, San Carlos Apache Indian Reservation, date unknown. The four upright posts with crosses on top mark out a "holy ground" where Edwards's followers danced and prayed, sometimes carrying snakes.

He [Silas John] said, "That's in case you see a snake close to your feet. If you see one, nothing will happen. It won't do nothing to you." It must be true, 'cause we never seen a snake or nothing that bites with poison.

   We used to go over there to the holy ground. Four mens and four ladies danced with snakes. Some of them were rattlesnakes, big ones. Eugene and his wife were picked to go after the snakes. They got a big basket, a burden basket, and they went with that to look for them. They put all of them in there. Then they brought them back. The next day, in the morning before they started dancing, they put their hands out and that man [Silas John] made signs on their hands with yellow powder. He told them, he said, "Don't be scared. When you put your hand in there to pick one up, don't hold back. Get it right away. Get it behind the head and take it out." So that's what they did. Eugene's wife was scared of *anything*—a spider, even a little bug. But she had to get those snakes and pick them up. I don't know how she did that! She just put her hand in there and got one. She held it while she was dancing.

Before they started dancing, he [Silas John] told them, he said, "Don't say anything about how it might hurt you! Don't even *think* how it might hurt you. Think of it as a friend. Don't be scared, 'cause they know when you're scared of them." He said, "If it goes up around your arm, don't drop it. If you have to bring it down, hold it close to the head and turn it around." Then he told them, he said, "If it bites you on the hand or somewhere else, don't say, 'It bit me.' Just say, 'The snake put yellow powder on my hand.' That way, it won't hurt you. Even though it put poison in your skin, it still won't hurt you." That's what he told the ones that were dancing with snakes.

And I guess that's what happened to one of the ladies that was dancing. The snake bit her finger. I guess she squeezed it a little too hard. I guess she was scared of it. She started crying 'cause she thought it was gonna make her sick. But he told her, he said, "Don't cry." Then he said, "Put the snake back in the basket and take it inside the four posts." Then he put yellow powder around her arm four times. He told her, "Nothing will happen to you." And it didn't! It didn't swell up or nothing. He told her, he said, "If you had said, 'It bit me,' that poison could have gotten you right away. But you didn't say that. You remembered what I told you." Then he told the rest of the people. He said, "Now you know why I told you to do that."

One night, everybody slept over there by the holy ground. My mother fixed a bed for us. My brother Eugene came over and told her to get us up before sunrise. "Be ready," he said. Early in the morning, he went and got some water. He put it in a pan. He told us to wash our face. We got ready. We went over there. Everybody was lined up in a circle around the four posts. Then the dancers went in there, four mens and four ladies. Each of them had a snake. They went around and held the snake to your hand. There's yellow powder on your hand and the snake puts out its tongue and eats it. They did that for everybody that's standing in the line.

There was one girl—she's about seventeen or eighteen years old— that was standing there. She was standing there with her hand out and that snake turned its head away from her. The next dancer did the same thing and the snake turned its head away again. The third one and the fourth one did the same way. And the fourth one, when they brought it close to her, snapped at her hand. They said that girl was not gonna be with us very long 'cause the snakes wouldn't eat the powder on her hand. So they started praying for her. About two or three weeks later that girl died.

Another time, there were lots of people over there at the holy ground. Silas John told them, he said, "Somebody's gonna come here. Somebody's gonna come and visit us pretty soon"—and he pointed to the snakes in the basket. Then he said, "If you see the visitor, don't chase it away. Just leave it alone. Get out of its way. Let it stay."

We forgot all about it. Everybody was taking their shoes off. They were putting yellow powder on their feet and in their shoes for the summer. They were all lined up in a big circle around the holy ground, lots of people and their kids. He [Silas John] was going around to them. The reason they put yellow powder in their shoes is that they leave them on the ground where there's lots of poison things—bugs, spiders, scorpions, snakes. If you used that yellow powder, those things wouldn't hurt you. That's why they put it in their shoes.

Eugene's wife was helping that man [Silas John]. She went to one of the posts to get more yellow powder. It was in a bag hanging on the post. That's when she seen it! The snake was up there! It was wrapped around the post on top. She hollered but she's not scared. He [Silas John] came over to where she was standing. She said, "I think this is the one you were talking about. The visitor is already here." That's what she told that man, Silas John.

That snake was all wrapped up around the post and its head was *way up* over the top. Then that man put some yellow powder in his hand and put it out to the snake. And you know what? The snake put its tongue on the powder! It did it again and again! Then everybody started doing that, putting yellow powder in their hand and holding it out for the snake. The snake was eating it. Everybody was feeding the visitor. Then they started singing and dancing, and its head started going back and forth. Its head was *way up*, going back and forth. It kept on doing that. It was still there when they got finished, still wrapped around the post on top.

I wondered why the snake did that. And how did that man know that one of them was coming? I asked my brother Eugene and he got after me. He said, "We don't talk about it. Don't say anything. Think about it and don't say anything."

Silas John cured a lot of people. There was a person that fell off a bridge and hurt his hip. It never would get well. The doctor told him that his bone was cracked and out of place. He was in the hospital at San Carlos but his relatives came and took him out 'cause he didn't like it in there. He just stayed home. He wouldn't stand up, he wouldn't sit up. He just laid on his bed all the time. And that man [Silas John] told him, he said, "If it cures sickness, it should cure you, too. 'Cause you're not really sick, it's just your bone."

He [Silas John] got four men to help him. They put a canvas around the four posts. Then they put that man in the middle in there. My brother Eugene said that they took his clothes off from the waist down. Then they made him point to where it hurts the most. Then they put a snake to that place. The snake licked it. Pretty soon, they had four snakes on that man. There was a snake around his leg, and another one around his other leg, and another one where his belt was at. And there's another one below where his hip joints are at. All four of them were wrapped around him while they're praying.

Then they made that man stand up. None of the snakes fell off! They just stayed on him. And Silas John told him, he said, "If none of the snakes fall off, you're gonna be well. Walk to the first post, then to the second post, then to the third, and then to the fourth. Turn around and walk back. Then we'll take the snakes off." So he did that. My brother said it was *really hard* to take them off when he came back.

And then—I think it was the same day—they [Silas John and his assistants] were eating lunch. He [Silas John] told that man they were praying for to come and eat. He got up and walked over there. He walked! He walked good! And from that time on, he never did get down anymore. Silas John told him, "From now on, don't be afraid to walk."

"When Is My Sister Coming Back from Heaven?"

My sister died at San Carlos. They sent her back from St. Johns. She was very sick. She died in 1925.

That was when my mother got throwed in jail. What happened was, me and Dewey went somewhere with my grandmother Rose. We were digging those little sweet potato–looking plants, the kind that grows in sandy places. We were digging those and my grandmother left us. I

guess she thought we're right behind her—but we're not. We kept digging those plants up. We got a big sackful and we started going home.
We had to go through a wide open place where the train stops. I guess
the policeman was riding around and he seen us walking there. I guess
he watched to see where we were going. He followed us home.

He came there. He said, "Why aren't those kids in school?" My
mother said, "They're not supposed to go to school over here. We want
them to go to school at St. Johns. Their brothers are there already.
The priest is gonna be taking them." That policeman told her, he said,
"Well, while they're waiting, they can go to school over here." He was
getting smart with her. Then he told my mother that she's got to go to
jail. "Let's go!" he said. So he marched her across to the jail.

Only the day before, my sister Donna came back from St. Johns.
They brought her home 'cause she was very sick. She was there with
us. When she seen my mother go off with the policeman, she got
scared. She got up from under the shade and ran across to get the
priest. She's not supposed to be running, but she ran all the way to the
church and told the priest that my mother was in jail. He went over
there right away. He got her out. He told them, he said, "Those kids
are my children. I'm taking them to school at St. Johns. I have their
mother's permission." He said, "I'm gonna take them as soon as my
car gets fixed—the brakes is no good." They told him, "Take those
kids down there as soon as possible." My mother and sister came back
home. When my sister got back home, she went to sleep. She was sleeping for a long time. The next day, she didn't feel right. She said it hurt
up around her neck. She wouldn't eat anything.

Two days after the priest got my mother out of jail, he came and
asked her, he said, "Are your children ready to go to St. Johns?" Me and
Dewey were ready. My sister was sick but she wanted to go with us.
My mother tried to tell her to stay. Then the priest said, "If she wants
to go, it's all right. I'll take her to see another doctor in Phoenix." So
my mother said, "Take her, if she wants to go. Maybe she can see her
friends and her brothers down there. It might make her feel better."
Then my sister said, "No, I want to make sure that my sister and my
brother get there all right. They never have been to school before."
So my mother let her go. The priest took her. My sister Donna went
with us.

She stayed at St. Johns only three or two days. She stayed in the clinic there. Then they took her to see a doctor in Phoenix. The doctor said that her tonsils were enlarged. He said they're so big they need to be out, an operation or something. I guess they called from St. Johns to San Carlos 'cause the priest came over and talked to my mother. She told him that she didn't want an operation on her daughter. So they brought my sister back home again. She was very sick.

After my sister got back, my grandmother Rose said, "There's a doctor here that works on children. Maybe he can help her." That doctor's name was "Porky." He's a *big* man. They took my sister over there and that doctor told her, he said, "I can't help you now, it's too late." She stayed there in the hospital. That stuff went up to her ears and one of them opened up. It was draining but her neck was real big. Her face swelled up. Pretty soon, where she swallows came together. It won't open up. The doctor put a tube in her. They gave her just nothing but liquids.

I think she died in September—September 1925. My mother wanted her kids to come back from St. Johns. She wanted us to come back for our sister's funeral. But the priest told her no. He told her, he said, "It's better that they don't see her like this. They can remember her all right but they won't remember her the way she looks now. It's better to keep them over there in school. They're well off over there." My mother was really sad but she just let it go.

They buried my sister. About a week later, I think it was. The priest came from San Carlos to St. Johns and told my brother Jack. He told him his sister died. He told him, he said, "Don't show that you're really sad about this. Talk to your brothers and sister but try to keep them out of it." So Jack told us that our sister was gone. He said something like, "Well, the priest said that she's in heaven now." I thought, "She must have gone to a different hospital, some other place where she can get cured." I didn't know what heaven is.

And that's how I hurt my mother when we got back home. When we came back from St. Johns—that was in May, I think—I still didn't understand what it was all about. So I asked my mother, I said, "When is my sister coming back from heaven?" That was all it took to make her real sad all over again. Jack didn't know how to answer me himself, so he went to go get the priest. He said, "Will you come over and talk to my sister and brothers?"

So the priest came and talked to us. Then he took us to the grave.

He told my brother Jack, "It's better this way. It's better to show them where she's at." And that's when I *really* found out. That's when we *really* understood. That's when I knew that my sister was gone. My brother told us, he said, "Don't mention nothing to our mother anymore. Just pray for her. You know how to pray, so just pray for her."

I lost three sisters. Two of them were just babies. My sister Donna was seventeen when she died. That was in 1925.

Chapter Five

My grandmother Rose belonged to the Catholics for a long time. She was young when she got interested in that. She put all her family through that church, even my mother and father, so we were really acquainted with the Catholics. That's why we went to school at St. Johns. They took care of the children down there and tried to help them out. They were strict, though. I went to St. Johns from 1925 'til 1929. That was it. I had to come home and look after my mother 'cause she got blind with trachoma again. I never went back to school after that. They were strict down there at St. Johns, but I liked it.

Arrival at St. Johns—"This Is a Church"—Orphans, New Names, and English— Boys on One Side, Girls on the Other—"It's Just Like in the Army"—Music— A Near Disaster—Company E—Chickenpox!—Jobs and Crusty Bread—"I'm Not Going Home"—No Shoes and Hot Cement—Rebellions and Runaways—Farewell to St. Johns—"I Liked It Down There"

Arrival at St. Johns

My sister Donna was with us when me and Dewey went to St. Johns. She didn't have long to live. We went down there on a little car with the priest. There's two seats up front and the back seat pulls out. Me and Dewey were in the back seat—no shade, nothing. The priest tied us in there. He put a rope around us to keep us in there. I guess he thought we might stand up while he's driving, so he tied us down so we don't fall out.

We stopped at Superior, right where the town is at, down in the bottom of a big wash. There's a water tank down there, close to a sycamore tree, and that's where we ate lunch. My brother wouldn't eat it. It's a ham sandwich—I guess the priest made it before he left San Carlos—and Dewey wouldn't eat the meat part. He just ate the lettuce. He told the priest, "You're supposed to boil this." He thought it was like *it'qq*, that wild spinach we eat. That's what he was thinking about. "You're supposed to boil it first," he said. My sister was laughing.

We stayed there for a few minutes and then we took off again. He took us to St. Mary's Catholic Church in Phoenix. We stayed there for a few minutes 'cause he wanted to call to St. Johns and tell them that we're coming. Phoenix was a little town then and in Mesa there's just a few houses. And there's nothing but trees, lots of cottonwood trees, and houses here and there not too close together. We stopped and the priest bought us something to drink. Then we went on to St. Johns. I was kind of scared. I was wondering what school is.

When we got to St. Johns we went all the way to the girls' dormitory. We got off over there. All the girls that knew my sister came over and hugged her. They're real glad to see her. Then the priest took Dewey back to the boys' side. He said, "You can't stay here with your sisters. You have to go to see your brothers, Jack and Joe." Dewey started crying but the priest said, "Your brothers are over there waiting for you." So Dewey got back on the car and went with the priest to the boys' side.

They put me with a group of girls. They're younger than the group my sister's in. I had Virginia and Sadie Stevens in my group. They're my close cousins from San Carlos. When it was time to eat they took us to the dining room. Everybody's real nice, even the girls that don't know you. They just grabbed you and took you around and showed you the dormitory, the clinic, the playroom, everything.

"This Is a Church"

There was a Catholic priest that used to come to Cibecue. He's a *real* old man. His name was Father Nevadas. He rode horseback from San Carlos to Cibecue. He used to come there and visit different houses. He came about once a month. I seen him lots of times.

I seen him again at San Carlos two days before we left to go to St.

Johns. After we got to St. Johns, the next morning, we all got up and
went to church—and there's that priest again! My sister was sitting at
the far end of the bench. I jumped up and hollered at her, "Look, that
priest is here! The horse man!" They all started laughing at me. One
of the Sisters came over and told me to sit down. And a girl from San
Carlos—her name was Terry Hoffman—she told me, she said, "This is
a church. You're not supposed to talk loud in here. You have to be quiet
'til it's over with. You can talk to your sister after you get out." So I sat
down. Then we all got out.

We went outside. We all lined up and marched to the girls' dormitory. I asked my sister, I said, "Did you see the priest in there? Did
you see him?" She said, "I know, he was at San Carlos. He goes everywhere to different churches. The church at San Carlos is not the only
church. They're all over, everywhere." She said, "That's what he does.
He goes and visits the churches." That priest was *real old*. You can't
hardly hear him talk.

Orphans, New Names, and English

There's lots of different tribes at St. Johns. It's mostly Pimas and Papagos, but there's Apaches from here [White Mountain Apaches] and
from San Carlos and Bylas and Camp Verde. There's kids from Mescalero, too, and Mojaves, Navajos, Hopis, and a few from Zuni and Laguna.
Some of them were orphans. One of them was an Apache girl from
Camp Verde. Her name was Hattie Jones. I always ask about her to see
if she's alive and has any family. Nobody knows. That poor girl was the
only one in her family.

Some of the boys that came to school had real long hair. They cut
it bald-headed the first time, not right down to the skin but real short.
They cut the girls' hair, too. It's short on the side and bangs. And they
sent the kids' clothes back to their families. They gave each of them a
bag and they told them to put their clothes in there. Then they sent it
back to their family. Then they gave them all new clothes.

Some of the kids had only Indian names, so they gave them new
names, English names. My sister told the Sisters that my name is
Eva—Eva Tulene—so that's what they called me. And some of the kids
don't know how to use a knife and fork. "What's this for?" they said.
The bigger girls, the older ones, showed them how to use those things,

Students at St. Johns Indian School and Mission in their school uniforms, 1928 or 1929. Back row, left to right: Michael Antone (Pima), Lewis Machukay (Western Apache). Front row: Jack Tulene Case, Andrew Logan (Western Apache).

Western Apache students at St. Johns Indian School and Mission, 1928 or 1929. On special occasions, these young men performed a version of the Apache *gáán* ceremonial as entertainment for visitors to the school. Left to right: John Burnette, Jack Tulene Case, Joe Tulene Case, Andrew Johnson. The boys in masks are unidentified. Except for Burnette, who is holding a drum, all are wearing wigs.

and there's a Sister that went around all the time in the dining room. "You're supposed to do it this way," she said.

All the kids talked English, the little ones just a little bit at first. See, nobody understands you if you talk your own language, so the kids have to learn English. They learned real fast! The girls' advisor told the older girls to teach the younger ones. "Show them what the names of different things are," she said. "Show them what they want to know." My sister used to try to teach us at home, just a little, not very much. But we learned fast, me and the other kids, 'cause everybody talked English all the time. After you catch on, you're not supposed to talk your own language anymore. If they catch you talking your own language, they punished you. They made you do extra work.

The girls that got punished had to strip the dormitory. The day they changed the sheets they had to strip every single one of the beds.

They put all the sheets in a cart and brought them to the laundry. It's hard work 'cause they had to carry them downstairs, go upstairs and get some more, carry them down again, go upstairs again—'til they're done. That's *hard*! There's about two hundred girls—two hundred beds—and it takes a long time. They got *tired*!

It's the same way with the boys. If they did something wrong, they gave them extra work. They made them milk the cows at three o'clock in the morning. My brother Joe said that they whipped the boys, too, but only if it's *real bad* and they can't control them. Mostly, they just gave them extra work.

Boys on One Side, Girls on the Other

They separated the boys and girls. They *always* kept them separate. The girls' dormitory was on this side, the boys' dormitory was on the other side, and there's other buildings in the middle. In class, the boys didn't mix with the girls—there's boys on this side, girls on that side. They're in the same place but they're separated. It's the same in the dining room, boys on one side, girls on the other.

At first I tried to go over to the boys' side and see my brothers, just to talk to them. I tried to go over there and I got caught every time. "I have to see my brothers," I said. Then somebody told the priest and he took me to a room where I could visit with them for a little while. Jack was the one that told me, he said, "Look, you're supposed to stay on that side. Girls don't mix with boys. The boys live over here and the girls live over there." He said, "We're not supposed to go on the girls' side and the girls are not supposed to go on the boys' side. You're supposed to stay over there."

After I got used to it, it was like being at home. To me, it was. I don't know how everybody else thought about it. My brothers liked it, too. If I want to see them, I have to go to the office first. The priest went after my brothers and brought them over there. It's a little room with chairs and books. We sat there and talked. I did that about twice a week at first. Then I got used to being with the girls on the other side. "Why don't you come see us no more?" my brothers said. "I'm all right now," I said. I made friends with some of the girls, especially Zema Early. She was Kenzie Early's sister. She was from Cibecue.

"It's Just Like in the Army"

They grouped the kids by size, boys and girls both. They called them by "company." There's five of them—Company A, B, C, D, and E. Company A was the big girls, the older ones. Some of them were twenty years old. The girls in B were sixteen or seventeen, something like that. I was in Company D at first, then in C. The little girls, the youngest ones, the ones I used to take care of, were in Company E.

Everywhere we went, we had to line up and march to where we're going. There's two leaders up front and the rest line up behind them. We marched to the schoolroom and then we marched back to the dormitory. The girls had school in the boys' dormitory downstairs, so we had to march over there. When it's time to go and eat, we marched to the dining room. Then we marched back to the dormitory again. In the morning, we marched to church. It's just like in the army.

They used to teach us all kinds of stuff, mostly prayers. We're praying *all* the time! We prayed to eat, we prayed after we eat. Going to school we prayed, after school we prayed. And at recess time, some of the kids went to church to pray. They didn't have to do that, only if they wanted to.

In school, after everybody got to their desk, they prayed. After they prayed, they sat down and started their lesson. They started wherever they left off yesterday. When they're finished with a book they put that one aside and started on a new one. They're teaching us to read and teaching us numbers and teaching us English. And in the afternoon, from two 'til three, they had Bible class. It's nice. They don't preach against Indians' religion. They told us that each nationality has their own way of praying but still they're praying to the same thing.

They had lots of things to play with over there. They had lots of games, like checkers. And when it's raining, or when it's cold outside, the girls went to a big playroom. They can do whatever they want in there. They can iron their clothes, if they want to, or do beadwork. The little ones used to play dolls. The bigger girls helped the little ones make doll clothes. They gave them dolls on Christmas. Then they made dresses and clothes for the dolls. The little girls liked that.

Music

They were teaching us music, too. The boys had a band, horns and drums. My brother Joe played the one that sticks out on the side [a flute], and Jack had the one that you push back and forth [a trombone]. My brother Albert was a drummer. The girls played the instruments with wires—violin, guitar, mandolin, and that round silver one [banjo]. Some of the girls played organ and piano, too.

I played piano and organ. When you're just starting, they gave you a long card. It's got pictures of the keys on it. The Sister that's teaching you reads out the letters—A, B, C, E—and then you know which fingers to put on the card. At first, that's how we played—we put the card on the table and played the card. There's no music. After that, we took turns at the piano and organ. They had two pianos and three organs in the music room. People from Phoenix donated them to the school.

There was a Pima girl that learned real good. She played in church. I played in church, too. On Sundays, we had to take all our music books and go up there. The organ was upstairs and that's where we played.

The best music teacher was Sister Mary Joseph. She was old, real old. I used to go with her to the music room and she used to sit there and talk to me and teach me how to play. "Just take your time," she said. Sister Teresena was a music teacher, too, but she was mean. If you didn't catch on fast enough, or if you made a mistake, she got mad. She was very impatient. Sister Mary Joseph wasn't like that. She never did get mad, so the music came out OK.

A Near Disaster

My uncle, Robert Beatty, went after my mother in 1926. He went down to Rice and brought her back to Cibecue. Augustine was about four years old. I was at St. Johns when they brought them back home. The first time me and my brothers came home for summer vacation, we stayed with my mother and my uncle across from the old school in Cibecue. My mother wasn't married to my stepfather yet. In the fall, we went back to St. Johns. There was lots of kids going that year. We had a whole truckload. They took us back in a little black truck.

The kids from San Carlos were supposed to get there the same day as us, but they had bad luck. The driver got all the way to Phoenix. Then he started taking his time. They spent the night somewhere down there, Mesa or Tempe. There's a big canal close to St. Johns, and the next day, in the morning, they were driving along that canal to get to the main road. And then that driver—they said he was drinking—went and spilled the kids in the canal. My cousin, Henry Stevens, jumped out and got hold of the truck. Some other boys helped him hold it up while the kids crawled out from under it. Then they let go and the truck turned over on its back. Those kids from San Carlos lost all their stuff.

Company E

I used to take care of the little girls, Company E. That was my job. I stayed with them in the morning while everybody went to church at six o'clock. They stayed in bed until all the other girls were gone. After that, I helped them put their clothes on, put their shoes on, fix their beds. And then, when each of them was ready, I made them sit down in the middle of the floor. When they're all together there, when everybody's ready, we marched downstairs to the washroom. I helped them wash up and comb their hair, and I seen if their stockings are tied up good. See, they wore those long stockings and they used to lose their garters. I used to tear rags and tie their stockings up for them. And then, when everybody's ready again, I marched with them to the dining room. They went in there and sat down. The older girls that work there fed them right away. They usually gave them oatmeal, prunes, and bread.

In the evening, I played with them, the little ones. They didn't mix with the other girls. Like I told you, they went by size and age at St. Johns. If the different sizes mixed together, they didn't like it. They didn't want the little girls to hear what some bigger ones might be talking about. In the evening, the big girls used to play with a tennis ball or just visit with each other. The middle-size girls used to play volleyball and baseball. The little ones learned to march. I made them march around. They liked that, they liked marching around. So I was teaching them. If one of them didn't do it right, I picked one that's perfect— perfect in marching—and put those two together. They marched back and forth. "Keep time!" I said. "Start off with your left foot, all the time with your left. It's on this side." And I used to put a number 1 on their left shoe and a number 2 on their right shoe. "One, two!" I said. "One, two!" That's how those little ones got started marching.

At the end of school, in May, they had a contest—boys and girls both—to see who marches the prettiest. The ones that won got to have a party. And you know what happened? The little girls marched perfectly, better than all the bigger girls. And on the boys' side, the full-grown boys won over the younger ones. So the full-grown boys had a party with all those little girls. The boys said, "I thought we were gonna get big girls over here." Everybody was just laughing!

Chickenpox!

The second year I was there I got chickenpox. I got it *real bad*! There's no doctor at St. Johns. There's a nurse, though, a Pima woman. Her name was Mary Jose. That lady went to nursing school. She was really nice. When somebody was sick in the clinic there, she always tried to take care of them real good. She took care of me.

I was just *covered* with sores—my face, my head, even my eyes. The nurse had to shave all my hair off. Other kids got it first. They told us to stay away from them, so we tried to stay away. I got it from a little girl I was taking care of. See, when they went to bed I went over there and helped them—fix their beds, cover them up, show books to them. And this little girl wouldn't go to sleep. Everybody else went to sleep except her. So I laid in the bed with her, showing her books. Finally, she went to sleep. She's the one I got it from.

They took me to a hospital in Phoenix. The doctor kept me there for one week. My hands were just *sores*—and my face, my neck, my body. I was laying there with no cover on, just a wet rag over my eyes. While I'm laying there, the sores stick to the pillow, and when they peel it off it hurts and bleeds. So they put a rubber cover on the pillow and some kind of oil on the sores. The medicine they used was something like sulfur. It's yellow. They mixed that with honey and gave it to you, a spoonful in your mouth. And the doctor put something in the water in the bathtub. It's purple. They put me in there for about an hour. They put a wet rag over my face and head. At one time, I thought I was *gone*! It made me swell up all over! There's lots of kids with chickenpox, but not as bad as I was.

They kept me in the hospital for a week. Then they sent me back to St. Johns when the sores were drying up. But they wouldn't let me stay in the dormitory, so I stayed in the clinic for about three months. Finally they said, "Do you want to go back to school?" I said, "Yes." So I went in there and the kids were afraid of me. They looked at me funny 'cause I was bandaged all over. They were sitting far away from me. When I came out of school at lunchtime I went back to the clinic. The nurse told me, she said, "You're supposed to eat in the dining room with the rest of the kids." I said, "The kids don't want me. They're afraid of me." So she went after some food and brought it back. She said, "Do you want to go back to school this afternoon?" I said, "No, I don't think so." Then, finally, the Sister that's in charge of the girls came over there with books and papers. After that I went to school in the clinic. I stayed there 'til everything was dried up.

A lady from Camp Verde came over there. She told the nurse, "My daughter was like that. A doctor told me to put castor oil on her sores. Wherever the scars are at, rub castor oil on there. That's how the scars went away." I did that. I had castor oil all over, especially my face. Even so, it left a whole lot of scars.

Jobs and Crusty Bread

All the kids had different jobs. In the morning, after they ate, the little girls went outside and picked up paper—you know, litter—and the middle-size girls cleaned the yard. The older girls cleaned the play-room, the laundry room, the dining room, the washroom. Some of them worked in the dormitory. They had to sweep the floor *real good*. And whoever didn't fix their bed had to go back and fix it!

Lots of girls worked in the laundry. The bigger girls did all the hand ironing. They used those old irons, heavy ones, and they stacked them up on a woodstove in the laundry. It gets *real hot* in there. I used to fold clothes all the time. And I worked on that big roller thing—you put the flat sheets in there and it irons them. Some of the boys worked in the laundry, too. They ran the washing machine and kept the woodstove going.

They used to teach the girls sewing. About twenty of the grown girls made dresses for us and shirts for the boys. The dresses were all the same color, made from the same material. They're gabardine with stripes, blue and white stripes. They were kind of stiff so they had to wash them after they made them. Underneath, the girls wore bloomers. One time, some people from California sent a whole lot of material—flannel material—and we made pajamas for the boys. The girls slept in nightgowns, long ones, and we made those, too. We had gray blankets and white blankets. They're wool. They looked like army blankets.

Half of the boys went to school in the morning and half of them worked on the farm and dairy. Then they changed places—the ones that were working went to school, and the ones in school that morning went to work. See, they grew their own vegetables there. They grew potatoes and corn, squash and watermelons, honeydew, all those things. They grew them by irrigation. The boys worked in the fields. They got the weeds out and everything. They took the vegetables over to the dining room and cut them up and gave them to the cooks.

The boys took care of the cattle, too, and the pigs and chickens. One time, somebody from California brought a whole lot of turkeys down and they used to look after them. Jack and Joe and their cousin Jimmy Stevens helped take care of the cattle. They're dairy cattle, milk cows. They had a pasture for them—I think it's about a mile from the school, maybe more—and that's where they kept their feed. There's a water trough over there and a water pump and a barn. The boys' swimming pool was over there, too. They used to go swimming on Saturdays and Sundays. The girls had their own swimming pool behind the dormitory.

Every morning my brothers went to milk the cattle. Some other boys went with them. They ran up there early in the morning—they race!—and whoever got there first opened the gate. There's about forty milk cows, I think, and those boys milked them every morning. They milked them in the barn. They called them by numbers. "Number One, get in here!" My brother said they came right away. Those cows gave lots of milk. We drank milk all the time.

The Sisters made butter and Brother Narciso—I think that was his name—made bread. They had a bread cutter inside the dining room. You put a loaf in there and then another one and that machine cut the bread. It slices by itself! The girls always liked to get the end of the loaf—they're just *itching* to get that. It's crusty and tastes real good

Western Apache students at St. Johns Indian School and Mission about to depart for summer vacation, 1928 or 1929.

with milk. About all we drank is milk. Sometimes they put honey on the bread. That crusty bread was real good with honey and butter and milk. And sometimes they let the girls make tortillas. They took two halves of an oil drum and put the fire inside. Then they put a screen on top. The girls made tortillas on that.

"I'm Not Going Home"

The second year I went over there, I wasn't supposed to stay during the summer. I was supposed to go home to Cibecue for vacation. But I stayed.

The day the trucks were coming to take the kids back home they told us to clean our suitcase and pack it. Then they locked it up and put it in a corner. It had a tag with your name on it. After that, the Sister came in and said, "Now it's time for you to go run around and play outside. Go get your balls and play outside 'til the trucks get here." Everybody went outside.

I was in the washroom. I got my suitcase from off the pile. There's a restroom in the back and way on the far end there's a sink, a deep sink. It's dark over there—you can't hardly see—and that's where I put my suitcase. I put it under the sink. Then I went outside to play.

About fifteen or twenty minutes later, the bell rang. Everybody ran. They ran to their company and lined up 'cause the trucks were coming. But I didn't go. I stayed behind. Nobody noticed me. I went past the grotto and through the gate and then to the graveyard. In the middle of that graveyard there's a big cross standing in a flat piece of concrete. I was sitting there, leaning back against the cross.

I seen those buses come. They picked up the kids. I counted three of them going by. One bus stayed behind in front of the girls' dormitory. It stayed there for a long, long time. I guess they were looking for me. I guess my brother Jack told the Sisters and Fathers, he said, "It's all right if she wants to stay. I think she's hiding someplace. She's got nobody to be with at home except her mother, and her mother's always working, so maybe she don't want to be there." He said, "It's all right for her to stay. I know my mother would let her stay, too." So that truck with the Apache kids went by.

I was down on the ground behind that cross in the graveyard. After a while, I walked back the same way I came. I was sitting there close to the grotto. One of the Sisters seen me. She came and said, "We were looking for you. Why didn't you get on the bus?" I said, "I don't want to go home. It's too far. I won't get home for two or three days." She said, "But how are you gonna go home now?" I said, "I'm not going home. I'm just gonna stay here." Then she said, "Your brothers were feeling bad 'cause you didn't get on the bus. You should have gone with them. I don't know if you'll get a chance to visit your mother this summer. It's all right—we're happy that you're here with us—but your mother needs you, too." I didn't tell her what I was thinking. See, my mother had married that man, Charley Marley, and I never had seen him before. That's the reason I didn't want to go home. I didn't want to be there when my mother was with another man.

So I stayed at St. Johns. Some other girls stayed there. We cleaned the dormitory. We washed it and scrubbed it and took the sheets off the beds. We piled the mattresses all in one place and then we covered them up. We took off the pillowcases and washed them. We washed all the sheets and put them away. And then, in the dining room, the same thing. We washed and scrubbed all the tables, and if some people put chewing gums underneath we had to take those off. We put all the dishes away. We piled the tables on top of each other on one side, and the room was all empty except for that. Then we washed and scrubbed the floor. We slept upstairs. They paid us for that work. They kept the money, though. If you wanted something—paper, books, lotion, stockings—they bought it for you. It didn't cost you nothing 'cause they deduct it from what you made working. I guess that's the first money I ever made.

When my brothers came back to St. Johns in the fall, they asked me, "How come you didn't come home?" I said, "My mother's with that man." Then they told me about him. My brother Jack said, "He's all right. He's a very kind man. He's been taking good care of everybody. He's taking good care of our mother, too." Then he said, "Are you gonna stay here again or go back home in the summer?" I said, "I don't know, I don't know what to think. When the time comes, I'll let you know." Then my brother said, "You should go home for a while, maybe only a month. If you don't like it, the priest can bring you back here."

So the next summer I went back with them. My stepfather was a kind man. He talked to me and I answered him. He laughed all the time. He made everybody laugh. He used to tell us stories, too, stories of his young life when he was a boy. By the end of the summer, when we were getting ready to go back to school, I was used to him real good.

No Shoes and Hot Cement

They didn't mind visitors coming to the school. They could come anytime to visit their kids. They had a place for visitors to sleep. It's a long building and every morning the girls watched that building to see if their parents or relatives came out. If they're out there, they went to the dining room and ate with their kids. One time, my brother Eugene and his wife came down to visit us. They took us to Phoenix. We stayed there all day and came back in the evening.

Another time, Sam Stevens and his wife came to see their kids. Sam Stevens's wife was a *big* woman. We used to laugh at her 'cause she never wore shoes. Ever since she was a kid, she never wore shoes.

Anyway, they came to see their children at St. Johns. They came over there and then they went to Phoenix. And while they're doing their shopping, that lady was running around like that—*hot cement* without no shoes on!

Willie Stevens felt sorry for her. He felt sorry for his daughter-in-law, so he bought her a pair of shoes, tennis shoes. She put them on and walked a little ways. Then she took them off and put them in the sack on her back. She started walking again. And Willie Stevens said, "How come she's got no shoes? What did she do with her shoes? Why did she take them off?" He tried to tell that lady to put them on again. She said, "No, I feel better without my shoes. I don't like to wear shoes." And he said, "I bought my daughter-in-law a new pair of shoes and she just throwed them away." Everybody was just *laughing*.

That's the way that lady was. She was like that. She ran around everywhere with no shoes. "This thing I'm walking on [the cement sidewalk] is not even hot," she said. Under her foot, under the sole there, was like *plastic*! It's hard! And the back of her heel was *thick*! Her heels were just cracked all over. Even in the wintertime, that lady never wore shoes.

Rebellions and Runaways

I never did think about home too much, but some of the girls—like Sadie Stevens, my cousin from San Carlos—used to get real lonesome. She used to go in the corner by herself and start crying. She won't stop. Mostly, I missed my grandmother Rose 'cause she was the one I went with all the time when I'm home. We used to go everywhere together.

Pearl Martinez's daughter—her second daughter, Martha—was stubborn. If she don't want to do something she won't do it. She won't pick up her clothes, she won't fix her bed, nothing. That's why she had a fight with one of the Sisters. The Sister told her to pick up her dirty clothes. She won't do it! She just laughed and throwed some more clothes on the floor. Then they left, those two. They went out of the room and closed the door on us, so when they started fighting we couldn't see what happened. There were some big girls—twenty years old, twenty-one—and they went in there and pulled them apart. They said they were really fighting. They punished that girl for fighting with a Catholic Sister. She had no shoes on and they made her walk from here to the gate [approximately 25 yards] for a long time—back and forth, back and forth, back and forth. And in church, when everybody's praying, she had to sit up front and face the people. Everybody knew that she done something wrong. She sat there and cried and cried, facing the people.

A lot of girls tried to run away. One time, two Papago girls ran off. Everybody went to mass at six o'clock in the morning, and I guess those girls took off to the end of the playground. They were hiding over there while everybody went into the church. Then they took off again. They went to Guadalupe, then down to Chandler. They knew where to go. There's desert on the other side of Chandler and that's where they went. They got back to their own country. Somebody from St. Johns notified their parents before they got home. So they [the parents] were looking for them. They knew where to look and they found those girls. They [school authorities] brought them back to St. Johns. They wanted to know why they ran off. They said they didn't like the food. Those girls got punished. They cut all their hair off. They were *bald-headed*! Boy, that was awful!

Then they found out that one of those girls was pregnant. She was already pregnant when she came to school. I guess she was scared that she might have her child there. She wanted to go home. She didn't say nothing about it, but they took her to the clinic and that's where they found out. So they had to send her home. Her mother came to St. Johns to visit the other girl who ran away. "My daughter has a baby now," she said.

Another time, four Apache girls ran off. They were from San Carlos. They got caught over there at Superior. They were going towards Globe. They got caught close to that hole that goes through the mountain [Queen Creek Tunnel, Arizona State Route 60]. A priest took three Apache boys from the school and they went looking for those girls in a car. They were looking for them, going towards Globe, and that's when one of the boys seen something. Those girls were hiding under a big rock. One of them had a big cut. I guess she got cut crawling over those big rocks. They brought those girls back to the school. They made them do *all the laundry*, working by themselves, for a long time. That's how they got punished.

Farewell to St. Johns

I left St. Johns 'cause my mother got blind from trachoma. She caught a cold, she said, and it started up again. She was living with my step-father. They were staying with my uncle, Robert Beatty, across from the old school at Cibecue.

When they found out that my mother wasn't getting better, Victor Beatty [Robert Beatty's son] wrote a letter to one of my brothers, Jack or Joe. One of them showed it to the priest. His name was Father Fideles. He talked with my brothers to see if they wanted to go home. They didn't want to go. He said, "How about your sister, maybe she can go. I'll fix up the papers for her, the lessons, and she can work on those while she's over there."

So my brother Jack talked to me. He asked me if I wanted to go home. I said, "I don't know. What about school?" He said, "Well, you can take school with you." Then he said, "Our mother is sick. It's her eyes. She can't see very good and she needs somebody to help her around. Us boys, we want to go, but we can't. It's got to be a girl, so it's up to you." I said, "Okay, I guess so." Then that priest told me, he said, "Your mother is suffering. She needs your help. That's why you should go home. Ask her what she wants. Do whatever she wants. Do that for her."

So I went back home to take care of my mother. It was close to Christmas. Her eyes were just *bloodshot* and covered with that stuff. She couldn't stand to see the light. She said it hurt her. I was washing her eyes out real good, cleaning them every day. I was using that green bushy stuff [an alga] that grows in the river [Cibecue Creek]. They told me, "Boil that one and use it to wash her eyes out." So I did that. The redness went away and all that stuff stopped coming out. But still she can't stand to see the light. It hurt her too much.

So they took her to the trachoma clinic at Fort Apache. She was in there for more than a month. When she got out she had to go back for treatment every day. Lots of people had trachoma. They put medicine in their eyes, drops. In the morning, they dropped in one drop. It's red. In the afternoon, they put in another kind. It's brown. It looks like io-dine. If they didn't do that, my mother said, your eyes really hurt from the sun. In the evening, before they went to sleep, they put some kind of oil in their eyes. Then they soaked a washcloth in icy water—they got it *real cold*—and put it over their eyes. They laid there for a long time 'til the rag gets warm. Then they put some more oil in their eyes and covered their eyes again with the same icy rag. Everybody's *brown* from that iodine-looking medicine. Their faces turned brown all over.

My mother stayed over there at Fort Apache for about a month. She got better and then she came home to Cibecue. She could see. She was well. They showed her how to take care of her eyes. Her eyes were clear. "I can still see," she said. They told her to stay out of the light and that's what she did—she stayed in the shade as much as she can. I stayed home with her. I couldn't go back to school. I couldn't do nothing. I had to stay there. My mother got better. But sometimes, if a person was coming, she didn't know who it is 'til the person got close. She could see things all right but it's still kind of blurry. It was blurry the rest of her life.

"I Liked It Down There"

Augustine was the last one in the family to go to St. Johns. He was only five when he left home. My mother tried to tell him to stay. He wouldn't do it. He wouldn't do it 'cause his brothers were going and he wanted to be with them. Jack told my mother, he said, "He should go now—with us. It's better that he goes while we're all still over there." So my mother let him go. He went down there with us. And when the boys lined up to march somewhere, Augustine was always standing on the end. He was the smallest one, the smallest one of the boys, standing on the end.

That same year my mother got blind with trachoma and I went back to Cibecue. After that, I never went back to school. I liked it down there at St. Johns 'cause there's always something to do! Nobody just sat around doing nothing. I liked looking after those little girls, especially the orphans. I felt sorry for them 'cause they're the only ones in their family.

Part Two

"A Really Good Place"

(1930–1944)

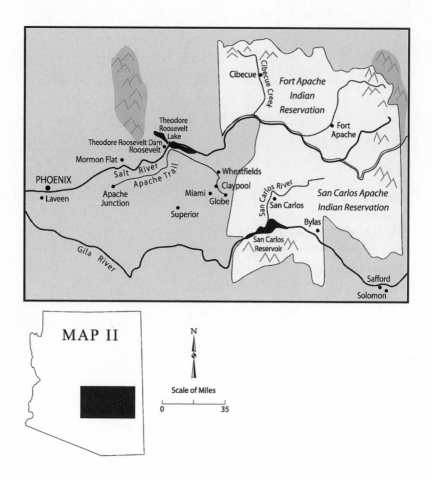

Map 2. San Carlos Apache Indian Reservation and vicinity.

Chapter Six

When I came back from St. Johns, my mother was already married to Charley Marley. He was a nice man. He was just like a father to us. My mother and him were living at Chediskai, right there by the river [Canyon Creek]. They lived there for a long time. It's real pretty down there. My stepfather built a log house, and we made an irrigation dam, and him and my brothers made a long ditch to get water to the fields. That was a *good* farming place. We grew lots of corn and beans and squash. We used to go back and forth to Cibecue, and back and forth to Oak Creek and Spring Creek. Mostly, though, we stayed there at Chediskai. There was bears down there, and lots of deer and wild turkeys, and mountain lions too.

People don't live like that no more. So when I think about those days—you know, the people down there and all that they used to do—it's like going somewhere good. We had lots of fun 'cause we were always doing something. And you know, it seems like every day something different happened. Nothing down there was always the same. Chediskai was a really good place.

"That Was My New Stepfather"—Charley Marley—Floods and Fish-head Soup— An Irrigation Dam—Bears—Looking for Metate Rocks—"You're Just Lucky!"— *Baby Eagles Dancing*

"That Was My New Stepfather"

We came back from St. Johns with a priest, Father Fideles. He took me and Joe and Dewey to Cibecue. We stayed there for about an hour while the priest went to see another person. When he came back, he said, "Let's go find your mother." Well, I thought she was just around there someplace, in the fields or with her relatives.

That priest took us *way out*! I was wondering where we were going. Then I knew we were going to Oak Creek. When we got over there, he drove down real slow, down that steep winding road, all the way down to the bottom. Then we went down to Tsééyaa Goltsogí [Yellow Below The Rocks]. We went right to where the corral is now. That corral wasn't there then. The people used to live there under those cottonwood trees.

My mother was there, so we went over and talked to her for a little while. Then she said, "Are you hungry?" We ate. It was already about to get dark. That night, real late in the evening, that man [Charley Marley] came in. He just looked at us. Then he said, "Who are the visitors?" And my mother told him, "These are my children. They were in school down in the desert but they're home with us now." And pretty soon, my mother said, "There's something for you to eat inside." Joe and Dewey jumped up. They said, "We'll go help him." They went and followed him in there. I guess they liked him right away. That was my new stepfather. He killed a beef for us the next day.

Charley Marley

My stepfather had only one eye. He said that when he was young, when he was around fourteen or something, he was wrangling horses. He was shoeing a horse and it kicked him in the eye. It kicked his eye out. You could tell. There was a mark like a horseshoe on his face. You could see that hoof mark on his skin.

He said that he was working with a horse when he was still a young man. He was getting ready to shoe it. His uncle told him, he said, "That horse might kick, so be careful." And he [Charley Marley] said, "It's tame enough. I think I can do it." So he got the horse and tied it to a post. He was putting a horseshoe on. He put a nail on one side and another nail on the other side to hold it even. Then he put a third one on the tip, and that's when he got kicked *right* in the eye! It knocked his eye out. It was still hanging by the veins, and his uncle went and cut them with a knife. Then they took a hot iron, a branding iron or some-

The wickiup of Ann Beatty and Charley Marley (behind parked cars belonging to Eva Watt's older brothers) after a snowfall at Cibecue, Fort Apache Indian Reservation, about 1930.

thing, and used it in there to stop the bleeding. Then they washed it out with some kind of pain medicine and put it in there. And then they just prayed for him. It didn't bleed or nothing. You could see the horseshoe mark right there on his face. It was a dent on his face like a horseshoe.

It didn't stop him, though. He was a horse wrangler at D. V. Marley's ranch for a long time, many years.[1] Him and D. V. Marley were real good friends. He worked over there in Cherry Creek 'til he married my mother. He met her at Spring Creek. My uncle, Robert Beatty, had a big field there, and that's where my mother and Augustine were living. My uncle knew that man [Charley Marley], and I guess he brought him home and introduced him to my mother. He was married before. He had one daughter. His wife died when that girl was being born. She looked just like him, too.

My stepfather was a funny man. He made us laugh. He got his English name from D. V. Marley. He told us about it. Right after he went to work over there, he said, they were making out checks. And D. V. Marley said, "What's your name? I got to use your name for your check. That's how I pay you for what you're doing for me." My stepfather's name was Tsééda'í [Edge Of The Cliff]. He didn't have no En-

D. V. Marley (left), cattle rancher and friend of Charley Marley; location and date unknown.

glish name. So he said—I don't know why, maybe he heard it some-where—"Chalee." He kept saying it, "Chalee, Chalee." Then D. V. Marley asked him, "What's your last name?" He didn't know. "Chalee, Chalee," that's all he said. "Chalee, Chalee." So D. V. Marley told him, he said, "Well, you're working for me. I'll just put 'Charley Marley' down there." So he did. That's how my stepfather got that name. He was "Charley Marley" for a long time. It was funny how he told that story.

He had two of those square leather bags for horses [panniers] that he got when he left D. V. Marley's ranch. D. V. Marley gave him those bags to put his things in and pack them home. He took care of them for a *long time*! Finally, they started having holes. He patched them up. He put deer hide on them and sewed it all the way around. Those bags were old but he was still using them. They were a present from D. V. Marley.

Boy, he [Charley Marley] was a person that didn't like people tak-ing his picture. He didn't like it. "You gotta pay me some money!" he said. He used to run away and hide. Every time we tried to take his picture, he put a hat or towel over his face. That's why there's no pictures of him.

He was a good old man. He was just like a father to us, nice and kind. He talked to us, told us not to do this, not to do that. "This is the way to live," he said. "Don't say things like this to nobody." I guess he was the one that kept us straight all the time, him and my mother. Not any of my brothers—I don't think any of them—had any trouble with people.

Floods and Fish-head Soup

When my mother and Charley Marley went to live at Chediskai, they lived on land that belonged to him. It's a big field. Then my mother made another field up above that one. It was just cedar trees and brush. She dug all those trees out and gathered all the rocks. She took the rocks to the river in her burden basket. When they first went over there, there was a fence around my stepfather's land. It was old and falling down. But then McQuillin gave them a whole truckload of barbed wire.[2] He said, "You can have this. If you need some more, I'll bring it to you." So my brothers started cutting logs for the posts. Then they made a new fence around both the fields. After that, they made an irrigation ditch all the way down from the dam. There's no ditch before that one—my brothers made the first one at Chediskai. After that, the cowboys from Oak Creek came in and made their camp, right there at the end of my mother's field under some trees. They put a table there and made that their camp.

That old man [Charley Marley] built a log house down there at Chediskai. My brothers helped him. It's one room but it's big. In wintertime, everybody slept in there. The beds were on the ground. I used to sleep behind the wood stove. There were big boxes in there, too, and that's where we kept the dry food. We kept meat in an icebox that my brothers built in the ground. My mother had a wickiup and a shade outside. She cooked out there 'cause it got too hot inside the house. And there's trees all around, lots of trees, plenty of shade.

We used to have about five apple trees and peach trees. Those apple trees were close to the river [Canyon Creek]. There was lots of

Ann Beatty with unidentified children at Chediskai, Fort Apache Indian Reservation, about 1935.

apples on them when they got washed out. One time, it was raining *hard*! My mother was over there getting all the apples down. They were ripe, so she wanted to get them off. I think she got four washtub loads during the rain. She was soaking wet but she didn't care. My brothers were helping her. They got most of the apples off. Then those trees washed out.

The river used to flood lots of times. In those days, there was lots of grass and trees up on the hills. Mostly the rain soaked in instead of running down. But now there's hardly no grass, so the rain runs down to the river. When there's a flood, my stepfather won't let us go near the water. When the first one went by [the first rush of floodwater carrying debris] you could smell the powder smell, that gunsmoke smell. Terrible! He said, "If you inhale that, you're gonna get sick inside." We believed it 'cause my brother [Paul Tulene] died from that. So we just stayed away from the river when it floods. When the water was high we didn't go close to it. "Stay away," my stepfather said.

There was lots of fish in the river in those days, mostly *łóg łikizhí* [trout]. When we made the dam and irrigated they went into the ditches and you could catch them in the fields. My mother caught one like that, way out there in the field. She brought it back. She said to the boys, "There's some more up there but I can't catch them." She told them where to go, and they went over there and got four more.

My stepfather wouldn't throw the fish heads away. He made soup out of them. What he did was chop the head off and get it real clean. He got all that gluelike stuff off with a scrubbing brush. Then he put the head in a pot and boiled it. After he boiled it real good, he put it through a sifter that he made. Then he took all the juice part out and throwed the bones and everything away. Then he made cornmeal dumplings and throwed them in the soup and boiled it. He ate it like that. I tasted it once, it was good. He put chili in there—cayenne powder, about half a teaspoon—and that made it better.

My stepfather said that D. V. Marley made that kind of soup. He used to go fishing in the Salt River and bring the fish back to his ranch below Cherry Creek. He cooked them and made that fish-head soup. That's where my stepfather learned how to make it. D. V. Marley showed him how.

An Irrigation Dam

We built an irrigation dam close to where the trail goes to Red Lake. We were all up there. We got cottonwood branches—small ones, some old ones—and chopped them up and stuck them in the river. We got grapevines, too, we got *lots* of grapevines. We gathered those and tied them up and put them in there with the branches. Then we put rocks in there up against the grapevines. Then my mother and three other ladies—they were in the water—pushed gravel up against it from the bottom. When they got the gravel above the water, we got our baskets, our burden baskets, and we carried them on our backs to a place where the mens were digging sand and dirt. We stood there and let the mens fill up the baskets. Then we walked back and dumped it on the dam. Then we went back and got some more. That's the way we did. We made that dam across the river. It's hard work! It took about four or five days to get it finished. And then, when a flood comes, it goes out! Then we had to do the same thing again.

Bears

There were bears down there. I seen them lots of times, taking a bath and playing in the water. They never bothered me at all. I'd be getting water early in the morning and those bears were sitting in the river. There's a *big* rock in the river there and they liked to sit on the other side where there's a big pool, a deep pool. That's where they went to take a bath. They didn't go in shallow water. They knew I was there but they paid no attention to me at all. They just kind of growled a little bit, talking to each other the way they do. Mostly, they came around in the summer, when it's hot, to get cool and take a bath. They liked to scratch each other's back. One turned away and another one stood up and scratched its back. They were about from here to that tree [approximately 15 yards], not very far. After they got through, they started marching up to the top of the mountain [Chediskai Mountain] across the river. I used to sit there and watch them.

They used to teach their babies how to swim. That's another reason they liked that deep water. I watched them for a long time. The mother swims around and the little ones try to follow her. Then she takes them back over to where they can stand on their feet again. She scratches their back for a while, and then, after that, she swims again in deeper water. They follow her and try to swim. Then she goes back to that same place again and they sit down. She growls at them, talks to them. Then she wants to go swimming by herself, I guess, 'cause when they try to follow her she growls at them and they sit back down. Then she goes around and swims by herself. She goes all the way under the water and comes back up. Those babies learn fast! They're swimming in no time!

One time, I was going up the hill to where we parked the wagon. My mother left a box of shells [bullets] up there. She told me to go get it, so I was going up there. It was way late in the evening. And I saw a cow, and then a bunch of them, right around a big oak tree, all of them bunched up. All their faces were out and their hind ends all were close to the tree. They were really hollering, too.

I was wondering what was going on. I was looking around, wondering what was wrong with them. I was looking around, looking around. There were two big old bears sitting across the wash from those cows. "No wonder," I said. "I bet those bears are chasing them around." It's a good thing I had that .30-.30. I shot at them. They took off up the hill. I went and got the box of shells and when I got back those cows were gone. Those were Oak Creek cattles. When I went out at night, I usually carried a rifle. Sometimes I carried firecrackers, too, just for the noise.

When you go down to Oak Creek from Chediskai, you have to cross the river seven times. And after the second crossing there's a big black rock sticking out and it's sandy all the way around it, like a beach. One time, two big bears were fighting right there. My mother and my stepfather were going down to Oak Creek. I was in front of them. My horse wouldn't go. It was making noise and jumping back, really jumping around. "Why is it doing that?" I thought. I looked up on the cliffs to see if there's something up there. Then I went around those rocks and looked over there. Two big bears were *fighting*! They were standing up! They were standing up, scratching at each other, grabbing at each other, falling down, rolling around on the sand. I don't think they saw me 'cause they just kept on fighting.

My mother and that old man [Charley Marley] were coming behind me, so I turned around real fast and went back and met them. I told them, I said, "Stop here, wait here. There's two bears fighting out there. Right close! You better stop 'til they get away."

And my stepfather said, "Ah! They won't bother me. They're my friends." My mother was yelling at him. "They're not your friends! They'll be your friends when they chew you up!" My stepfather had a can. He always had screws and nuts and shells in there, and he always kept it in his saddlebag. He grabbed that can and started shaking it. He was trying to scare those fighting bears. Then he said, "Well, I'll go over there and show them my gun." He said that before he got over there his horse did the same thing—it started jumping around. So he got off his horse and got his gun and walked to the edge of the river. Then he went and shot his big old gun. Boy! It was *real loud!* You could hear it a long ways off! He said those bears took off, chasing each other, towards Dǫ' Bi Gową [Flies' Home]. He had a real long gun. He used to put only one shell in it. It was a .44. Those shells are *long*. I don't know where he got that gun. He said that somebody gave it to him. He couldn't hardly get shells for it anywhere.

Looking for Metate Rocks

My mother and my stepfather were just like bears. We used to laugh about it. They used to go up and down the river all the time. They were just like bears, turning rocks over to see which one they could take home and make a grinding stone with. That's what they were looking for, walking up and down. Every time there's a flood, after the flood when it's dry, they went up and down the river turning over rocks. "There go the bears," my brothers used to say.

Sometimes people went to those old stone houses [prehistoric Pueblo ruins], but they don't pick up nothing except beads that they find on the ground. If they seen something else in the ground, right there where the house is sitting, they leave it alone. But if they seen something *away* from the house, then they could take it and use it. My mother got a grinding stone that way, one of those metate rocks. Lots of times, when there's a flood, the water washes things out and brings them down the river. She found that metate rock after a flood. It's not very big. It's volcano stone. I still have it. It's still good. I still use it.

A Western Apache woman grinding corn outside the old day school at Cibecue, Fort Apache Indian Reservation, about 1923. As preparation for adult life, Apache girls began grinding corn when they were five or six years old.

You know, if you had a real smooth grinding stone, you had to pound on it all over to make it sharp again [i.e., roughen its surface]. Then you had to wash it real good to get the dust and dirt off. My mother didn't like that. The one she had, that volcano stone, had lots of little holes in it. She said it was natural sharp, so she didn't have to pound on it. She didn't have to do that 'cause when she's grinding something—you know, like dry corn—those little holes open up by themselves, and then they're sharp again. My mother just treasured that grinding stone. Every time we went acorn hunting she put it in a sack that's hanging from the saddle. And when we got there and gathered the acorns she used to grind them. She got a lot of use from that grinding stone. She didn't want nobody to bother it.

One time, my mother took Lucinda Cooley to get a metate rock. She was a big, tall woman. We took her 'cause she was blind—not too blind, she could see things that were moving around, but she couldn't see the ground very good. My mother wanted a metate rock, too. So she said, "We never look down that way. We'll go on the trail all the way down and come back up on the side of the river." Usually, my mother and my stepfather went up the river when they're looking for things. I guess they did that 'cause there's not so much brush.

They found a rock that's kind of square, and that lady liked it. She was just feeling of it and she liked it. So my mother said, "What are you gonna do? It's heavy. How are you gonna carry it?" And she [Lucinda Cooley] said, "I'm gonna put it in this gunny sack." So they pushed it into the gunny sack. Then they tied a rope on one side of the gunny sack, and then on the other side, so she could get under it and carry it on her back. "I think I can get up with it," she said. So we put it on a high rock. We sat it up there and that lady was gonna get under it.

That lady was always joking and she said something real funny. She said something about an old story from long years ago. It's about somebody that carried a log, a real heavy log. And those two ladies started giggling and giggling and giggling. They were just sitting there, giggling away. Finally, they quit. And then that lady said, "OK, let's go." So she got under that gunny sack and put the rope over her head. She was getting up. She was getting up but then she started giggling again— and she fell over on her back! And she's still just giggling away, I guess she can't stop. So we pushed it back on the rock again and my mother got under it. She said, "I'll take it for you." She got under it right away and carried it all the way back home.

We had a big pot of beans boiling in the hole in the ground that we cooked in. My mother said, "I wonder if it's done." I said, "I think it's done already." And she [Lucinda Cooley] said, "Well, I'll make the bread. Go ahead and mix the dough and I'll make it for you." So she did, she made the bread. Then we started digging out the bean pot, and that's when my brothers came in. They came back from the irrigation dam. They were hungry! So they got the beans out, cooked real well done, and they got those tortillas that lady made. They're dipping out the beans with that fresh bread.

And then Engel Hanna brought in a deer. I guess he killed a white-tail just across the river. We heard him shooting. He killed it and brought it back. He said, "I got two." He said, "I'm going back after

the other one. I'm giving this one to you, so go ahead and skin it." He
went back across the river with his wife. They were looking for the
other deer. They found it. I guess it was trying to jump between two
branches of a cedar tree and got stuck in there and died. That's what
he said when he came back to get his ax. He took it back over there.
They had to chop off one of the branches to get the deer out. It was a
big whitetail.

That bean pot was a big one, too. There was enough beans in there
for everybody, more than enough. So everybody went over to where
my mother was, and they built a big fire and skinned that deer and
butchered it. They were roasting the meat and eating beans, and then
somebody made some more bread. They had a feast *all night*!

"You're Just *Lucky*!"

There used to be mountain lions down there, too. Their tracks were
there all the time. They used to crawl around in those big boulder
rocks, the big ones. One of them jumped down on Edith Hanna's horse.
I guess it hit the horse right here [on its withers]. Part of its skin was
torn off. They knew it was a mountain lion that done it. They sewed the
skin back on and pretty soon that horse was all right.

One time, I took some horses up towards Iron Mine. My brother
Jack and his family was up there. I left the horses there 'cause he
needed them to bring his family back to Chediskai. He asked me,
"Which way are you going? You better go home before it gets dark." I
said, "I'll go the way I came. I guess it's better that way." He said, "OK,
hurry up." After we ate lunch, I started. But instead of going up high
on the hills, I thought, "Well, I'll go along the river."

So I went down to the river. I walked and walked. Then I found
a place where the water was real deep. It was just *blue* right there. I
started fishing. I had the string and a hook in a little bag, but I didn't
have a stick. So I got me a stick and tied the string on the end of it. I
started fishing and caught some *lóg likizhí* about that big [16–18 inches
long]. I caught four of them right there. And I forgot about the time.

I started walking down again. I walked, I walked, I walked. I walked
over those big rocks, those big old boulders along the side of the river.
I had to crawl over them and between them. I didn't think nothing of

it. I kept walking down and I found another place where there's lots of fish. I started fishing again right there. I caught some more. I was carrying them with that string I had. I kept walking. I walked all the way down to Chediskai. I got down to the fields. It was probably about nine or ten o'clock. The moon was coming up. It was dark with only the moon. Then I saw a fox! It was following me. I kept going. I went down to the house. Finally, I got home.

I came in the house. Everybody was still up yet. My stepfather and my mother were sitting there. They were making leather, stretching it, next to the fire. My stepfather said, "Where have you been? I thought you were gonna come back with your brother tomorrow. We were about ready to go to bed." I said, "I caught lots of fish." He said, "So *that's* what you were doing! You came back along the river!" I said, "Yes, I came back that way. I started back after lunch." They got up. They didn't say nothing. And I thought, "Well, it's my own fault."

The next day, my brother Jack came in early. I guess he just piled his family on the horses and came down from where they were camping. When he came in, he said, "Who got all the fish?" I said, "I did, last night." I got another scolding right there. I was thinking I should shut up! My brother said, "There's mountain lions around here! There's lots of them! They live in those big rocks!" He said, "If you're quiet and come close to them, real close, that's when they get scared, and that's when they jump on you from the rocks. You better watch out!" That's what he said.

The next morning, he got after me again. I got another scolding. He said, "You're crazy to go that way! I told you to come back the same way you came!" I said, "Well, I'm here. Nothing happened to me." He said, "You're lucky! That's what it is—you're just *lucky*!"

See, I was raised with boys. I guess that's why I was like that. I never did get afraid of very much. I guess I just didn't think about it.

Baby Eagles Dancing

That time I seen those two bears fighting close to the rocks, I was in a hurry. That's why I was in front of my mother and my stepfather. I was trying to get over on a high hill real fast. "What's up there that's so important?" my mother said. I said, "I want to see those baby eagles up there. They're only there in the mornings."

There's a high hill—Dził Nabaa [Hazy Mountain] they call it—
down there, and when you got up on top and looked down you could
see the baby eagles. They were on the branch of a pine tree. It's a tall
tree but it looks short when you're way up there. Those baby eagles
acted like they were dancing—just dancing away! They were holding
their wings out, going back and forth. They jumped around and went
this way, jumped around and went that way, dancing back and forth on
the branch. I don't know why they do that. It's cute the way they do,
all of them dancing together.

Chapter Seven

Chediskai was a real small community. Only a few families had land down there. Some of them came just for the summer. There's hardly any visitors, too, so it was real quiet. All of us liked it down there. I worked with my mother in the fields, and my brothers went hunting for deer and worked with my stepfather. We always had plenty to eat, even in wintertime. Sometimes, maybe once a month, we went to the store in Cibecue, and sometimes we went to visit my uncle, Robert Beatty, at Spring Creek. For me, going to Cibecue was like going to a town.

Six Families at Chediskai—"Each Corn Was Like a Person"—Lots of Turkeys —Old-timer Beans—"I Shot the Deer"—Salt Banks—An Icebox at Chediskai— A Food Cache at Spring Creek—"Not Many People Had Money"—Trickery at Cibecue—"Thank You, Kate"—Lots of Ruts—Sorghum Syrup and Sheepskins—A Christmas Party

Six Families at Chediskai

Besides us, there was five other families down there at Chediskai. They used to come and go. They didn't stay there like we did. We stayed there permanent, almost all the time, except when we had to go somewhere like Cibecue or Oak Creek. William Taylee was the leader at Cibecue then, and William Lupe, my grandfather, was leader of Oak Creek.

Ralph Dazen's father had a farm there [at Chediskai], but he never

William Taylee (C-1), leader of the Western Apache community at Cibecue, Fort Apache Indian Reservation, about 1925.

came up after his son killed a lady in Oak Creek. He shot her from the
back. He killed her grandmother, too. After that, the Dazens moved to
Whiteriver.

Engel Hanna—that's Edith Hanna's father and Lee Hanna's father
—had a field there, too. Lots of times, they used to plant it and then forget about it. They went off, usually to Cibecue, and didn't come back
'til harvest time.

Ned Machuse came but he didn't have a field. His family just stayed
there for the summer. And there's Charley Stago's family. They had
land down there but they traveled a lot. They just came and went. That
old man Stago had two wives.

And there's James Johnson's family, too. James Johnson was Pearl
Martinez's brother. He had land there, a space, but it had a lot of brush
on it. He cleared that off himself and made it a farm, a little one. At
first he planted only squash and vegetables, but he kept on digging and
digging—digging all those roots out—and he made it bigger. Then he
planted corn.

All those families were close related, so everybody tried to help
everybody else. If one of the mens killed a deer, he gave some of the

meat to the other families. They shared tools, too, like axes and shovels, and sometimes they loaned their horses to each other. And if a family made lots of barbecue corn, they kept enough for themselves and gave the rest away. That's how they used to do.

In those days, people were *busy*. They were always doing something—working in the fields, cooking, grinding corn, making baskets and moccasin shoes, hunting, fixing fences, taming horses, all that kind of stuff. And making woods [firewood]. They had to make lots of woods and drag it back home, especially in wintertime. They used their donkeys and horses for that. In those days, very few people had wagons.

Everybody was friendly, too. They hardly ever thought of fighting. There's lots more fighting nowadays. People get jealous of each other, jealous of what they own, and they get mad and say mean things and then they want to fight. There's no reason to be around them when they're like that, no reason at all.

"Each Corn Was Like a Person"

Every morning—early in the morning before the sun comes up—my stepfather got everybody up. We went outside and lined up. Then he prayed with all of us. He prayed *for* us, too, and he blessed us with yellow powder. Then he said, "Go your own way and don't say anything mean. Don't do anything that's not supposed to be done." Then he said, "Go check the gates!" He got mad if somebody said, "No, it's not my turn." He said, "Don't say it's somebody else's turn!" He said, "Everybody get up and go! We grow lots of corn. We grow lots of beans. We got work to do!"

He had only one eye, and I think it was getting pretty bad. He can't see very much but still he was always working. He said, "Don't ever say you're tired, or you're feeling lazy, or anything like that. What has to be done has to be done." He said, "It don't matter how sick you are or how bad you're feeling. What has to be done has to be done."

I was in the fields all the time, me and my mother, looking after the corn. In those days, when people planted corn, they took care of it. I mean, they took *care* of it! My mother used to go to the fields every morning from beginning to end, from planting time to harvest time. After they plowed the ground and put in the seeds, she stayed there.

If she seen any weeds, she pulled them out and throwed them away, especially that morning glory plant. She said you should pull that one out right away. "Clean it up!" Every day she cleaned up the fields, and going around, going back and forth, she prayed for the corn. And when she knows it needs water, she irrigated. She told the boys, she said, "Go check the ditch and let the water come through." So they did that. And then, after they irrigated, about three or two days later, we went back again and pulled out the weeds coming from the irrigation. "Clean it up!" And when the corn was growing, if she seen a little piece growing off the bottom, she pulled it off. "If you leave that one there," she said, "there won't be no corn." So she pulled it off when she saw it. It seemed to me that she looked at each corn—each one, row by row—and she *knew* it. She knew each plant like it was a person and she treated it that way. But nowadays, it seems like to me, very few people do that.[1]

At plowing time and planting time and harvest time, everybody helped everybody else. And of course they always had *túlbáí* [dull-color water], so everybody knows they're going to get some of that to drink.[2] But they didn't get drunk, not even a little bit. It just kept the hungry away—that's all it was. It was made thick, like malted milk. It's food! They drank it while they were working and they didn't get hungry. In the evening, if there's any left over, they drank it and practiced singing, just to see who knows the prettiest songs. They used to sit in a circle with a five-gallon can in the middle. Somebody starting singing, and it went around this way [clockwise], each person singing a song. That was real nice! Nobody got drunk.

Lots of Turkeys

One time, we barbecued corn down there. Next morning, we got up early and started digging it out of the pit.[3] We got it all out and put it on a canvas. The corn was cooling off, so we went back home to eat something. After we ate, my mother and Engel Hanna's wife said they were going to watch the corn. They didn't do that. They went to their fields and started pulling out weeds. And while they were doing that, a whole bunch of wild turkeys started eating that barbecue corn. My brother said, "I'll bring those two ladies some coffee." He went over there and came back. He was laughing. He said, "There's nobody sitting over there, but there's *lots* of turkeys getting fat!" Those turkeys were in the middle of that barbecued corn, just eating away.

Old-timer Beans

We used to plant lots of beans. They always came up good. Oh! I just remembered those yellow beans—I wonder if anybody has that kind of beans anymore. My brother found them, my brother Jack.

He was fishing along the Salt River. He was there with some other boys. They were going along, he said, and he seen a big slab of rock hanging down toward the river. He got on top of it and was walking on it. He jumped off to the side and there was a hole. He said it looked big enough for one person to go through. So he did. I guess he had matches and everything.

So he went in there. Jack was never afraid of anything like that. He didn't even think there might be a mountain lion in there or snakes. He said you could see everywhere inside. He was looking around. He saw an old part-burnt corncob laying on the floor. Then he knew that somebody must have been in there before. He put it back down the way it was.

He looked around some more. He found pots and bowls. And those braided shoes—sandals, or whatever you call them—he found a pair of those. He said he wanted to take one of the pots but he didn't 'cause it's so pretty. He said it was too rocky to bring it back—if he fell he might break it. He said there was a grinding stone in there, a metate rock with the top part [mano] on it.

He said there were holes in the rock on the floor. Big flat rocks were on top of them and straw was on top of the rocks. He was thinking, "What's in those holes?" He took one of the rocks off and opened it up. He found parched corn in there. Then he opened a hole closer to the door. That one had the beans in it—yellow beans, kind of orange-looking. He put two handfuls in his pocket. He thought, "Those beans might grow. I wonder what it looks like when it's growing."

He opened another hole. He said it was lined with grass. He said it had cooked mescal in it. It was all pounded up and already made into cakes. There was grass in between the cakes—grass, a mescal, grass, a mescal, like that. He picked out one of the cakes and looked at it, and then he put it back the way it was. It's probably still there unless somebody found it. I think Apache people must have used that place — you know, 'cause of all that cooked mescal and the parched corn. I was thinking they must have used it.

When my brother came back — it was way late at night — he gave those beans to my mother. He said, "That's what I found over there." He said, "There's lots of them over there. There's lots of other stuff, too." He said, "I took this little bit of beans to see if it will grow."

My mother planted those yellow beans. They grew. She made about two rows from the ones he brought. We didn't eat any of those. My mother just let them get ripe so we could use them again for seeds. The following year, we planted a big piece of land. We put all the beans in there. They grew. They grew without much irrigation. I guess that's the reason they grew so good. Old-timer beans! It looks exactly like the other kinds of beans, the leaves and everything, but it grows *big*, way up high. It's a big bush and all the beans are underneath. The beans taste almost like pinto beans.

"I Shot the Deer"

Everything grew good down there — corn, beans, squash, everything. And then again, there's no hunting seasons on the reservation in those days, so the mens could hunt deer and wild turkeys at any time. My brothers used to hunt a lot on the mountain [Chediskai Mountain] across the river. There's lots of whitetails that run back and forth up there. All you had to do is run up the mountain and shoot at them. And there's rabbits and wild turkeys all over the place.

Sometimes I went hunting with my brothers for birds and rabbits. They used a .22 for that. "Come on," they said, "let's go." One time they had my stepfather's gun. That was a powerful gun, that .44, and they're not supposed to use it. The boys told me to try. Joe was standing right behind me. He said, "I'll catch you if you fall down." I didn't believe it. When I shot that .44, I just *flew* backwards! My mother got after us. She told us, she said, "You shouldn't be playing with that thing."

I shot a whitetail with that gun right there where we used to park the wagon. We came back from Cibecue and were getting ready to take our things down below to the house. I was standing on the wagon and didn't see the deer 'til I looked up. There was two of them. They were watching us. I told my stepfather, I said, "There's a deer standing right behind us. There's two of them. They're right close, so don't move. They're just looking at us." I said, "Where's your gun?"

He didn't turn around. He just went past the wagon and got to his old blue donkey. He had his gun tied on so tight! He had to untie and untie and untie. Finally, he got it loose. Then he took his little bag—it's like a little purse—and took out two shells. He put one of them in the gun. Then he said, "Where's it at? Where? Where?" I said, "It's right next to that stump. It's standing there, looking over the stump at us."

I guess he seen it 'cause he said, "Yeah, I see it now." But then he said, "I can't see it! I can't do it! Here, you shoot it." I shot that deer. I shot it here [in the neck below the jaw]. It fell. I said, "It's down." And that old man was just standing there. He kept saying, "Where's my eye! Where's my eye!" Then he said, "Let's go see."

So we went over there. He said, "You have to do it this way." He took me by my right hand and put it on the right leg of the deer. "Turn it over," he said. I did that. "Step over it." I stepped over it. Then he started praying for it. After that, he cut the neck and started draining the blood out. I said, "While you're doing that, I'm gonna take our stuff down to the house." I took it down there and dumped it off. Then I came back up. He wasn't even halfway done yet, so I went over there and helped him. Finally, he took the insides out. Then he put the meat on his donkey. That donkey was about to run with it—I guess he smelled the blood—so I throwed a canvas over it. I said, "If it falls, it will fall on the canvas."

We got to the bottom of the hill. He took the meat off the donkey and was hanging it up. He said, "I'm gonna hang this up here so everybody can see that I killed a deer." My mother was laughing. He hung it up. And those little bees, those yellowjackets—boy, can they eat meat! There was *lots* of them! So I put a canvas around it. My stepfather said, "That's what I don't like." He said, "I don't want you putting that canvas around it." I said, "Why?" And he said, "It's got to be dry. It's not drying when it's covered." So he stood there with straw in his hand and tried to shoo those things away. He did that for a little while. Then they got mad at him 'cause he was chasing them away. He got stung. He got stung again. He got stung several times.

The boys came in about two days later. They were working at the sawmill in Cibecue. They wanted to know who killed the deer. My stepfather said, "I did! Can't you see? I'm the only man around here." He was always teasing my brothers.

Salt Banks

They used to kill deer at any time, and sometimes they got too much meat. My mother used to make jerkies from that meat or put it in the icebox in the ground. When she made jerkies, she used salt from Salt Banks. She put it in a pot, about two handfuls, and filled it up with water. Then she boiled it. She kept on boiling that salt. Then she split the meat, sliced it real thin, and dipped it in there. She took it out and hung it up to dry. It tastes good! It lasts a long time. It's not too salty. It's just right.

My mother used to get salt from Salt Banks. She went down there in the fall. There's lots of salt then. In the summer you can go down there but there's not very much. She used to get four sacks of salt. When you get the salt it's wet, so you have to put it in a sack, like a flour sack. Then you have to keep squeezing it and pounding it on something hard, like a rock. The salt keeps going down, going down, 'til it gets real tight in the bottom of the sack. And when the bottom gets real tight you start on the top part, doing the same thing. You keep squeezing the sack and pounding it 'til the salt gets tight all over. Then you set the sack next to the fire and turn it around and around, not too fast. You do that for a long time 'til it gets dry, real dry, and then you cut the sack off. Now it's a block of salt, a hard round block. As long as it's hard like that, it stays clean and white. But if you keep it loose, it gets dirty real fast. When you need salt for cooking, you just get a sand rock [a piece of sandstone] and scrape it off the block. It tastes kind of like that salt they give to cows. It's *good*! My mother kept two or three of those blocks in the place where we stored our winter food.

Salt Banks was real pretty once, but then two whitemen destroyed it. I think it was around 1932 or 1933. They were camping close to the salt cave. There's a little spot there, a flat spot on the north side where the road goes down now. It's not very big but it's big enough for a camp. That's where those two men were living. They had a tent up.

My brother Albert saw them down there. I guess he thought they

Entrance to the salt cave on Salt River, Fort Apache Indian Reservation, 1904. In the 1930s, this sacred site was destroyed with dynamite by two non-Indians who may have been searching for gold. A short time later, the vandals were killed by lightning at their camp nearby.

were just doing some fishing or something. He went down there with his uncle, Robert Beatty, to get salt. When they came back to Oak Creek, they told F-1 [William Lupe], they said, "Some whitemen are living down there. I guess they're just fishing."

But they destroyed the salt cave. It used to be kind of like a porch and the roof was way up high. There's water dripping down from the roof and you could see the salts hanging down from up there. They looked like pipes, white pipes hanging down. Those were the salts and water was dripping out of them. The water was kind of milky-looking. It was real salty. We used to stand there and it dropped in our mouth.

Those salts were a long way up high. Even with a ladder, you can't get them. So when my mother went there she always took one of the boys, usually Joe, and he took the bow and arrows. He went in there and shot at the salts. If he hit one, it fell, and my mother ran over there with her basket and picked it up. That's the way she used to get salt.

It was kind of dark inside there. It was slippery, too, from the water dripping down. You're supposed to dip your hand in the water and bless yourself—one, two, three, four times—and then put some water on top of yourself. The first time I was there, my mother told me to follow her. She said, "Stay behind me and watch what I do."

Like I told you, those two whitemen destroyed the salt cave. They destroyed the porch-looking part. Now it's all down on the ground. It's all chopped up. They used powder—dynamite—to destroy it. I don't know why they did that. I don't know what they were looking for. Long years ago, people were crazy for gold—maybe that's what they thought.

Those two whitemen lost their lives. They were struck by lightning. They were struck by lightning right there at their camp. Some people going after salt found them. I guess they were dead about a week. When those people came back, they told F-1 [William Lupe] what happened. He told them, he said, "We have to go down there and pray all night. The water might flood and just wash the whole thing out. The water might take it away from us. That's why we have to go down there and pray for our salt place." So they went down there and did that. Only mens went. They went down there and prayed.

Then, after that, some people went to Whiteriver for a meeting. Just the old mens went over there. F-1 went and Carter Johnson and

Lee Declay—he was a policeman—and Rufus Lupe. They had a meeting about what happened at that place. They said, "Nobody's supposed to fool with our salt place. It's not supposed to be touched. That place is sacred. It was used by Indian people long years before us. We still get our salt there. We still pray and bless ourselves when we go down there. From now on, that place must be protected." My mother told me that's what they said.

An Icebox at Chediskai

My brothers built an icebox down there at Chediskai. They dug a hole in the ground, kind of square. It's almost from here to there [7–8 feet wide] and it's about that deep [6–7 feet]. Then they used boards to build a box in the hole, about that much away from the wall [8–10 inches] all the way around. And under the box, down there at the bottom, they put pieces of tin. They put a whole bunch of snow around the box and under the tin, and they packed it and packed it. They packed it real good so it won't melt fast. They put a heavy door on top and a stepladder going down. When they killed a deer or something, they hung it in there. And wild turkeys, if they had any, they put them in there, too. My mother put green corn in there. She boiled it for about five minutes and then she put it in there. It lasts all winter. McQuillin used to laugh when he came down there to Chediskai. "Got something good in the icebox?" My mother said, "We got some deer meat and turkey meat. Go cut the pieces you want." She let him go in there and cut it.

People from Cibecue always used to say that we stole cattle. "You hide the meat in there [the icebox]," that's what they told us. So we made McQuillin go in there and check to see if there's any beef. He said, "I don't see no beef. It's all deer meat." My mother said, "That's what I told you."

We had to go to court 'cause of those Cibecue people. James Johnson went over there and told them off. He said, "We don't steal nothing from you. I don't see why you accuse us. Come over there and look for yourself and see if there's any beef. Go around in the brush and see if there's any meat hanging up in the trees. Did you see someone putting meat down in there [the icebox]? I want to know where you seen me with beef. And where did I butcher it before I put it in there?"

Nobody answered him. They just said, "So-and-so said this, so-and-so said that." He told them, he said, "We don't believe in *ch'idii* [gossip]. Just 'cause we live away from you, it don't mean we steal things!"

A Food Cache at Spring Creek

My mother stored some of her food in a hole above my uncle's camp at Spring Creek. It was a *big* hole on a hill away from his log cabin. Only the people that used it knew where it was. If somebody wanted to steal something and came around the house, that's all they could see, the house. The hole was in a secret place.

My mother and my uncle's wife made a big basket. Big! It was this big across, from here to there [6–7 feet]. After they got through, before they put it down in the ground, they had to seal it. My uncle, Robert Beatty, brought clay—you know, that real sticky clay from up towards White Springs—and they made it into paste with water. Then they put that clay on the inside of the basket all the way around. When the inside was dry they put the paste on the outside, and they left it for a while 'til it was real dry. Then, finally, they put that basket in the hole. They put two canvases underneath it and that's how they lowered it into the ground.

Then somebody went down inside and put the food in. Dry corn was put in first. Each family marked their corn with a different color material. They tied it on the sacks to keep them separate, to mark them as their own. They did that with everything. Dry corn was first, and then, if they had some, *dijíízhi* [roasted corn]. And then acorns, walnuts, *dinos* [manzanita berries], *diltałé* [juniper berries], *ch'ink'ózhé* [skunkbush], all of those. And *nadah* that's been made into cakes, they put that in there, too. Everything had to be dry, real dry. And then, finally, they put in *gogíshé* [beargrass]. They tied that together with *igáyé*—they made it look like curtains—and they put it down between their sacks. That's how they knew that this side belonged to somebody and that side belonged to somebody else.

Then they covered it up. They got cedar bark and rubbed it 'til it was real soft. They put it all the way around on top. Then they put down flat bark—it's cedar bark but they didn't soften it up, they just left it the way it was. And then, if they had any canvas or gunny sacks, they put those down and covered the whole thing. And after that, if they had any pieces of tin, they put those down with rocks on top to hold them. Finally, they put dirt on top of that. They covered everything with dirt.

It keeps! The food keeps a long time. Sometimes it keeps for two years. No water went in there. Even in wintertime, when there's lots of snow on the ground, nothing went in there. So the people could go anywhere—go, come back, go, come back—and their food was still there.

"Not Many People Had Money"

There used to be a store at Grasshopper. It stopped a long time ago. It still stands, right there by the water tank—that stone house there was the store. The Grasshopper cowboys use it now. And there used to be a store in lower Cibecue close to where Minnie Narcisco lives. That was the first store in Cibecue.[4] It stopped a long time ago, too. And then, later on, they put up another store—Knapp's store. Mostly we went there. Cooley's store was after that. And then, just lately, they put up the commercial center.

We didn't get much from the store—sugar, coffee, flour, lard, baking powder, a few things like that. That old man [Charley Marley] used to get horseshoes and horseshoe nails, and my mother got material and thread for making dresses. If she had money, she paid for it, but mostly she traded with the baskets and beadwork she made. In those days, not many people had money. And when they got some—like after they sold their cattles or got paid for fixing fences—they spent it right away. It didn't bother them much, not having money. If everybody helps everybody else, you don't need lots of money.

I used to ride horseback from Chediskai to the store in Cibecue. I left early in the morning when it's still dark. I got there early and got what we needed and then I started back. I got back to Chediskai around two or three o'clock in the afternoon. I liked doing that.

In wintertime, my mother and my stepfather wanted to go to the store, but sometimes it was too cold for them. I could hear them talking, "We need this, this, this." I told them I was going just before I left. I knew that if I told them before—like if I said, "I'm leaving for Cibecue tomorrow"—they might say no. "Don't go alone. It's too cold.

Cibecue Creek with Western Apache homes on both sides, 1919.

Stay home." So I told them I was leaving just before I left. Then I took off!

Trickery at Cibecue

My mother used to go to Knapp's store in Cibecue. Once in a while, she went to the other one, Cooley's store. But then that man [Don Cooley, Sr.] did something she didn't like. She said that when she went over there, he always gave her whatever she wanted and packed it up for her real good. He always took it outside for her and put it in the wagon. But then, when she tried to pay for it, he didn't take her money. I mean, he *took the money* and he changed it all right, but he gave her back the *same amount* in change! He didn't take anything out! And she really didn't know.

Somehow she found out about it. So she went over there to the store and told him, "I gave you *that much* the last time I was here and you didn't take your money out." He said, "I know, I know." She said, "Have you been doing this before?" He said, "Yes, yes." See, he knew

Members of a Western Apache family at their home near Cibecue, Fort Apache Indian Reservation, about 1925.

that she usually went to Knapp's store, and he was trying to help her out so that she would go to *his* store. But my mother didn't like it. She said, "He was tricking me and I didn't even know." So she wouldn't go over there after that. She said, "From now on, I'll go to Knapp's store to get what we need." So that's what we did.

"Thank You, Kate"

That old man was crazy, Mr. Knapp. He didn't keep enough drinks for himself, so he used to run around looking for homebrew. Sometimes he sent somebody to get him a gallon. They took it to the barn behind his house, and then they told him where they put it. Then he went over there and got a drink. He did that a lot. That man would go to Globe and he wouldn't come back. He started drinking down there and forgot to come home. So his wife was there by herself. She didn't like it, staying there all by herself.

One time, she asked me, "Are you busy, are you doing something?"

I said, "No, I'm not." She said, "I wonder if you can stay with me tonight. My husband went to Globe. I don't know when he'll be coming back." I said, "Yes, I can stay with you."

They had a bunch of dogs outside. That night we fed them. Then that lady said, "How many cans of dog food do we have?" I said, "There's two more cans on the shelf." I put them on the counter. She said, "OK, we'll feed them that in the morning." Then we went to bed.

After we went to bed her husband came home. He came in the house. Then he went back outside. He was drunk. He was talking to one of the dogs: Kate was her name. He said, "Thank you, Kate, a can of hash for me. I'm sure glad for that. I'm hungry. I have to eat it now." He was sitting outside, talking away to that dog, and I could hear the spoon scraping against the can. "Thank you, Kate, that was *good.*" Then he came back in and put the can in the trash can inside.

The next morning, he was still asleep when we got up. His wife wanted to know what he ate. She said, "I usually put a can of hash out for him. When he comes home he opens it and eats it. I put it on the counter. That's what I usually do."

But this time it was dog food! That old man didn't know the difference! He ate one whole can of dog food! We found out by looking in the trash can. There's no can of hash in there, only one empty can of dog food!

Lots of Ruts

Mr. Knapp used to go to Globe in his car. There were dents all over it. Cooley [Don Cooley, Sr.] had a car, and I think he had a little truck, too. McQuillin had a car and the schoolteachers had one, and I think the Lutheran church had a car, too. In those days, the road was rough—lots of ruts—and when it rains there's nothing but mud, real sticky mud. So the ones that had cars can't go nowhere 'til the road dried out good. I don't know how many times that road washed out.

I think the first car in Cibecue [owned by an Apache person] belonged to Shirley Endfield's grandfather. He bought it but didn't drive it. He just parked it at his house. He used to sit in it parked, not moving. He lived on the hill where Violet Caddo lives now. Everybody came to look at it, but he just sat in there, still not moving, Finally, some man tried to drive it for him. He wrecked it for him right away. I guess he thought of it just like a wagon that could go anywhere. He got it going on that rough dirt road, and then—where the road was washed out deep—he just *ran* it in there! That's how he destroyed it. All he did was steer. He didn't know about brakes.

Arthur Naklanita had a car, too. It was a little one. I remember he took my mother and me over there to Whiteriver once, when he first got it. I think it went only about thirty miles an hour. We started early in the morning. We got there about twelve o'clock. The road was still dirt all the way. He was careful 'cause of the road. Ruts, lots of ruts!

Sorghum Syrup and Sheepskins

For a while—I think it was around 1931 or '32, somewhere in there—they gave out rations at Cibecue. Rufus Lavender used to give them out. He gave them out to anybody that comes along. There used to be a little house there and a little field and an apple orchard. He kept those things in that little house. It's not very far from where Judy Dehose lives now.

He gave out flour, beans, coffee, sugar and bacon, corn flour and cornmeal, and sometimes potatoes and onions. He gave out beef, too, chopped up in pieces. He cut it himself according to how many kids there are in the family. If you had a big family, he gave you a big piece. He gave out sorghum syrup, too, but you had to bring your own container. And when the apples were getting ripe—they didn't belong to nobody—he just told the people to take them off the trees. He stored them inside that little house and gave them out when people asked for them. He was there all the time, taking care of that place.

Sometimes, if he couldn't make it or had to do something, that farmer, McQuillin, gave out rations. We never went there every week like some people did, so he gave us enough for more than a month. He gave us three big pieces of salt pork and beans and flour and sugar and sorghum syrup. We got a lot of canned milk, too. We had no container for the sorghum syrup. My mother said, "I don't know what we're gonna put it in." She said, "All we have is that *tús* [water jug]." It was a big one. And McQuillin said, "That's good, that's good, that's something to put it in." So we emptied out the water and he poured the syrup in there. He filled up the tús with sorghum syrup! It lasted a long time.

One time, Rufus Lavender gave out sheepskins. It comes by the bundle, big bundles. I don't know where he got them. We went to Cibecue and my mother got some of those sheepskins. She took them back to Chediskai. She cut them straight, square. She cut all the crooked parts off and then she sewed them together. She made a big mattress out of them. We didn't have no beds, so she put it on top of the straw and put blankets on top of it. It keeps you real warm!

Then my brothers wanted some, so they went to Cibecue and got a bundle for themselves. They soaked theirs in a washtub. They put a lot of yucca soap in there and washed them real good. Then they took them into the river and rinsed them and rinsed them. And then they spread them out on top of some big rocks to let them dry. When they were dry, they brought them home. They used a sandy rock to rub them, scrape them, and that made them real soft. After they were soft, they cut the crooked parts off, like my mother did, and sewed them together and put them down on the straw.

A Christmas Party

The family stayed at Chediskai during wintertime. My mother liked it down there 'cause my brothers all stayed home. She knew that in Cibecue they wouldn't stay home. If somebody came and asked them to go with them somewhere—they're *gone*! They didn't come back 'til way late in the afternoon or in the evening. She worried about them.

One winter we stayed in Oak Creek. My stepfather had a little log cabin down there. The next winter we went back, but it was hard to get firewood—it was scarce and far away to get—so we left and came home to Chediskai. It got cold at Chediskai but it wasn't windy very much. In those days, it snowed a lot, a lot more than now, especially up at Cibecue. Cibecue was *cold*!

At Christmastime people used to have Christmas parties. That was lots of fun. They sang and gave things away. I went to one of those parties with my mother and my stepfather. It was in Cibecue. It lasted all night. I remember it 'cause my mother sang a real funny song.

It was cold, so everybody was inside a wickiup. It was a big one.

They all gathered in there, sitting all the way around, and they all brought their own blankets to sit on. They had lots of túłbáí for people to drink and a big pot of coffee. And they had lots of wood—oak, chopped in little pieces—that they put on the fire in the middle of the wickiup. They put those pieces on there and it kept burning all night. The smoke from the fire went straight up through the hole at the top. They passed the túłbáí around in a bucket and they ate whatever they had to eat— cornbread, walnuts, mescal.

Some of them had Pendleton blankets, those cotton Pendleton blankets, and some had moccasin shoes. And some were carrying deer-skins, already soft, and some were wearing beads around their necks. Those things were valuable to them. Close to midnight, a man started singing songs, social songs. Everybody just listened. Then the mens started taking turns singing. And then somebody said, "Everybody sings in here, one song. If you know a song, you can sing. If you don't know a song, you have to choose somebody to sing for you. Even the ladies, they have to sing, too."

While they were singing, they started giving presents to each other. The person by the door starts and it goes around this way, always to the right [clockwise]. The first one makes a present, and then the next person makes a present, and it goes all the way around. And if they want to choose somebody to give something to somebody else, they can do that, too. What they really do is exchange stuff, 'cause when they *give* somebody something they *take* something, too. If you had a blanket and somebody put a blanket over you, they could take your blanket. And if they took your moccasin shoes, they could put their moccasin shoes on you. Beads was the same way—if they took your beads, they could put their beads on you. They kept on going like that, singing and giving stuff away.

My mother sang a song—I guess you could say it's about an old lady. It's about a *real* old lady and my mother was singing it. And every-body was just *yelling* 'cause it's funny! It's so *funny*! She sang that song, she finished it, and they tried to tell her to sing it again. "No," she said, "I already did." Early in the morning, they asked her to sing again. "It's for the closing song. Can you sing that one again?" She said, "If you know how to sing it, I'll sing it. If you don't, I won't sing it for you." Some of them said that they knew part of it, so she started singing again. She did all the motions, too—you know, what that lady in the song is doing—and all of them did that, too. She told them, "If you don't do the motions with me, I'm not gonna sing no more." It's lots of fun doing that. They made her sing that song two or three times before she quit. They *loved* that song!

Chapter Eight

The family always had horses. We rode them all the time—Oak Creek, Spring Creek, Cibecue, Salt Banks—we rode those horses everywhere. And my stepfather had his donkey, that smart blue donkey. Whenever he had to go somewhere he always took that donkey. My mother was always looking after animals, all kinds of animals, feeding them and raising them 'til they got big. She raised a pig. Oh, that pig! My stepfather didn't *like* it. I raised a bear. It wouldn't hurt nobody but it almost got us into trouble.

"Come on Down!"—Taming Horses—Catching a Wild Horse—"Ride 'em, Cowboy!"—Killing Horses for Fish Food—A Car-Wagon—A Blue Donkey—Blue Learns a Lesson—Blue Sounds an Alarm—"Blue Was Real Careful with Me"—Bichįh Nteelé (Wide Nose)—Raising an Orphan Horse—"They Slept on Her Head!"—Tommy

"Come on Down!"

I started riding horses when I was living at Chediskai, that's when I really started. The fields were on this side of the river, and that big mountain—Dził Cho [Chediskai Mountain], they call it—was on the other side. My brothers made a big pasture on that mountain. They built a fence all the way around it with barbed wire. A trail went up and around the mountain, then it went down, then it went up to the top. Every time you turned the horses loose they went up there.

My stepfather used to talk to the horses. He talked to them in

Apache. They understand, too. They stood there and listened, looking at him. Whenever he let them go, they went way up the mountain on the other side of the river. They went *way up* and you could see them from the house. But my stepfather didn't see very well—he's just got one eye—and he always asked Augustine or Dewey, "Do you see the horses somewhere?" They said, "They're way up there"—and they pointed to them. "Well," he said, "it's time for them to come down."

They [the horses] knew my stepfather better than anyone else. They knew his voice. So he called them to come down. He stood in the middle of the field and started hollering. "He-e-e-ey! Come on down! Come back here! We got a job to do!" They put their heads up when they heard him. Then they started marching back. They came down the mountain and went across the river, coming this way. Then they stood by the gate 'til somebody went over there to open it. They came right in and went to the shade and stood there. Then he put ropes around their necks and gave each of them a dipper full of corn. They ate. Then he told them, he said, "It's time to go to work." He said, "It's time to start plowing."

Taming Horses

Everybody was always doing *something* back then. The mens don't hardly drink, so they're ready to do something all the time. Like working with horse hair, hair from the horse's tail. They shaved those off and soaked them in yucca soap for about two days. Then they rinsed them off and made the horse's bridle. It's real pretty. They used different colors for their design. My stepfather used to make those. He used deer hide, too. He cut it in strips, thin strips, and then he braided those and made ropes. Lots of times, he made bridles that way, too. He made hat bands with horse hair, and he made those violins, Apache violins.[1]

They made ropes out of yucca, too. They got those *igáyé* and pounded them a little bit—not too much, not to break the strings, just to make them soft. Then they rolled them on a rock. Then they shook them and all the green skin came off. Then they soaked them in water and after that, when the water turns kind of white, they took them out and hung them up to dry. When the leaves were almost dry, they tied them together at the ends and made long strings out of them. They tied them real tight. The knots were real small. Then they put three of those long strings together and tied them with igáyé to a post. Then they started working. They twisted it—pull and twist, pull and twist, pull and twist—'til it gets real tight. They used to make three or four ropes at a time. They're strong!

In those days, they used to eat horse meat. If they got real hungry somewhere, they killed one of their horses. They cooked the meat and ate it. They took the hide off. They used the hides for bags, saddlebags or anything they want. Some of them left the hair on and tanned it real soft. They used those hides for moccasin shoes, too.

That old man [Charley Marley] was good at taming horses. To make the young ones take the bit, he used a stick. He took the bark off and cleaned it real good—you know, to wash the taste off. Then he tied a string to one end of the stick. The string went over the horse's head and down the side to the other end, and he tied it there, too. Then he put the stick in the horse's mouth, all the way across where there's no teeth on the side. He left it there for a while, about two or three days. "They get used to it fast," he said. Pretty soon, the horse knew what to do. It opened its mouth by itself and then it was easy to put the bridle on.

If the horse was bucking hard, he tied a cowhide or piece of cardboard behind it. It kicked at it and kicked at it. Pretty soon, the horse got tired of kicking and started walking around with it. It walked around but it didn't kick at the hide no more. Then my stepfather knew it was ready. It was easy to get on and ride. That's the way he used to tame his horses.

We used to take young horses down to the river. We took them to a rocky place and rode them there. That way they don't buck very much. It scares them—I guess they're afraid the rocks might hurt their feet. If you keep on riding them there—back and forth, back and forth— they get used to it fast. Then you can ride them on smooth ground and they won't hardly buck at all.

I was about sixteen years old when I started taming horses. My brothers were doing it, so I tagged along with them. I was raised only with boys. I had no sister. The older sister I had, Donna, I didn't get to know very well. She died.

Catching a Wild Horse

Paul Martinez gave me a horse. It was his father-in-law's but he gave it to me. The mother of that horse died or got killed somewhere. That horse he gave me was *wild*!

They thought we never would catch that horse, but we did. Joe and Jack and me and Paul Davis, we found it right away. It was up there on the mountain with the others. Paul Davis said, "I know that horse. Maybe I can make it come down." So he went up there. He got on his horse and went up there. Then he led his horse all the way back down, taking his time, and that wild horse followed him. They came down. They crossed the river. The gate of the corral was wide open. Paul Davis came through the gate, leading his horse. The other one stood there for a long, long time. It didn't see us. It was just standing there, just scratching on the ground. Paul Davis's horse started hollering. It was hollering for the other one, the wild one, so finally it came inside the corral. That was it! Everybody ran to the gate and closed it.

"Ride 'em, Cowboy!"

We used to go and pick acorns.[2] We all went together—Dewey, Joe, Augustine, me, my mother, and my stepfather. Sometimes we made a hundred pounds in one day. All of us just picked and picked.

There's lots of acorn trees down below Oak Creek. We were going down there. We were getting ready to go, and I just don't know what *happened* to that horse. I think a wasp or a bee stung it. My mother got on it all right, but then my brothers stirred up the nest and those things were flying all over the place. I told her to get away from there right away, but one of them stung the horse and it started *going*! Those boys were running alongside, and Dewey was teasing my mother. "Ride 'em cowboy! Ride 'em cowboy!" He kept running alongside the horse.

Then Joe ran in front of it and caught it by the bridle. He caught it but it was still kicking and jumping around. Joe told my mother, he said, "You take my horse and I'll take this one." So she got off and got on Joe's horse. Then Joe got back on the other one—and it started all over again. That horse started *going*! Joe fell off. All his brothers were making fun of him. "You're not a cowboy," they said. "My mother is!" They made fun of him all day 'cause he fell off the horse.[3]

Killing Horses for Fish Food

They were killing horses. They were killing wild horses for fish food.[4] Somebody told the cowboys from Cibecue that there was lots of wild horses at Oak Creek and Chediskai, so they came over there looking for them. If they killed one they got paid. When my stepfather knew the cowboys were down there, he called to the horses. "Here! Here!" They all came down the mountain by themselves and stood at the gate. He told them, he said, "They're hunting you, so don't show yourselves out here in the open." He said, "Go to Dǫ' Bi Gową and stay there." So they did. They understood. They marched down there and stayed 'til all the cowboys were gone.

See, sometimes they don't know if a horse was wild or if it belonged to somebody. That's what happened to us—they killed one of my stepfather's horses. He went up to Grasshopper and told the white stockman there, he said, "How come you're killing good horses? You should know which horses to kill. You and your cowboys killed one of mine." He said, "You got no horse yourself, so you ride all the horses that belong to the Indians. Why don't you kill *those* horses?" He said, "I can't plow my fields 'cause you killed one of my team. One of my team is *gone*! You got to pay me for that one. I don't care how many horses you're killing, I want you to pay for that one." He kept on and on.

I guess that stockman got scared 'cause he got a mule from somewhere and gave it to my stepfather. But that mule just jerked around. It won't go straight. "I'll make it quit," my stepfather said. So he cut a pair of real old jeans and made a strip. He tied it around the mule's head and put it over its eyes. He used that mule all day that way. After that, it quit jerking around. It went straight.

A Car-Wagon

My brother Albert made a wagon. He made it out of a car. It was just the bottom part that he used 'cause the upper part was gone. He asked some man in Cibecue, "What are you going to do with that?" He said, "I'm just about ready to take it to the dumpyard." My brother said, "Well, if you don't want it, I'll take it off your hands." And that man said, "OK, go ahead. Take it."

My brother pulled it back to Spring Creek with a horse and he put it under the shade. He started working on it. He took the tires off. He got new tires, four of them. And the tubes that go in there, he got those, too. Then he made the front part—you know, the long pole that goes between the horses. Then he put a seat on there. It was an old car seat that was left behind by the Oak Creek cowboys. After that he got some boards and made the back part, the part where you put your stuff. Then he put the wheels on again.

He said, "Who's going to town?" My mother said, "Where to?" He said, "Cibecue. Let's go. We'll get there around noontime." She said, "It takes longer than that." He said, "Not in this car, not in this car-wagon." So everybody got ready and got in there. That wagon went fast! It's not very heavy and the horses didn't get tired. We got there around noontime, just like he said.

A Blue Donkey

My stepfather plowed with horses and mules and sometimes with his donkey. Him and his donkey! He called it Blue, Túlgayé Dotł'izhí [Blue Donkey]. That donkey was smart! He was strong, too. He was a donkey but larger than donkeys, almost like a mule. When he got in the corral with the horses, he hollered and hollered *all day long*. He didn't want to stay in there. Every time he seen somebody moving around, he hollered. He wants you to open the gate for him. When you did that, he quiets down right away. And he only let one person ride him—*one person*! If it's two, no, he bucked them right off.

He did that to my mother one time. We were going to pick acorns and another lady was coming with us. We were getting ready to go. My mother was sitting on Blue. That lady said, "I'm gonna put my grand-daughter up there with you. She don't like to walk and I hate carrying her on my back. Can she ride with you?" My mother said, "I can ride by myself but I can't put nobody else up here. This donkey don't like it." And that lady said, "Well, that's OK. There's a place right behind you. I'll put her up there." My mother said, "No, it's no good. This thing will start jumping with us. Your granddaughter's gonna fall off." But that lady didn't believe it. She put the little girl up there.

We started off. We were going towards the gate. My brother's

Blue, Charley Marley's donkey, ridden by Jack Tulene Case at Cibecue, Fort Apache Indian Reservation, about 1930.

horse was on this side, the donkey was in the middle, and my horse was on the other side. We kept it crowded like that so it won't start acting up. Then somebody hollered for me. My brother and I went over there, and *right away* that donkey started to buck. That little girl fell off and my mother's saddle got sideways. When me and my brother got back, Blue was eating grass. We fixed the saddle for my mother. She got back on and went home. She told that lady, she said, "I told you not to put the little girl up here. This donkey don't like it."

Blue Learns a Lesson

The horses used to come right away when my stepfather hollered for them, all except that stubborn donkey. That blue donkey liked to hide! I don't know how he did it, but he rubbed his bell against a tree or a rock and pushed it up under the rope that went around his neck. He pushed it up in there and then it wouldn't move. His bell wouldn't ring! When he did that, you couldn't find him.

He used to go to a place—it's so hard to get to—and hide there on a cliff. I used to go up above there and throw rocks at him. One time, I almost made him slide all the way down. He saw me standing up there. "You better come here," I said. I threw a rock at him. I couldn't help it, I was so mad at him. He started running along the cliff into a smaller place. But then I threw a rock in front of him and he swung around—so fast!—and he just went over. He was sliding down and, I don't know, somehow he put his hoofs in the ground real deep and stopped. He crawled out of there. Then he turned around real slow and came back up. He came right to me.

I put a rope around his neck and started walking him to the trail. We stopped up there on a flat spot and I patted him on his head. I said, "You almost killed yourself acting so smart. You know you can't get away." There's a big rock there. He stopped right there in front of that rock. That means he wants me to get on and ride him. So I did. I got on the rock and jumped on his back and went down.

I told everybody what happened to him. My stepfather took him to the shade and gave him his corn. He was standing there talking to Blue. I don't know how he made him understand, but he did. He told him, he said, "That's what happens to somebody like you." He said, "You try to hide 'cause you're lazy. It's no use, this is life. We got to work all the time." He said, "We're your friends. We're not your enemy. We feed you corn. We give you something that's good for you."

And you know what? That donkey never went back up there. He just stayed on the side of the mountain with the other horses. He never went back to that cliff.

Blue Sounds an Alarm

We went to Cherry Creek to gather those plants they make baskets with. We went over there and cut and cut and cut. We got four bundles, four big bundles, and we put them on the donkey. We piled those bundles on Blue.

I started home. I was ahead of the others and something spooked my horse. I never did know what it was. He started jumping around with me. I thought I was gonna fall. I almost did. And then that horse took off, running on the trail. That scared horse ran with me for about two miles, maybe more than that. Finally, I got him stopped. I tried to turn around and go back, but his ears were way up high—I guess he smelled something—and I couldn't make him go.

My mother and Joe were back there behind me. They said that Blue started hollering his head off and that's when they knew that something happened to me. So they came running! They came with their horses running real fast. I was sitting there under an acorn tree. My horse was tied up. They said, "What happened?" I said, "I don't know. Something spooked that horse and he ran with me this far." Then Blue came running with those bundles on his back. He was really hollering his head off! And you know, when he seen me and that horse, he quieted down right away. He just stood there. I guess he knew we were all right.

"Blue Was Real Careful with Me"

I only got hurt one time. I was going back to Chediskai. My horse slid on the ice. He fell. I was going to get the horses. I don't know why, but whenever we stayed down at Oak Creek the horses ran back to Chediskai. So we were down there at Oak Creek. It was wintertime.

My brothers looked for the horses. They couldn't find them. So they told me, "They're probably back at Chediskai. Go get them." In the morning, I went back. We had to cross the river seven times. The last crossing is where I got hurt. The horse I was riding fell to the side. He slipped on the ice and I fell off. There was a stump there with sharp pieces sticking up. I fell on it and the horse fell on top of me.

I tried to get up but I couldn't. The horse was pinning me down. Then he got up. He was standing there. He kept putting his head down, so I got hold of his bridle and he pulled me up. Then I felt something hot down there on my back. I reached down there and it was bleeding real bad. I didn't know what to do.

I couldn't go. I was just sitting there. So I put my hand out and patted him on the neck. Then I took his bridle off. See, if you took that horse's bridle off, he always ran back to Oak Creek 'cause that's where he grew up. But if you left it on, he won't go nowhere. I told him, "Go home!" He ran off, making that noise he does. He ran all the way back to Oak Creek.

My brothers came about an hour later, Jack and Joe. They took me up to the house at Chediskai. They went and got a horse. They asked me if I could sit on it. "I guess I can," I said. I tried. I tried so hard but I couldn't—it hurt so bad. I said, "I can stay here at Chediskai." But they said, "We can't leave you here. You're all alone." Then Joe went and got the other horses. He chased them down from the mountain. Then I said, "That donkey, I might ride that donkey 'cause he don't shake you like a horse. I think that donkey might take me back down." So they saddled him up for me. I finally got on and I went with them to Oak Creek. Blue was real careful with me. He didn't shake me hardly at all.

When I got there they wanted to know what happened. I said, "The ice, the ice. There's ice along the edge of the river. It was icy."

Bichįh Nteelé (Wide Nose)

My mother raised all kinds of animals. She was always looking after them. She raised turkeys and quails and horses. There used to be animals all over the place! She raised a pig, too.

She called that pig Bichįh Nteelé [Wide Nose]. It was a little tiny one when she got it. Somebody was living on the other side of Salt River and whoever it was left their camp. They left everything and the pig was there. My brother Albert was fixing fence over there and he heard about it. He brought two of those pigs back home and gave them to my mother. He said, "There was a bunch of them but the mother ran off with the big ones. These two little ones were left behind."

So he brought them back. My mother raised them for about two weeks. Then another man saw one and he wanted it. So my brother, without even asking my mother, went and gave it to that man. He came to get it but she wouldn't let him have it. When my brother came home, he said, "I just gave him one of them." And my mother said, "Why didn't you ask me? You gave it to me first. Why didn't you ask me before you did that?" She didn't want to give it up but she did. So she raised only one of those pigs.

Dewey and Augustine used to play with it. They had a washpan and a bucket of water outside the house. They had to wash their hands there. But if that pig wanted a drink, they wouldn't let him have it. They kept teasing them. They put the washpan down and started washing their hands, and then, when the pig came running, they went somewhere else with the water. My mother told them, she said, "You better let that pig drink. You better give it some water."

They didn't listen to her. They kept teasing that pig. And you know what happened? He *bit* both of them on the leg! They hit him somewhere and he was dragging his back leg for a while, about a day or so. My mother got mad at them, so she picked up the pig and wrapped it up in a blanket. She put it behind her where she was sitting. She kept it there, and when she moved she took it with her. She kept on doing that. She kept that pig with her all the time. My brothers said, "I bet when we were babies you didn't treat us like that."

My mother kept that pig until it was *big*! She used to go get walnuts under the trees at Oak Creek. There was lots of walnuts over there. She brought them home and filled up a big old box. Then, in the wintertime, she took a couple of walnuts and a cup of corn and fed it to the pig. He got bigger and bigger and bigger. He was just *fat*!

My stepfather used to get mad at that pig 'cause he won't leave my mother. If you put him in the corral, he won't stay there. He cried and screamed all night. So my mother got up and went over there and opened the gate. He came running after her. And when she went back to bed he went to sleep beside her. That's when my stepfather got mad. "What are you doing with your husband?" he said. "What's your husband doing now?"

We called that pig Bichįh Nteelé. My mother raised him 'til he got real big. Then McQuillin came down there and said, "You have to kill that pig or sell it." So she sold it to him. I think she got only five dollars for that pig. After that I guess he felt bad about it, 'cause he gave part of the meat back to my mother. She wouldn't eat it. She wouldn't even take a bite out of it. One day, my brothers boiled beans and put some of the meat in there. She wouldn't even eat the beans.

Raising an Orphan Horse

My mother raised a horse, too. Its mother died when it was being born. She was lying up there on top of the cliff at Chediskai. I guess she was chased by a fox or a wolf or maybe a mountain lion. She stopped running 'cause she was giving birth. She was really screaming, so my mother and stepfather went up there to look. They came back. They said, "She was right at the edge of the cliff. She was trying to get up and fell over. She broke her neck. The baby was already born." That's how my mother got that little horse.

We had lots of canned milk. My mother mixed it with cornmeal or flour and fed it to that orphan horse. She boiled it first. It was kind of watery-like. That horse would drink it from a bottle. She fed it that way for a long time.

It grew up good, that orphan horse. My mother started taking it around, going with it to get grass. It followed her wherever she went. She seen what the other horses were eating and she grabbed those kinds of grass and brought them home. So she raised that horse and pretty soon it started going with the rest of the horses. But they were kind of mean, they won't let it come around them.

McQuillin came down there and my mother told him about that horse. "The mother died," she said. He said, "I got some dry milk at home. I'll bring it to you tomorrow." So he brought a whole big box full of it. My mother used that for a while. It didn't take long for that horse to start eating grass, though. It grew up good and the other horses quit being mean to it.

"They Slept on Her Head!"

I used to eat quail eggs a lot. My brothers said, "You're gonna have a face with spots on it." I said, "That's OK, they'll go away." There used to be lots of quails in Oak Creek. I took a bucket and went out and looked for quail eggs. They're out in the open, that's where you find them. They lay their eggs right there. They don't sit on them to hatch, it's the sun that does it. When you see a bunch of little quails running around and you run toward them, they're gone in no time and you can't find them. They change their colors when they go close to the ground. They're *there* but you can't see them.

My mother raised two of those quails. She got two of them in Oak Creek. She threw her basket on top of them. She said, "Another one ran off. I looked for it. It was *right there* and then it disappeared." It didn't disappear, she just didn't see it.

Anyway, she got those two quails. She brought them home to Chediskai. She kept them in a little box covered with a veil. She fed them 'til they got big. She ground corn and sprinkled it in front of them to eat. Pretty soon, she could handle them and pick them up. And every time she went to get water, they followed her. They followed her around wherever she went. And when she went to bed, those two quail sat right on her head. At night, they slept on her head!

Tommy

I took some horses to my brother up there close to Iron Mine. I got there around lunchtime. I thought I was supposed to go back to Chediskai Farms with him and his family, but he said he's not going 'til the next morning. He said, "You can go home now, if you want to, or stay here for the night." I said, "No, I'm going home."

I got on my horse and started back. I was going down, going towards Chediskai, and I heard some babies crying. It sounded just like babies. "I wonder whose babies those are!" Then, when I got closer, I heard it was coming from a tree somewhere up high. I was looking up there. Finally, I found out it was baby bears, two of them. I got the lower one off the tree but the upper one was sitting way up high. I couldn't catch it. So I just got that one.

The horse I was riding wouldn't stand still. He was jumping around with me. I put my jacket around the bear and wrapped it up. I guess the horse couldn't smell the bear no more 'cause he quit jumping around. I kept going. When I got home nobody was there. I put the bear down and got something to eat.

Then I went up on the hill where they parked the wagon. There was a big box there where they usually put corn. There was nothing in it, so I spread some grass in there and put the bear inside. We always kept water up there, so I got some water and put it in a pan and put the pan in the box. Then I came back down.

My mother was under the shade. She said, "Where have you been?" I said, "I was just walking around." She said, "We thought you might have fallen off the horse and it came back by itself. The old man [Charley Marley] went looking for you." I said, "I was right here." She said, "Well, he went back up there looking for you, so you better get on your horse and follow him and tell him to come home." I went after him. He said, "Where did you go?" I told him, "I was home." He said, "We hollered! Why didn't you answer us?" I said, "I was way up on top." I didn't tell him nothing about the bear.

I kept the bear up there for a long time. I was taking it things to eat. Then my brother Joe found out about it. He said that he was going hunting for wild turkeys. He went up there towards the wagon, and I guess he heard the same sound as I heard before. He stopped. The bear was in the box. He came back down. He didn't say nothing about it. I was putting some corn gravy in a coffee can. I put it in there and closed it. Joe said, "What are you going to do with that?" I said, "I'm just going to put it up. I might eat it later." Then he said, "Are you going to take it up there?" I said, "Take it up where?" He was just smiling— he knew what I was hiding—but still he didn't say nothing.

Later, my mother and my stepfather went off somewhere. Joe asked me, he said, "How come you didn't go with them?" I said, "I'm going after them in a while. I have to make bread first." "Oh," he said. "When are you gonna take that gravy up there on the hill?" He said, "I know about it. I know how that old man is gonna get mad, too, if he finds out. You better let it [the bear] go 'cause the mother might come over here and bother us." I said, "I don't know. She might go up there, but not down here. She'll go up there first." Then he said, "Can I take the gravy up there for you?" So I gave it to him. When he came back down, he said, "That thing was starving! He ate it all up." I guess Joe put some canned milk in his pocket and mixed it with water. He gave it to the bear. He said it was really drinking it!

Then my mother and my stepfather found out about it. I went to the river for water and the old man went to get the harness. The harness was up there by the wagon. It was hanging on a tree. He usually put it in the box. He decided to put it back in there so the rain won't get to it. He tried to put it in there—and *there's the bear*! He just dropped the harness and came running back down. I didn't say nothing. He was telling my mother about it. I took off!

When I came back, I told them what happened. I said, "I got it a long time ago. It was small then but now it's getting bigger. I don't think it will hurt nobody." So they went and got the bear. My mother liked it right away. She put a red rag around its neck and tied it to the shade on a long rope. She started feeding it different things. It was real friendly. When she untied it, it followed her around like a dog. It followed her around wherever she went.

But people were scared of it. They used to come around on horse-back, but they quit doing that 'cause the horses don't like it and started jumping around. They called us the Bear Family. I told my mother, I said, "Somebody's gonna report on us." That's what they did. They told McQuillin. So he sent somebody down there. That man said, "Bring the bear to Cibecue."

So my brother made a cage and we put the bear in there. We took it on the wagon to Cibecue. When we got there we took it out and tied it up. That's when lots of people found out about it—that's when they seen it for the first time. I guess they were talking about it. When my brother came back from the store, he told me, he said, "People over here are afraid of it. You better turn it loose." He said, "When you get back home, you better turn it loose."

McQuillin came over the next morning real early. We were already packed and ready to go when he came. He said, "What are you going to do with that bear?" I said, "I'm going to take it home and turn it loose." He said, "You can't." He said, "I already reported it to the zoo. The zoo is coming after it, so put it back in the cage." I put it in there. It just *cried* and *cried*! I was walking away from it and it just *cried* after me.

So I took it home. I told that man [McQuillin], "If you want it, you can come and get it at Chediskai." I said, "I'm not gonna let it stay here. If it gets loose, it's gonna scare the people." He said, "We'll come down there tomorrow." So we put it in the cage and left.

The next day, McQuillin came with another man. I guess that man worked for the zoo. He looked at the bear and fell in love with it right away. He said, "What's his name?" I said, "Tommy." They took it. It cried and cried when they were taking it away.

Chapter Nine

In those days, if somebody got sick or hurt real bad, people knew how to cure them. Different people were good for different things. Some were good for this kind of sickness, some were good for that kind. Some of the ladies, like my mother, used herbs. The mens used yellow powder and other things, but mostly they cured with their prayers. Those prayers were strong! Usually, they sang them at night, thirty-two of them. Other mens helped them sing. Those medicine mens had to be careful not to make mistakes. Their songs had to be perfect. Even when I was the one they were singing for—even when I was sick—I thought those songs were wonderful.

No Doctors, No Nurses—"Making Him Strong"—A Difficult Birth at Oak Creek—Izee sidogí (It Heats You Up Plant Medicine)—Bikee' Delichí'é (Pink Foot)—"He Tells You What Made You Sick"—"Your Footprint Is Bear's Footprint"—"They Were Taking Away Her Sickness"—"It Was Almost Real"—"He Shrinks the Distance"—"This Is Your Last Chance!"—The Death of William Goshoney

No Doctors, No Nurses

No doctors and no nurses ever did come to Chediskai or Oak Creek. There were no doctors down there. There was a hospital in Whiteriver but it took a long time to get over there 'cause of the road. It's a dirt road, lots of ruts, and you can't go fast at all. And when it rained the road was real muddy, so you got stuck. You can't get through. Lots of times that road used to wash out, too.

If somebody in my family got sick, my mother and my stepfather just made them go to bed. They made us go to bed and we stayed in there 'til they brought something—herbs—and fixed it for us. They said, "Drink this and go back to bed." And they felt of you wherever your pains were at—your chest, your neck, around your stomach. You know, constipation was one of the worst things at that time. "That's what's wrong with you," they said. So they went and got herbs for that—you know, to wash you out. After that you feel a lot better.

When my stepfather had a cold, when he had that fever, when his temperature was high, he went to the river and got in there. He went early in the morning. He just sat in the river moving his legs, his arms, like exercising in the water. He stayed there 'til he got real cold. Then he put his clothes on and came home. "Don't give me nothing hot to eat or drink," he said. "I don't want nothing hot." He sat there and drank water or something else that's cold. He sat there for a long time—'til around noontime—and then he asked for something to eat, like cold cornbread.

One time, my mother got a cold herself. She had it real bad and her throat was just *sore*. He [Charley Marley] took her down to the river and put her in the cold water. He said, "I want you to stay in there for a while. That cold water is good for you. After you come out, don't get in the sun or sit next to the fire. You have to warm up slowly, not too fast." So my mother did that. When she came back home, she sat out there under the shade for a long time. Finally, she asked for *ch'ink'ózhé* [skunkbush]. "Have you got any of that juice?" I said, "Yes, there's some in the house." I went and got it for her. She was sitting there sipping on it. She got well.

They used to do that with Augustine, too. When he was small, they took him right away to the river and put him in there. He screamed his head off. "It's *cold*! It's *cold*!" Even in the winter when there's ice around the edge of the river, they put him in there. "This is good for you," they told him. "You have to feel the cold all over."

"Making Him Strong"

When a boy's voice started to change, the mens took him off somewhere. They showed him how to do everything on the man's side. They made him strong for life. They showed him how to hunt and do everything for himself. He has to know how to get woods [firewood] and how to break branches off trees. And he has to know how to run in case something chases him. He can't crawl up a tree; he has to outrun whatever is chasing him. They showed him all those things.

They sang for him every morning. He had to get up before the sun and run. They made him bring woods for the fire in the morning. He can't do that the night before, he has to do it in the morning. And the pot, or whatever they use to carry water in, it had to be empty at night. In the morning, after the boy built the fire, they made him get the pot and run to where water is. He filled it up and brought it home and put the coffee on.

Like I said, they took the boy a long ways off. There's no ladies, no children, just him. He's the only child in the group. The rest is grown mens. The person that prays for him is with them. The others are that medicine man's servants. The songs he sings are *gozhǫǫ sįh* [goodness songs]. He sings other songs, too. Those are *na'iyee' sįh* [strength songs], and they make him [the boy] strong in heart and strong in mind. They're not supposed to sing that kind of songs where there's lots of kids and ladies around. That's the reason they took him way out there.

See, they used to sing those na'íyee' sįh when mens went to war. They sang for them to make them mean, so they're not afraid of *nothing*. When they came back from war, they asked the person that prayed for them to take it away from them, so they won't stay mean. Some didn't do that. They stayed mean.

Anyway, they kept that boy out there four days. When it's the fourth day, he had to run to the river and jump in. Raining or snowing, it don't matter. He still had to jump in the water and take a bath and clean himself good. They had a name for what they did when they took a boy away like that. They called it *nalwod go'áíleh* [it makes him strong]. It means that they're gonna strengthen him—strong in thinking, strong in heart, strong in his body, strong wherever he goes.

Now they've done away with it. The last one I heard about was in 1927, maybe '28. They did that to my cousin, Victor Beatty. I asked my uncle [Robert Beatty, Victor Beatty's father] why they were doing that to him. He said, "You don't want no lazy man around you, do you? He's got to be strong if he's gonna be a man and take care of his family. That's what they're doing for him out there." Like I told you, the boy has to hunt, and I kind of think that's why they stopped doing it—'cause they couldn't hunt at any time no more. They had to get a license and all that, and they had to wait 'til a certain time of the year to go hunting. But they're not supposed to wait. They're supposed to do that right away, as soon as they notice that the boy's voice is changing.

My brother Eugene had that done for him. I think somebody prayed for my other brothers, but I don't know for sure. I think my father went with a medicine man down to St. Johns. Albert was there and Jack and Joe. I kind of think that man went to pray for them.

A Difficult Birth at Oak Creek

The Apaches always told a woman that's going to have a baby *never* to eat intestines. That's what they told them. "Don't eat that," they said. "Otherwise, if you do, the cord on the baby will get too long. So stay away from intestines." And they told her, they said, "Don't let the sun step over you. Get up early and walk around outside. And during the day, don't lay down too much, don't sit too much. If you sit all day, the baby's head gets bigger and flat on top. So don't do that. Keep walking. You don't have to run or go someplace fast, just keep walking. That way, when the baby is born, it will be small." That's what they used to say.

One time, they sent for my mother to go to Oak Creek. A lady over there was going to have a baby. She was my stepfather's niece. Oh, that was *awful*! That lady had a real hard time.

See, that lady's husband was working for the cowboys, and when they killed a beef he brought those things home, those intestines. And that lady went and ate them. Her mother got so mad at her. "Don't eat that!" she told her. "These people know what they're talking about. They know why they tell you not to eat that." But she won't listen. So when it was time for the child to be born, she stayed in pain for about a week. They didn't know what to do! Everybody was just sitting around crying 'cause they couldn't do nothing for that lady.

So they sent for my mother. She went over there to Oak Creek. I went with her. Oh, it was awful the way that baby was born! The cord was too *long*! It was wrapped around his neck and down around his leg, and up around his neck again and down under his leg. It was real *long*!

So they asked my mother, they said, "Will you try and help us?" She said, "Yes, I'll try." Then my mother cut her sleeves. They used to wear long sleeves, all the ladies did, way down to the wrist. She cut both sides and rolled them up and tied them way up here [above her biceps]. Then she washed her hands real good. Then she went to that lady. She told her, she said, "Your baby is just tied up. The place where he's supposed to come out is open, but he can't come out." She said, "What do you think?" That lady said, "You're the only one. We depend on you to help. Do the best you can."

They wanted my mother to cut that cord. But my mother said, "No, we can't do that." What she did was loosen a part of it and straighten out one of the baby's legs. Then she turned him around in there. Then she said, "Now we can try to help her." She started pushing him towards the place where he's supposed to come out. She got part of him out. "We might as well get him all the way out," she said. She pressed— not too hard, just kind of easy—and pushed the baby down. Finally, she pushed him out. He was just wrapped up *all over* with that cord! Everywhere! That cord was just too long. He lived, though. He was born.

Then my mother hollered at me. "Come and help me!" So I got the baby and put him on a cloth. Then she said that everything was out of that lady, even that afterbirth thing. "Everything is out now," she said. So she cut the cord and wrapped him in a blanket and put him aside.

Then the mother fainted. She fainted. We worked on her for a long time. Finally, we got her out of it. She was real weak. She said, "I'm hungry. I'm starving." My mother had gravy ready. She already made it, water with flour and just a little salt. She poured it for her. She told her, she said, "Drink this, it's the only thing that's gonna help you." She drank that. "I want some more," she said. She drank some more. Then she said, "Is it all right if I drink some coffee?" We gave her some coffee. Then she said, "I think I'm through it now. How's the baby boy?" My mother said, "The boy's OK." That baby was *big*! He was about ten pounds. His mother used to tell my mother, "I would have been gone a long time ago but you gave me my life back."

Pregnant ladies are not supposed to look at not-human-looking things. They're not supposed to eat rabbits, 'cause if they do that the baby will have a split lip. And pictures—like pictures of a monkey—if they look at those the baby's face deforms.

It's the same way with *gáán*s [crown dancers]. One baby was born at San Carlos—boy, it was awful. He was alive all right but he didn't live very long. He lived about an hour. But anyway, his face was just *plain*. It looked like it was all covered up—just two little holes here, where the nose is, and his eyes were like that, too, just two little holes. His lips were there but they were sealed together. That's the way he was born. And they asked his mother if she had ever looked at the gááns. She said that after she got pregnant, about a month or two, she went to a dance. She seen them, and that's why her baby imitated them. Its face was just *plain!*[1]

After that baby died, they took it to a doctor. He didn't know what to think. He said there's really nothing wrong with it except for the face. He asked them, "Why don't this happen to other people. Other people don't have these things." And they told him, they said, "'Cause we're Apaches, that's why. Our people know the reasons for this." So he told that lady [the mother of the deformed child], "You should listen to your people and do what they tell you."

Edith Hanna had a sister, a younger sister. She was born at Oak Creek. But her father was trapping raccoon when her mother was pregnant. He brought them home. When the baby was born, her feet were like raccoon feet and her hands were like that, too. And when she cried, she sounded like a raccoon. Charley Marley told that man, "We told you about this. We told you to leave those coons alone. Look at your child. She's crying like a raccoon."

A lady that's gonna have a baby is not supposed to eat liver. If they eat liver, that afterbirth thing gets real big. They're just supposed to eat plain meat—no liver, no intestines, nothing from the inside. And they told them, "Don't ever sit with your back to the sun." They said, "You have to face the sun every time you sit down." They said, "If the sun hits you in the back, that afterbirth thing will stick to your back. It won't come out." That's why they told them to sit facing the sun. They faced the sun all the time.

I seen a lady like that. She had twins over at Mormon Flat, two boys. They were born all right—they came out—but that afterbirth thing was stuck inside to her back. That lady's uncle—he was blind—

kept praying for her, but it didn't do no good. That lady's stomach was getting bigger and bigger, filling up with blood. Her sister's name was Malena, and an old man was getting after her. He said, "Malena, those babies are out already but not that other thing. Scrub your hands and follow the cord inside. Follow the cord and you'll find it. Try to move it around, if you can. Try to get it out." But she wouldn't do it. She just started crying. I guess she got scared. Then that old man said, "Ladies used to do that a long time ago. They washed their hands and tried to get it out." So my mother did that. She put her hand in there. It was stuck all right. Then she put her hand back in there, and it moved. She said that when it moved, that lady fainted. Then she pulled it out, all of it. That lady made it, she was OK. Her blood was just filling her up.

My mother taught me all those things. When she went to take care of some lady, I had to go with her and see what it was all about. She explained those things to me. That's why I know.

Izee sidogí (It Heats You Up Plant Medicine)

There was one medicine that my mother called pneumonia medicine. There used to be a lot of it over at Hawley Lake. It's probably all gone now, I don't know.

My mother gave that to a lady. She was just *coughing*! Her chest sounded like it was clotted up inside. She couldn't hardly breathe. She told my mother, "I have a hard time breathing. I growl at night."

So my mother made some of that medicine. When it cooled off she filled up a one-gallon jug. When she got over there to where that lady lived, she warmed it up. Then she put it in a one-pound coffee can. She had a cup. She told that lady, "This is my measuring cup. I always use this one." She told her to drink it down. She said, "You don't have to drink the whole thing. Just sip on it 'til it's gone." Then she said, "If you go to sleep, as soon as you wake up, drink another cup. And if *that* puts you to sleep, drink another cup when you wake up." Then she said, "Don't take more than three cups." She said, "This will help you. It will loosen everything up in your chest."

I guess that's what that lady did. We went back over there two days later and she was grinding corn. She said, "My chest is all right now. I don't growl at night like I did before." She wanted more of that medicine. My mother said, "All you need is just that one gallon. Did you finish it?" That lady said, "I've still got this much." My mother said, "You've got plenty there. That will cure you. Do what you did before. Do it the same way. Take it the same way I gave it to you before. Drink up what's left." That lady said she would. Then she said, "That's the best medicine I ever had." She got well fast!

People around here call that medicine *izee libaahí*, but it's different than the one my mother used for that bad flu. My mother called this one *izee sidogí* [it heats you up medicine]. The reason is—if you're cold, if your feet are cold, if your hands are cold, if you're cold all over—it will warm you up in no time. It heats you up when you drink it. It heats up your blood and that's why it loosens that stuff in your chest. Pneumonia medicine. She called it izee sidogí.

One time, my mother used that medicine on Francis Bullock's wife. She had pneumonia real bad. She was in the hospital at Whiteriver. The doctor sent her home 'cause she was so skinny. The doctor said he couldn't help her.

That sick lady's mother came over and asked my mother, she said, "You're always picking out all kinds of medicines." She said, "I think you know something about this kind of coughing. You mentioned it once before, I heard you talking about it." She said, "Can you give my daughter some of that medicine to see if she can clear her lungs?" My mother said, "Yes, it could help her."

So we went to Oak Creek. My mother knew where to get that plant, that medicine, so we went down there. We got it and the next day we came back to Cibecue. She boiled it that morning and then she strained it. She put some of it in a bottle. Then she took it over there to that sick lady.

When my mother got over there, she poured some of it in a cup. And she told that lady, she said, "This will warm you up." She told her to sip on it but she went and poured the whole thing down! It made her sweat. She was *sweating*! She said, "I can feel the medicine doing that to me." My mother covered her up so she won't get too cold. She told her to wait there under her blanket. That lady went to sleep. She slept for about two hours.

Finally, when she woke up, she said, "I'm hungry." She wanted some dumplings—plain, just like noodles. They were making that for her. My mother said, "She might not eat 'cause she hasn't had nothing for a long time." See, that lady didn't eat in the hospital—just a little sip of coffee or something—and she stayed that way when they brought her back home. They gave her those dumplings and she ate the whole thing, a big bowl. Then my mother told her, she said, "Be sure to drink some more of that medicine." That evening, I guess she did. Then they made some more of those dumplings for her and she ate the way she did before. Then she went to sleep. She stayed in bed.

About two days later, my mother was sitting outside making a basket—and here she comes! That lady came over there. My mother was surprised. "He-e-e-y, you're walking now!" That lady said, "Yes, you made me walk." Then she said, "My husband bought some meat. He's gone somewhere, but he told me to come and tell you to come and get that meat." My mother said, "Don't walk too far, just this far and that's all. Wait 'til you get more strength." And that lady said, "That's what I'm doing, I'm trying to get my strength back." She said, "I'm feeling a lot better. I didn't cough all last night. I used to cough real bad as soon as evening comes. I started coughing and coughing and coughing. I was coughing 'til morning. But I didn't cough last night."

About three weeks later, that lady was on horseback. "I'm going to get acorns," she said.

Bikee' Délichí'é (Pink Foot)

There was a lady that used to sing for people. Her name was Bikee' Délichí'é [Pink Foot]. I guess they gave her that name when she was just a baby. She knowed all, everything. She cured people. When she's singing, she said, the kind of plant she needs to get goes into her mind.[2] That's how she knows how to cure the sick person. She worked on everybody, ladies and mens and kids. She was raised in Cibecue. She was raised by George Button's wife.

"He Tells You What Made You Sick"

You know, Kenzie Early's father prayed for me. His name was Scott Early. He was a medicine man. There was something wrong with my gall bladder, something like that. It was hurting *bad*!

Like I told you, we used to go back and forth—Chediskai to Oak Creek, Chediskai to Cibecue, back and forth—and we used to drink water from all the springs and rivers. That medicine man told my mother, "Maybe she drank water from where a bear took a drink or a bath. That's what could do that." So my mother asked him to pray for me.

He did. He came over. He was singing that song. And in there, in part of that song, if you listen to what he's saying—if you listen *real good* to the words—he tells you what made you sick. And if you don't understand, then afterwards, when it's all over, he tells you the same thing. My mother was listening to that song he was singing and I guess she found out right away. "That's what I thought," she said. "That's what I thought." I said, "What are you talking about?" She said, "You'll know later on." She told me to go to sleep. I just lay there. I kept listening to the songs.

They sang all night. Towards morning, I went to sleep. I didn't wake up 'til they were already having breakfast. Then, after they ate breakfast, he [Scott Early] said, "It's time to get together now for what I know." He said, "This is what happened to you. You drank some water where a bear was drinking. It spit in the water there. It was still floating around when you drank the water. That's what made you hurt real bad."

That pain I had was gone. It was gone at breakfast time. And later, a lady told my mother, she said, "That man [Scott Early] said that your daughter has lived all over the country. He said that she always travels a lot, and she still will travel when she's an old lady with white hair. He says that when she's real old nobody will think she's her age." In a way, I guess it's true.

"Your Footprint Is Bear's Footprint"

My mother was hurting. She was at Chediskai. So that old man [Charley Marley] said, "You better get to Cibecue so you can find somebody to work on you."

We went to Cibecue. Kenny Dale's father prayed for my mother. His name was David Dale. He said that he was gonna draw on her stomach where it hurts. He said, "We're gonna put your footprint on your stomach." I was wondering what he was talking about. Then that man said, "Your footprint is Bear's footprint." Then he drew a bear's footprint with yellow powder on her stomach.

Before he did that, before he started praying, he told us to go and get water from the spring below Knapp's store. We went over there and got it and brought it back. He said, "Give me a cup of that water." He prayed for that water, just plain water. He told her to drink it. "Drink it up," he said, "this will clear it up." She drank it. After that he got some food for her. He prayed for that, too. She ate. Then he said, "This will make you sleepy. Go to sleep." And he told us, he said, "Don't wake her up for anything. If you want something from her, ask her now. Don't wake her up. She has to wake up by herself." Nobody said anything. She went to sleep.

After she went to sleep in there [a wickiup], everybody went outside. We sat under a shade. In the afternoon, around close to two-thirty, she came out by herself. She said she wanted a drink of water. They gave it to her. They said, "Do you want to eat?" She said, "No, is that man [David Dale] still here?" They said, "No, he went home. He said your pain will be gone." She said, "It is gone. I don't even feel it no more." That man cured her right away. He cured her with just plain water.

David Dale stuttered. He stuttered when he talked and it was hard for him to say the next word. But he didn't stutter when he was singing—he was perfect then. I don't know how people like him used to do those things that they did. In those days, long years ago, they used to cure people just by talking and praying for them. Nowadays, hardly anybody does that, not anywhere.

"They Were Taking Away Her Sickness"

My grandfather, William Lupe, was the main one that sang for the gáans, the crown dancers.[3] His brother, John Lupe, did that too. Their father, I think, was the one that taught them.

You know, those dancers never used to dress close to where they dance. They used to dress way up on a mountain somewhere. And you know how curious little boys are—well, sometimes they followed the mens going up to where they dress. They're not supposed to do that.

David Dale, Western Apache medicine man, outside the old day school at Cibecue, Fort Apache Indian Reservation, about 1925. Hampered when speaking by an acute stutter, David Dale was a flawless ceremonial singer.

The mens had food up there and pots and pans to cook with, and the little boys would sneak around and try to get a piece of bread or something. That's when they got caught! But the mens don't say nothing. They don't get mad. They just told the boys to eat.

And when those dancers were making their hats [ceremonial headpieces], they told the boys to go and get *igáyé* 'cause they need it for what they're doing. They told them to get it about that long [2–3 feet]. Then, when they brought it back, they told them to make it into strips. Those boys don't think nothing of it 'til just before the dance starts, 'cause that's when the man that caught them uses that igáyé to whip them all the way to the dance. They did that during the dance, too. One of the gááns had that whip tied to his hand, and every time that boy made a mistake out there he got another whack. He had to dance four songs with the gááns. If he didn't cry out for four songs they let him go. But if he whimpered or cried, he had to dance all night.

Nadah Nch'íí' [Bitter Mescal] is where they used to dress, way up there on that mountain. And right where Robert Henry used to live, right at that flat place there, is where they used to dance. They put four trees in the ground, one for each of the four directions. Whoever they're dancing for—the sick person—was already there. And when it started to get dark all the people built fires all the way around. It was a big circle of fires and the dance was in the middle.

The gááns start marching down from Nadah Nch'íí' when the sun goes down. They're coming down. They march towards Lonely Mountain. They have a lantern shining every once in a while. From Lonely Mountain they come down towards Cibecue, past where the graveyards are at and along the edge of the bluff there. They're there. They wait.

Gáán łibayé [Dull-color crown dancer] is the first one to come. He comes by himself. He brings the message. "They're coming soon! Be ready!" He goes around to all the trees and then he goes around to them again. Then he makes that *sound* with the thing he uses [a bullroarer] and starts running back to where the rest of them are waiting. When he gets back over there, the gááns start marching down again. They're coming down! They don't stop moving, they keep moving all the time. They're moving *every minute*, all the way down to where they dance.

When they get there, they have to go to the east side, the east tree. That's where they stand—and they don't stand still, either. They're moving, always moving. And then, when the first song starts, they go in there and start dancing. There's a big fire in the middle, and the medicine man and his helpers are sitting on benches or logs a little ways off. They're singing. For the second song, the gááns go in from the south side, the south tree. The next is from the west side, and the next is from the north side. After the fourth song, they line up facing east. They pray. Then they bless the fire. Then they go to the sick person, the one that they're dancing for—she's sitting down—and they pray for her. They do that [repeat the same sequence] all night long.

When the gááns go to rest around midnight, they go to Lonely Mountain. They go over there and stay for a while. Then Gáán łibayé comes again and makes that sound. If they're singing when he gets there, he has to stay and dance for a while. When he makes that sound again, it means he's gonna go back and get the rest of the gááns. And when he brings them in, they have to holler four times before they get there. It means they're coming, coming closer.

When the gááns get there, they go around the whole camp. Then they go back inside [the dance ground]. They bless the fire. After that, they go to the sick person. Then they tie—I think it's igáyé they use for that—they tie four strings around this arm and four around that arm. There's four strings on her legs, and on her body there's four tied around, and they tie one around her head above her eyes. Later, when they're dancing again, they go and cut those off. They don't lose any of those strings that she was tied with. They have to be careful with them. They have a container they put them in. When they finish doing that, the medicine man and his helpers keep on singing and the gááns keep on dancing. Then they go over to where the sick person is sitting. They get her up and dance with her towards the sun, the east. They hold her up for two songs and then, for the last two songs, she's dancing all by herself. That means she's getting well.

The gááns dance all night. Then, just before the sun comes up, they go away. They're gone. They don't come back.

"It Was Almost Real"

There used to be a well at Oak Creek. One time, we were gonna have lunch there. We had deer meat. We were gonna roast it on charcoal. So I built a fire and my mother went after water at the well. And somehow, when she lowered her bucket down in there, she caught a big old bull-frog. I guess she didn't see it 'cause she brought it back in the bucket. Then she seen it in there. "Aaah!" She poured all that water out. She wouldn't go back to the well. "That old frog already peed in there," she said. So she dug a hole in the wash, and after the water got clear she brought it back and used it. She wouldn't go back and get water from the well.

A long time ago, I heard, people used to dance by that well. It was a spring then, under those cottonwood trees, and that's where they were dancing. There's a tall hill there and nothing used to grow on it. The singer—his name was Má' bitsee' [Fox Tail]—made people dance from the spring all the way to the top of the hill. Then they danced back down. That man told the dancers what was supposed to happen when they got to the top of the hill. He said that a cloud was supposed to go underneath their feet and lift them up. That's what he said.

But it never did happen. There's always complaints about some-thing. "Somebody said this, somebody said that. Somebody did this, somebody did that." The singer said, "There's no reason it's not gonna happen. We'll just have to wait another few days and do it over again." But then it started raining—I guess it rained real hard—so they can't dance no more.

Mary Riley's mother was one of the girls that danced up that hill. She said, "Nothing happened to me." She said, "The wind was real strong up there. It felt like it's gonna lift you up. But it's not strong enough." She said, "What they were doing was almost real, but it never did happen."

My mother and Charley Marley told me about this.[4]

"He Shrinks the Distance"

There was a little medicine man. He was Bessie Lupe's uncle. He was a *small man* and he used to walk *all over*! One time, we saw him walk-ing way down near Cherry Creek. We saw him coming up, coming to-wards us. "Who's that coming?" We figured it was a little boy. "What's he doing?" We figured his family was probably down by the river. He kept on coming and pretty soon we found out it was that little old man. He's short—but *he walks*!

That man used to walk all the time. Everywhere he went, he

walked. They tried to make him ride horses but he won't do it. They tried to make him go on wagons but he won't do it. I don't know, he was kind of a funny man.

One time, we found him right there on Cibecue Mountain. We were right behind him on a wagon. We were going to a dance at Canyon Day—Arthur Naklanita, his wife, me and another girl. We saw him sitting under a tree way up on top. My uncle [Arthur Naklanita] stopped the wagon. He said, "Where are you going?" That little man said, "I'm going to a dance over at Canyon Day." And my uncle said, "That's where we're going. We're going there, too." He said, "I know." My uncle told him, he said, "Why don't you ride on the wagon? Get on the back and you can come with us." He said, "No, by sundown I'll be there. I'll see you over there by sundown."

They gave him a drink of *túlbái* 'cause they had some in the wagon. He drank some of that and started walking again. My uncle said, "It's a long ways yet to Canyon Day. He's got a long ways to go." And his wife said, "You don't know that man. He prays all the time when he's walking. The distance shrinks every time he goes somewhere. That's what he does—he shrinks the distance—it's something that he knows." She said, "That's why he don't ride horses or wagons."

That little man lived with John Lupe. The only relative he had was John Lupe's wife, Bessie Lupe's mother. When we came back from Canyon Day, we told my grandfather [John Lupe] about what happened. We said, "That man don't want to ride." And John Lupe said, "Look over there! I bought him that saddle, it's just his size. I got him a horse, a real small horse. He won't even *look* at them!" My grandpa was laughing. "He just walks. He never rides nothing!" They said that man never did get married.

Pain! That little medicine man cured mostly pain. People with a toothache went to him. He didn't put anything on it. He just prayed and rubbed it with his hand. And that's it! "Toothache's gone," they said. And when he prayed for people, close to the end, they went to sleep. It seems to me that all of them went to sleep.

If somebody got shot, he cured that, too. If the bullet was still inside, he prayed and prayed and then he put yellow powder on it [the wound]. If blood was coming out, he cleaned it off. Then, after that, he put yellow powder on it and sucked it. Pretty soon, he got the lead out.

He did that to a man who shot himself, I don't know for what reasons. He was a policeman somewhere. They came to get that little man. He went. He washed it [the wound] off first. He prayed. Then he put yellow powder on it. Then he put his head down and sucked the blood out. He spit it out. Then he put some more powder on there and sucked it again. He did that four times. Then he said, "Give me a pan, a wash-pan." They gave him a pan. He spit the bullet in there. You could hear that thing drop in the pan. He said, "This is what I have to save. I have to save this one." Nothing happened to that man who shot himself. Where the bullet went in didn't swell up or nothing. It just closed up.

If somebody was cut bad with a knife or something, that little medicine man cured it. He cured it the same way—with nothing. Nothing! He didn't use any kind of herbs. He just used that yellow powder and his prayers. That's all. He did that for my brother Joe.

Two men were fighting, stabbing at each other. They were brothers. My brother Joe jumped in there and got cut real bad. He didn't know 'til he got back home. "I'm sweating," he said. My mother said, "It's wintertime, it's cold." He said, "My sleeve's all wet." We didn't have a lantern or nothing, so we built a fire. Then we could see it—he got cut up high on his arm. It was bleeding real bad. My mother was talking to him. "Well, you got no business jumping in there. You don't even know how those men might have stabbed you."

That little medicine man was outside in the shade. He was talking with my stepfather. So my mother told Joe, she said, "You better go see what he can do for you." Joe went out there. That man prayed for Joe for a long time. Then he came back inside. There was a rag around the cut. He said, "It don't hurt no more and now it's not bleeding." He said. "A while ago, it was giving me lots of pain."

One time, that little medicine man heard a spirit. What happened was, my grandfather, John Lupe, had a son and a daughter. They died kind of young. His son was just about the same size as my brother Joe. They were born, I think, one day apart. I think Joe was born first. They were raised together. My grandpa wanted Joe to stay with him and his family. "I can raise two boys myself," he said. So Joe went to stay with them. He played with that boy all the time. They were always together.

When Joe went off to St. Johns, that little boy got lonesome for him. I guess that made him sick. He wasn't feeling good. John Lupe and some mens went down to his farm below Medicine 'cause they left some corn over there. When they came back, that boy was really not feeling good. He got worse. He was throwing up his food.

That little medicine man was in Whiteriver. Somebody came for him and he went over there. My grandfather wanted to get him [to treat the ailing boy] but he couldn't 'cause he was over there at Whiteriver. When that little man was walking back to Cibecue, he said that somebody called to him at Cowboy Springs. He stopped there to get a drink of water. He was sitting there eating some cornbread and somebody called him. He said it sounded just like that sick boy. That old man said, "Where are you? Come here! Come eat some of this cornbread." He thought that boy might be sneaking around on him, so he started looking for him. He couldn't find him. Then he thought, "Maybe there's something wrong with him—that's his spirit over here."

So he started walking again. He said that he just took about two bites out of his cornbread and put it away. He went across the river [Cibecue Creek] where Minnie Narcisco lives now and went straight by Lonely Mountain to Blue House. They told him when he got there that that little boy had died. He already knew it. "That's why he was calling me," he said.

He was a cute little old man. He really liked children. He used to play with them. He used to make them *laugh*! My brother Dewey wanted him for a playmate. Dewey said, "Let's take him home so he can play with me. Let's take him! He's got no mother, he's got no father, so can we take him home? I'm going to play with him!" I guess Dewey thought he was just a little boy.

He loved kids! He played with them all the time. When they asked him to do something he did it for them. Like dressing up with flowers. We were at Spring Creek. Dewey and his cousin, James Beatty, were playing with a little donkey. There was lots of purple flowers over there, and those boys made a long string of them and put it around the donkey's neck. They put another string around its ears and then they tied flowers on its mane and tail. That donkey was just *decorated* with flowers. They played with it and played with it.

Then they told that little medicine man to ride that decorated donkey. It was a real small one. "Ride it," they said, "and we'll take you back home." Those boys had flowers over their hair and flowers over their shoulders. There was *lots* of them, all hanging down in strings.

They were coming this way, coming toward the camp. My uncle [Robert Beatty] said, "He-e-e-y, look what's coming! The flowers are walking this way!" That little man was riding on that decorated donkey. He had *lots* of flowers on his hair, and those two boys were walking on each side of him. They dressed him up! They were playing with him!

They went by. They went down to where the peach trees are. My mother was down there scraping a hide. She told me to bring her some bread and some coffee. I took it down there, and that's when I seen that old man up in the tree. I guess those two boys pushed him up there to get peaches for them. They were trying to get him down. They couldn't do it. He was hanging onto the tree. He was *stuck*!

I told Dewey, I said, "You've got that old man stuck up there. He can't get down. If he falls, people are gonna get mad at you." I said, "Go get the stepladder, the short one." They went and got it. When they came back that man was still up there. He was eating peaches, those small white peaches. They finally got him down. I guess he got tired sitting up there, hanging onto the tree.

Bessie Lupe was raised by that old man. When her mother died, he was all she had. He took care of her like an old lady. She used to go with him everywhere. I don't think he had a name in English. His Apache name means something like "Looking Out For Enemies"—you know, a man with a gun in his hand or a bow and arrows.

"This Is Your Last Chance!"

Charley Marley was a medicine man. I'll tell you something that happened that I know.

We were going from Cibecue back to Chediskai. My uncle [Robert Beatty] and my brother Joe went ahead of us. My uncle was going to kill one of his cattles. They killed and butchered it. They were waiting for us to come with the wagon. It was getting dark. Joe told my uncle, "They should be coming along pretty soon."

We were coming all right, but then we had trouble with that pig, Bichįh Nteelé. He jumped off the wagon and we couldn't get him back up there. It rained the day before and he was just laying in the mud on the side of the road. My stepfather was beating on that pig. He was calling to my mother. "Do you want your old man back up there? He has more to do with you than me! You left me for this pig!" Finally, we got him out of the mud. I was trying to wash the mud off. When you scratched his back with a stick, he just *enjoyed* it. He stood right there and enjoyed it. So my mother said, "Scratch his back while I clean him off." I did that. She washed all the mud off. That old man [Charley Marley] said, "Is your husband ready to travel yet?" My mother was laughing.

It was dark when we got there. We heard somebody hollering at us. My mother said, "It sounds like Joe." So we stopped. We parked the wagon there. We got lots of dry wood and picked up a bunch of pine cones. If you strike a match to those pine cones, pretty soon it's burning real good! We made a big fire there.

Then Joe came. He said, "You're gonna have to spend the night out here with us. My uncle don't want to go back to Cibecue 'til tomorrow. He wants to spend the night here." So we took everything off the wagon. Then Joe took the wagon to go get my uncle and the meat. They brought the meat back and hung it up in a tree.

We spread a canvas on the ground for my mother. She fixed her bed on it. I put a canvas down and fixed my bed on that. They were all telling stories. I went to bed. I was facing the fire 'cause I was listening to them tell stories. Then I felt something *real cold* behind my back. I said to Joe, "I feel something moving behind my back. It's real cold." My uncle Robert heard me. He told me, "Don't move. Don't pull the covers back. Be still." Then he told me, "Slowly, take your hands from under the canvas and put them out." I did that. Then he said to Joe, "Get her hands and pull her out fast. I'll throw the covers off." They put more wood on the fire. It was like daylight all over, all the light from the fire.

Then my uncle said, *"Now!"* Joe pulled me out and my uncle Robert throwed off the blankets. I jumped up! And you know what? There was a big old rattlesnake in there, a diamondback. It didn't make a sound. It's got a big rattle, about this long [3–4 inches], and it didn't make a sound. My uncle said, "Wait, it might start rattling." See, when those snakes are friendly to people—when they smell them and want to be friendly—they're supposed to rattle. But that one didn't. It didn't rattle. It never made a sound.

Then my stepfather said, "Ínłgaashń [witch]! You know you're supposed to rattle! You didn't do that! You just came for trouble. That's why you crawled in her bed! You were gonna hurt her." Then he said, "Maybe you're the one that's gonna get hurt!" He was talking to that snake. Then he put his hand out like this—one, two, three—and that thing kind of curled up. I thought it was getting ready to jump but it didn't. Then my stepfather said, "This is your last chance! If you rattle, I'll let you go. If you don't, you're the one that's going!" So he put out his hand again—four!—and that snake stretched out and died. That's what happened. I didn't believe it for a long time.

Later, when I was older, I asked my mother. I said, "How did he do that? He didn't even touch it, not with a rock or a stick or nothing. It just stretched out and died." She said, "That's the way they did a long time ago. It's an old prayer that he knows. He can hurt those things with his prayer. It [the rattlesnake] was about to take your life and now it's gone in your place." I got scared, and from that time on I hoped I never would see one again. And you know, to this day I haven't seen but one.

That man [Charley Marley] used to eat charcoal, a burning red hot charcoal. He went like this three times and the fourth time he put it in his mouth. He chewed it up. It didn't hurt him. It didn't do nothing to him. Even a little fire will really hurt you, and it's *tender* in your mouth. If a person had a rash, a bad rash, he spit on his hands after he ate the charcoal. He spit on his hands and rubbed it all over the rash. The next day, it was already getting dry. That's what they call *kǫ'diyiní* [fire medicine man].

The Death of William Goshoney

A-2 [William Goshoney] lived down by the river [White River] below where the Baptist church is now. He had a wickiup there. I went to visit him for a week, and that was when he died. I was down there with Carl Altaha and his younger brother. They were related to A-2's wife.

We told that old man, "It's warm, the sun is shining." He said, "Well, I'd like to be outside. I want to rest in the sun." So we pulled a single mattress out of the wickiup. We put it there so he could lay on it. He said, "I don't want it like that. I want to sit up!" That old man was *never* satisfied. So we put some stuff behind the mattress so he could sit up against the wickiup. Then he wanted his table—it's a little short table—and we put it in front of him. Then he wanted his Mexican cards. He said, "Give me those and I'll play my games."

While he was playing there, I was just a little ways from him. I was washing clothes on a washboard in a washtub. Then, pretty soon, he was humming some kind of song. He picked up his cards and mixed them up and started playing again. I guess he won his game 'cause he was clapping his hands.

After I hung up the clothes, I looked at him again. I thought he was sitting there sleeping. I didn't know that he was already gone. He wasn't moving at all, so I went over there and felt of him here [his cheek]. He didn't move. He didn't say nothing, and usually, if you touched that old man, he really hollered at you. But he didn't say nothing. Then I told those two mens that were there, "Come over! I think this old man died." *"How?"* they said. *"How?"* I said, "Maybe a heart attack, or maybe he just went to sleep and didn't wake up." So they came over there. We tried to feel around for his pulse, but there's nothing.

So one of them jumped on a horse and went after the two ladies that lived there. They were down at Lee's store. He told them what happened. I guess Johnny Lee called the police 'cause pretty soon they came down. They had a pickup. They put the mattress in there and took that man to the hospital. They said he was already gone.

After that, they asked me all kinds of questions. "What did he say? What was he doing? What happened? What do you know?" I said, "He said he only wanted to rest. He didn't want to lay flat on the mattress. He wanted to sit up against the wickiup, so we put some blankets behind the mattress. Then he wanted his little table to play cards on, so we went and got that and put a blanket over it. He was playing cards right there, humming some kind of song, and every time he won a game he clapped his hands. I was just standing there, looking at him. Then I went to hang up the clothes. When I came back he was sitting there like this [slumped slightly to one side], and it looked like he was sleeping."

Anyway, that's how A-2 died. He was playing Mexican cards. He was clapping his hands. He prayed all the time, every day, every minute of his life. He was over a hundred when he died. He didn't *die*—he just went to sleep.

Chapter Ten

Maybe it sounds like we stayed down there at Chediskai all the time. It's not that way. We used to go to different places and stay for a while. You know how the Apaches are—they like to travel and visit their relatives and see different things and do different things. We were like that. But we didn't go too far away. Mostly, we stayed close to home. We went to Oak Creek, Cibecue, Cherry Creek, Grasshopper, Spring Creek—back and forth, back and forth, lots of times. And sometimes we went to Whiteriver and East Fork and other places over there on the other side of the reservation. We used to go to off the reservation, too, but not very much. See, in those days, people didn't know very much about the outside ways. There's prejudice against them off the reservation, and they don't talk English good, and they just didn't *know* what to do. Sometimes they got into trouble.

Tsééch'iizhé (Sandstone)—"I Don't Want to Waste It"—Murder at Oak Creek— Wild Kids—Trading at Snowflake—"Too Many Friends"—Wild Pigs—Gonatáhá (You Try to Find It)—"Help! Somebody!"—Outlaw!—Cattle Drives to Holbrook

Tsééch'iizhé (Sandstone)

My mother and my stepfather went to Knapp's store in Cibecue maybe once a month. There was another place above Red Lake somewhere. They called that place Tsééch'iizhé. It's off the reservation but it's the closest store to Oak Creek. Well, it's not really a store. People used to go up there and work for groceries. They worked for moonshine, too.

That man up there had a short arm. Something happened to his hand. They had to cut it off. He had a hook on it. He didn't know his Apache name. They called him Ndaa Bigan Nagodé [Whiteman With Shortened Arm]. Charley Marley made up that name for him.

That man had a little vein of asbestos, a mine. He used to work on it himself. He used to get big chunks of rock out of the mine and put them on the ground over there. He brought them out on a wheelbarrow. He piled them up outside and covered them up. And then, when people come around wanting groceries or moonshine, he took the cover off and told them to bust the rocks and take the asbestos out. They put it in buckets or cans. He made them work for groceries and moonshine. He had a lot of groceries in his home. He made it like a store in there.[1]

Once in a while, we used to go up there. That old man [Charley Marley] told Ndaa Bigan Nagodé, "We'll work for some groceries." He said, "OK, let's work." So my stepfather went to work, him and the boys. They were pounding those rocks, getting all that asbestos out and putting it in cans. They filled up eleven cans. That man was really happy about it. He said, "I never get that much when I work by myself." So he gave them whatever groceries they needed. We came home with lots of groceries from over there.

One time, we went up there and busted rocks. That short-armed man was selling butters, the big ones wrapped in paper, like in the store. And he told my stepfather, he said, "Charley, this is butter. It's not cheese." He [Charley Marley] said OK, so that man gave us about four of those butters. When we got back to Chediskai, my mother was making tortillas. She gave him one. She said, "Here, put some of that butter on this." And he cut a *big chunk* and put it in his tortilla and rolled it up and ate it. I said, "Look, you're not supposed to eat it like that. You're supposed to spread just a little bit on it." He said, "It don't have *no taste* that way!" Then he said, "Give me some more of that cheese." I said, "That's not cheese, that's butter." That old man didn't know any better. He didn't know what butter is. But that night he ran outside every few hours. There was snow on the ground. He had a hard time, slipping around in the snow 'cause he ate all that butter.

"I Don't Want to Waste It"

That man up there at Tsééch'iizhé, the one that was digging asbestos, made moonshine whiskey. Engel Hanna and James Johnson went up there. They stayed there for two or three days. And I guess that man was making it, that corn mash or whatever it was, and those two were helping him. That's how they learned to make that stuff.

So Engel Hanna wanted to start making it himself. I guess Ndaa Bigan Nagodé loaned him that stuff—it's a copper pot with copper pipes all the way around it—and he brought it back to Chediskai. He put it up under the trees. He didn't want nobody to see him 'cause they're not allowed to make that stuff on the reservation. If they got caught, they got throwed in jail.

So he went up there, Engel Hanna and his wife. They built a fire under that copper pot. They started making it. And he told her, "I'll go up high and watch." See, the cowboys used to come by—sometimes they worked along there—and he was wanting to see if they could see the fire. So he was up there while that old lady was under the trees watching the fire under the pot.

And I guess that moonshine started dripping out. He had a bowl under there and it started filling up. And you know what that old lady did? She took a little sip. Then she put the bowl back under there again. It started filling up again. She was thinking, "I don't want to waste it." So she took another sip. She kept on doing that. Her husband came down from where he was watching. He said, "How come it's not filling up? Maybe the fire's not hot enough." He put some more wood on there and went off again. When he came back that lady was all *drunk*! "I didn't want to waste it," she said. So he brought her out from under the trees and told her to go home. He said, "Go home and get something to eat." He went back up there. She started walking.

My mother and my brothers were irrigating the fields and that lady got into the mud! She fell down, I don't know *how many* times! She was crawling around in the mud! She was just *covered* with it—her hair, her face, her arms, her dress—she was covered with it, *all over*! My mother went back to the house for something and she seen her from there. She told that lady's daughter, "He-e-ey, Edith, look at your mother! It looks like she's drunk or something." So Edith went over there to see what's wrong with her. I was with her. We went a little ways and met her mother in the mud. And Edith just started giggling and laughing at her. "You *pig*! You *pig*! How come you don't leave things alone? How come you started drinking that stuff?" And that lady said, "Your father left me over there. The cup was getting full and I didn't know what to do with it." She was all *drunk*! She was giggling and laughing.

So we dragged her back to the house. There was a big barrel of water there, rainwater. We were trying to clean her off with that water. She kept giggling and giggling, laughing and laughing. We made her sit down right there, and we poured the water on her head. We were scrubbing the mud away from her face, but she kept picking up mud on the ground and putting it on her face again! So we were laughing at her and she was laughing at us. And then that lady started *dancing*! She's a big round one, and she was going back and forth, going back and forth, laughing and laughing. And we were pouring water on her, trying to clean her up. My stepfather was under the shade. He started laughing at that lady. "Go away from here," he said. "You're making too much noise, you little pig! We got enough pigs around here!"

Finally, that lady quit laughing and dancing. She told her daughter, "Your father said I had to make him some lunch. I came back to make lunch." Edith was still laughing at her. She said, "Go make lunch in bed." So she went to bed. She didn't wake up 'til the next morning.

Engel Hanna got caught for making that moonshine. He was in jail close to Chicago, I think. He stayed there for about six months. He never did speak a word of English before that, but when he came back he talked English real good.

Murder at Oak Creek

Ralph Dazen's older brother killed an old lady and her granddaughter. He was living with the old lady's granddaughter. That girl got together with some of the Stago ladies. They told her they were going to Young. She went with them and left that man behind. He didn't know where she went 'til old lady Stago told him. "She went over there with them," she said.

They didn't go to Young. They went to Tsééch'iizhé. I guess a bunch of cowboys was there and those stupid women started drinking with them. That's how they destroyed that young girl's life, it seems like to me. She was just a young girl and she didn't think nothing would happen to her. She passed out and that's when she got into trouble.

When they came back to Chediskai, those Stago ladies tried to blame everything on her. They said that she brought it on herself. That man she was with found out. He was kind of crippled—something happened to his ankles and his knees. He went to where that girl was living with her grandmother. She told him, "I don't know if I should go back with you." She said, "There's a story about me that I know you won't like. I have to tell you myself what happened over there. I don't want nobody else telling you. This is what really happened, but it's all changed in the story those ladies are telling." She said, "For me, I don't know what to do. It's hurting me the way the story turned out. I don't know if you want to come back to me or not."

I guess he was a jealous man. He shot her in the head from behind. She was sitting on the ground grinding corn. He was sitting behind her and shot her in the back of the head. She fell right into the flour she was grinding. Then her grandmother came running out of her house. She was kind of deaf but she heard the gun. She came out *yelling*! She hollered for her granddaughter. She didn't get no answer but she kept on hollering. That's when he shot at her. He killed her, too. He killed both of them.

He started walking towards Cibecue. He kept on walking. Then he crawled into some brush, some scrub oak brush. He dug a hole in the ground and buried himself in there. He just put the leaves over him and covered himself real good. Some mens were looking for him. They couldn't find him. Then it got dark, so he started walking again. He walked to Cibecue and crossed the river [Cibecue Creek] below Minnie Narcisco's house. He crossed there and came up again, going towards Whiteriver.

They were working on the road to Cibecue. There was a road camp there. He went to the road camp and told them what he did. He told them to take him to Charley Foster. Foster used to be the policeman at Carrizo. So they took him over there, and he [Charley Foster] called to Whiteriver. They came and got him in a car. They put him in jail in Whiteriver. Then they sent him off somewhere in Illinois. He died out there. I guess he's buried out there somewhere.

It was harvesting time when that happened. They put both of those ladies' bodies in a grave under a peach tree. It's right there in Oak Creek below the corral. That's where those two ladies are buried. That peach tree used to blossom all the time.

Wild Kids

Those Stago boys were wild kids. My stepfather never did like them. He used to chase them away when we went to Young to pick acorns. He said, "I don't want those boys to come along with us. I don't want to take none of them." Their mother said, "Go ahead and take them." He said, "No, I'm not taking none of those boys. Before you know it, I'll be in trouble because of them."

See, those boys went in people's gardens up there at Young. They had big gardens up there, beautiful to look at, and those boys used to go in there and help themselves. They went in the corn, squash, string beans, everything, and they used to come out carrying a whole bunch of those vegetables. That's why my stepfather didn't want them along with him. He told their mother, "If you want to take those boys, take them yourself. I'm not taking them for you."

There was a store at Young, a grocery store, and those Stago boys did the same thing in there. One time, four of us went over there— James Johnson's wife, my mother, my sister-in-law's mother, and me. We were going after acorns. We went to that grocery store to get some food. James Johnson's wife got a watermelon and took it outside. My mother got some potatoes, lard, and some small cantaloupes. Then she got a loaf of bread and some baloney. We went out. We were sitting outside the store, eating under a tree.

And here come those Stago boys! They went in the store. They came out with a whole bunch of stuff. Those kids were coming out with something every few minutes! Then they went back inside and came out with something more. James Johnson's wife said, "Let's get away from here. We're gonna get blamed for those boys. Look what they're doing. They're taking everything out. They're not paying for it! They're just grabbing it and running outside!"

So we got on the horses and started back to the camps. And I don't know why, but those Stago boys were following us. We got behind that hill there, all the way behind it, and then we came back to the store, and *then* we went back to our camp. They thought we went up on the hill and stayed there, I guess, so they went up there. We didn't go that way. We fooled them.

We were coming close to Pleasant Valley along with some other people. A policeman came over there. He said, "What do you know about what happened at the store?" James Johnson's wife told him, she said, "They were over there when we left. I think they got a fifty-pound sack of flour. They got watermelons, too, three of them. They got lots of other stuff out of there, and I think they got a pair of shoes."

That policeman got the shoes back. I don't know what he done with the food they took. They told those boys that they have to pay for it, and if they can't pay for it, they have to work. There's a field right there, close to where we were camping. Those Stago boys went up there and they worked in the field for several days. They worked 'til they paid for the whole thing. That policeman made them work for it.

Trading at Snowflake

There was a man at Snowflake that traded meat for corn. I think his name was Whipple. He worked in the slaughterhouse over there. We went over there—my stepfather and my mother and me. We put four sacks of corn on the wagon. They were big sacks full to the top. We left Chediskai and drove all the way to Snowflake on the wagon.

That man, Whipple, was cleaning up in there. I asked him if he could give us meat for the corn. He said, "They like soft corn over here. Somebody was in here last week and that's what they were talking about. Have you got some of that soft corn?" I said, "Yes, I think so." So he went over to the wagon and looked at the corn. He said, "That's the one, that's the kind they want." Then he said, "What do you want for that?" I asked my stepfather, I said, "He wants to know how much you want for the corn." He said, "I don't know. Just tell him I want meat. I'm hungry for soup." So I said to that man, "He wants to know if you can trade it for meat." Then that man said, "Well, I'll go and see what the main boss is gonna say."

He went back over there and pretty soon the main boss came out. He looked at the corn. "Yes," he said, "that's the one I want." So he took two sacks of corn off the wagon. He gave us a whole half of a beef for them. He gave us those neck parts, too. They cut them off from what they sold, and he had some of them there. He said, "If you want them, you can have all the necks." Then he said to that other man, "They know how to cook those things. They know how to barbecue them and make them tender." We took all of them.

It looked like we had a cow sitting on the wagon. That man, Whipple, gave us an old canvas to cover it with and we put all the necks in there. Then we went home to Chediskai.

"Too Many Friends"

We used to go to Pleasant Valley on horseback. We went over there for that celebration they have. It's in August or July. It's something they celebrate but I don't know what it is. My stepfather was always invited to come 'cause he's got lots of friends over there. He knew all those people, those ranchers and cowboys, from when he was working for D. V. Marley.

They had a rodeo over there, a rodeo and dinners. They had barbecue beef and that old man [Charley Marley] was always out there cooking and cutting up meat. They had a dinner each day. For three days they did that. They gave you a tag. It had a number on it. When you went up there, you had to show them your number. Then you could eat. Lots of people used to go to that celebration from Oak Creek and Cibecue. When it's all over with, they killed a bunch of cows and gave meat to everybody. And bread that's left over, they gave that to them, too. My stepfather always got lots of meat and bread 'cause he helped with the cooking. The ladies didn't go to the rodeo. We just went and picked acorns.

Charley Marley had too many friends, all those cowboys that he knew. Wherever he went—Young, Snowflake, Holbrook—they're real glad to see him. They always wanted to drink with him. "He's our friend," they said. "He worked with us for so many years. Let's buy him a drink."

One time, we went to Young to pick acorns. A man told us to go ahead and pick acorns inside his fence. He gave my mother the key to open the gate. He said, "Be sure to close it when you go in. When you get through, when you're ready to go home, you can open the gate and bring back the key." So that's where we were. That old man [Charley Marley] knows that we're safe, so he took off. He was gone for two or three days. When the man that gave us the key came in from Young, we asked him, "Have you seen Charley?" He said, "Yeah, he's having a good time over there. Don't worry, he's all right. He's coming home. He said he can't see good at night, so he won't be back 'til tomorrow."

The next day, in the afternoon, he came back leading his Blue. There was a big pack of something on the back of that donkey. He was just singing away and whooping every once in a while. I said to my mother, "It sounds like he's drunk." He was. So we threw a mattress down for him to go to sleep on. He sat down. Augustine said, "What happened?" He said, "Nothing happened." And then he started, he said, "I seen all my friends. I seen all my old friends from years ago." He started crying. "That's how come they gave me a whole bunch of vegetables. Take them off [the donkey] and give them to your mother." He was crying.

He was just sitting there for a while. Then the two other boys picked him up and put him in the tent. He went to sleep. Then, way late at night, he woke up. He said, "What happened to me? What did I do? Where did I go? I remember sitting in the bar with three men." He was naming them, but I don't remember their names. Then he mentioned D. V. Marley. "I seen him, too," he said. "I was sure glad to see him again."

The next day, he noticed that his jacket was all dirty. He asked my mother to wash it. "You better dig in all the pockets," he said. She was digging in there, digging in the inside pocket, and she pulled out an envelope. She opened it. There was *money* in there! There's writing on the envelope. It said, "I'm giving this to Charley Marley and his family. He can do whatever he wants with the money. I'm glad to see my old friend again." That man's name was on it, too—"D. V. Marley." That envelope was stuck in his coat pocket and he didn't even *know* about it!

Wild Pigs

Around 1935, I think it was, they were fixing the fences in different places and on the reservation line. Some of the fences were all down and the posts were breaking off. Everybody that worked got paid thirty dollars a month from CCC [Civilian Conservation Corps].[2] It's not much, but in those days, you know, things didn't cost very much. And there's no store out there, so you could save all the money. My brothers gave money to my mother. They only kept ten for themselves. There was three of them—Jack, Joe, and Albert—so she got twenty dollars from each of them. They got paid every two weeks, I think, maybe once a month. They got paid with money, not with a check. They tried checks once, but those Indians just tore them up and threw them away. They didn't know what a check is.

There were about ten families in that fence crew, maybe more. That was lots of fun, going around with them. The mens cut posts and dragged them with the horses to where the fence was gonna be. My stepfather took the barbed wire over there on donkeys. He had two donkeys, Blue and another one. He packed the rolls of wire on those donkeys and took them over to where the mens were working.

We moved from just below Blue House to fix the fence way down below Oak Creek. When we first got there we camped up on a hill close to some oak trees. The other families camped down below where there's lots of walnut trees. But there was a water line down there— you know, where the water goes up high when there's lots of rain. My mother said, "It's better to live up here." There was a big oak tree up there and we camped under that tree.

It was lunchtime, so everybody built a fire. My mother told me to go get some wood, so I did. I went down a little ways and I saw those things moving around. At first I thought they were dogs. They were wild pigs, javelina, a bunch of them. They had two little ones, little tiny babies.

When I came back home, I told my brother Jack. He was fixing the cinch on his saddle. I told him, "There's some pigs over there. There's a bunch of them." He grabbed his gun and took off on his horse. I guess he shot at them somewhere and wounded one. He shot it in the leg. He said he saw the blood on the rocks. So he went after it. I guess it went in a hole. He tried to crawl in after it. He shot it again. And he kept pulling and pulling and pulling, and finally he pulled it out. He brought it back to the camp and hung it up by the legs in that oak tree. The people came over there and were looking at it—kids, ladies, all of them. They

said, "He shouldn't have gone after it." They said, "Those things are
real mean. They're *mean*! He shouldn't have gone after it."

That night those pigs came around. The pig my brother killed was
hanging on that oak tree right there close to us, and the other ones
came back for it. The dogs were barking and barking, running after
them, and you could hear those pigs running around, all over, all night,
and everybody was hollering and shooting off guns *all night long*—and
still they won't quit! As soon as daylight came they were gone. Those
people told my brother to take that thing away. He did. He took it down
and threw it away somewhere.

The next night those pigs were doing it again! They came back
looking for it! I guess they smelled the blood. The dogs were running
around, running around, just barking and barking. Those pigs got one
of the dogs right here [the shoulder and rib cage]. Its skin was torn,
hanging down. So my mother got her sewing needle, and some people
held that dog down, and she sewed the skin back on it. She put it back
together again. She sewed up that dog.

Then those people said, "Tonight, let's play *gonatáhá* [you try to
find it] tonight. We should play that game. We'll be all together and
maybe they'll leave us alone." So that's what they did. They made a
big brush [a brush enclosure], and right in the middle was a big fire.
The mens brought their guns over there in case those pigs came back.
They started playing that game and they were singing and dancing
and hollering all night long. Nothing happened. The next night they
played again and nothing happened again. In the morning, they said,
"We better get back to work 'cause then we'll have to move. If we move,
maybe they won't come back and bother us."

So they started fixing the fence. I had my horse. I got everybody's
lunch and took it down to where they were working. I delivered all the
lunches to them. After they ate, I picked up those things, their dishes
and stuff, and brought them back to camp. When I got back to camp,
somebody said, "We saw one of those pigs again!" "Where?" I said.
"Over there!" They told me, "Leave it alone! They're gonna start running after us again. Leave it alone!" But it wasn't a pig, it was just a
baby deer. I went over there, and it was just a little deer lying in the
grass.

Finally, we moved and got away from those pigs. They're mean!

Gonatáhá (You Try to Find It)

I played gonatáhá quite a few times. That game takes a long time to finish 'cause it can go on all night. It's lots of fun, though. I played it that time in Oak Creek when those pigs were running around everywhere scaring people.

What they do in that game is hide something in a pile of sand. It's piled up kind of round and it's divided in four sections. They call that the mountain. There's two sides that play against each other. A person on one side puts it [the object to be hidden] in one of the sections of the mountain and covers it up. Then one of the people on the other side has to find out where it is and get it out. If they don't find it, they have to hide it, and then somebody on the other side goes after it. They keep going that way. They bet against each other. Sometimes they bet *lots*!

In Oak Creek that time, my brother Jack was sitting with us. He was a quiet boy. He never was loud. He was just sitting there watching. Then he bet a horse with a saddle on it. He bet against a man on the other side. He had a horse and saddle, too.

My brother Joe and an old man were playing against those people on the other side. That old man was looking at me. He said, "Get her! Get her! She's just a young girl." He said, "We're gonna be in luck pretty soon!" See, they say that if it's a pure girl, one that nobody's had anything to do with, she can see it in the mountain right away. And if she's the one that hides it in there, nobody on the other side will find it. That's why that old man wanted me in there. He didn't want Jack to lose that horse.

So they started singing that song—it's about an old man with foggy eyes that can't see—and they all started dancing. My mother said, "Go on, dance with them." So I went in there. *I saw it*! I saw it real clear! It's just like the mountain was covered with a glass bowl! I said, "Let me get it! Let me get it!" That old man said, "Go on!" He told me, "Go on! Go ahead! You'll probably get it right away!" And we were dancing— over there, over here, over there, over here—and pretty soon everybody started hollering. They got excited! So we kept on dancing and they were hollering again. And then, all of a sudden, I just jumped in there and grabbed that thing—I got it out! And boy, those people on the other side were *mad*!

Eva Tulene Case at the White Mountain Apache Tribal Fair and Rodeo, Whiteriver, Fort Apache Indian Reservation, about 1930.

I won that horse for my brother. He was just sitting there. But then he got excited and started dancing around. Jack came dancing in there! He was really happy I won that horse and saddle for him.

"Help! Somebody!"

Do you remember Fanny John? Her father was my brother Jack's friend. They worked together all the time on that fence crew. We were down below Oak Creek. It was wintertime, and somebody went after moonshine at Tsééch'iizhé and brought back a whole big gallon of it.

And that man got so drunk! He was sitting there all by himself, just singing away. My brother Jack said, "I better go and take care of my friend. It's getting dark. If he starts walking around, he might get lost." So he led him back to his tent and put him to bed.

When he woke up during the night, that man was real thirsty. He had a little pail of water, that's all, and he drank it all up. So he took his pail and went to get some more water. There's a pond over there—it's all ice—and he got too far away from the edge. He was on top of the ice, sliding around, sliding around, and I guess he couldn't get up. The ice was thick, holding him up, but he couldn't get up. He couldn't get back to the edge.

I guess my brother heard him, so he put his clothes on and took a rope and went over there. He said that man was *way* in the middle of the pond, sitting there singing, just shaking and singing away. Then, pretty soon he started hollering, "Help! Somebody! Where are you! Where is everybody! Come here! Help me! I'm thirsty!" My brother tried to throw the rope around him two or three times, but he said he couldn't get him.

Then James Johnson came over there. "Who's yelling?" My brother said, "It's that old man, your brother-in-law." James Johnson said, "Let me try it." He throwed the rope around him but he tried to take it off. He was fighting it, fighting the rope, trying to take it off. Then they pulled it tight on him. They kept pulling him, pulling him, and finally they got him back to the edge. There was blood on his shirt. They didn't know why. He said, "I just wanted some water." He left his pail in the middle of the pond, so they got a canteen and gave him some water.

Then they took him back up there to his tent. He said, "I'm cold. Build me a fire." So they did that. I guess that man went to sleep right away. When my brother came home, he told us, "I don't know who gave him that moonshine. He's not strong enough to drink that stuff. He was over there in the middle of the pond, singing and sliding around. We had to rope him and pull him in."

Then my brother said, "I better go check on him." He took a big dipper of hot coffee over there. That man was still asleep. My brother woke him up. He tried to make him drink some of that coffee. "I can't drink on account of my mouth." My brother was thinking maybe the ice cut him, so he said, "Let me see your mouth." That man opened his mouth. There was no skin on top of his tongue and it was bleeding. So my brother asked him, he said, "What were you doing out there?" He said, "I was thirsty. I was wanting some water. I was trying to lick the ice." He said that he got stuck to the ice for a long time with his tongue. When he jerked it, he pulled off the skin.

That moonshine made people crazy. It's not like *túłbáí*. In those days, people gathered to drink túłbáí but hardly nobody ever got drunk. That moonshine was different. It's strong! They didn't know how to drink it. They didn't know when to stop. It made them do real crazy things, like that man that licked the ice. That stuff is *bad*! I wish they never made it.

Outlaw!

They caught an outlaw down there at Oak Creek. My brother Joe helped them do that. He was living at Chediskai then, him and my brother Albert and my mother and my stepfather. Joe was supposed to get flour and coffee and sugar from my stepfather's log cabin in Oak Creek. He went and got the horses on the mountain and brought them back. And my mother told him, "You better go get me some water before you go." He took two buckets and went down to the river. That's where he seen the tracks!

He came back and talked to my brother Albert. He said, "Somebody with moccasin shoes got a drink out of our dipper just a little while ago. I looked around but I didn't see nobody." He said, "Somebody, whoever it is, was walking along the river. I followed his tracks. He was walking along on the other side, but when he seen where we get our water he jumped over to this side. When he seen our dipper there, I guess he got it and drank some water. It looks like he was standing there looking at us. Then he put the dipper back down and went on down the river." My brother Albert asked him, he said, "How do you know it was just a little while ago?" Joe said, "'Cause he poured water out of the dipper. He throwed it on the sand and the sand is still wet." He said, "I know he's down there ahead of me. He's somewhere down there where I'm going." And Albert said, "Don't tell my mother and that old man [Charley Marley] 'cause they're gonna tell you to stay here." Joe didn't say nothing to them. So that morning just my two brothers knew about it.

Joe got on his horse and started off. He said that man was hiding his tracks. He was following the trail but staying away from it, stepping way over on one side, jumping from here to there. Going to Oak

Creek we had to cross the river seven times. My brother got down to the last crossing. There's a dividing fence coming down from the mountain and there's a gate there. He got off his horse to open the gate, and that's when he seen him! He looked up to see if that man was up there somewhere. *There he was!* He was way up towards the top of the mountain. My brother just stayed there. He wanted to see what the stranger would do. He waited.

Then Joe decided to go another way. "I'll go on this side of the mountain, then over behind the high hills and from there over to Oak Creek." So he did that. When he got to one of the high hills he looked back again. He said that man was coming down closer, coming down to the bottom of the mountain. He was looking to see if he had a gun or something. He said he had a big stick. Then my brother hurried behind the hills again and went down into the trees and got back on the trail again. He was thinking, "That man might hurt somebody down there at Oak Creek. If he's hungry, he might hurt somebody for something to eat."

Paul Davis's father had the first camp in Oak Creek. My brother stopped there and told him about the stranger. "OK, I'll lock my door and go down with you to the people's camps." That old man got his horse. They rode down together. They stopped at each camp and told whoever was home. Most of the people lived way down below, close to where the corral is now.

Then some mens got their horses. They took all the ladies and children way down the wash to T'iis Sikaad [Cottonwoods Standing]. They told the ladies, "Stay down here. Hide yourselves and your kids on both sides of the wash. And if you have to get away fast, go through the wash. It's easier running that way."

Those mens that saddled their horses went back to a high place to see if they could see that man. He was *coming!* Finally, he came all the way down to the first camp, old man Davis's camp. The dogs scared him away. "The dogs were barking," my brother said, "so he got out of there *fast.*" Then he started walking again. Those mens got scared. His hair was long! He had a beard! He was wearing moccasin shoes. He had a pack on his back. He had a gun. He had two belts on. He had a wide belt with shells in it across his chest and another shell belt going the other way. So those mens knew that he might be dangerous.

Then the mens started back down to see if all the children were

Joe Tulene Case, Eva Watt's older brother, when he worked as a cowboy at Oak Creek, Fort Apache Indian Reservation, about 1935.

gone from their homes. One old lady was still there. They told her to
hurry up. They told that old man Davis, they said, "Take her down
below. Help her. She can't walk that far. Make her ride your horse."
His horse was a good one for that old lady—you know, real quiet and
gentle—so he put her on the horse and started leading it down. He took
her below T'iis Sikaad in the wash. He didn't see *nobody!* They were all
along the wash, sitting there in the brush. Finally, when he got close
to the end of where they were sitting, somebody called to him. "Did
you see anything?" He said, "I didn't see nobody." Then that person
said, "They're all behind you, they're back there behind you." He said,
"That's good, they really know how to hide." So he brought that old
lady down there. "Take her, help her," he said. She got off and went
with the others that were hiding in the brush. Then he got on his horse
and went back up the wash. He was looking around. He didn't see nobody.

That man, that stranger, went to all the camps. I guess he was looking for food. But the people left their dogs behind, and everywhere he
went the dogs were barking and he couldn't get in. Those mens on
horses were watching him. They were watching him, and I guess he
didn't even know it. He was coming closer! Then Clay Lupe shot one
shell—that means he's seen him somewhere pretty close. Those mens
gathered over there. They wanted to know where the stranger was at.
There's nothing but brush over there, scrub oaks, a whole bunch of
them, real thick brush. Clay Lupe told them, "He crawled in there."
They couldn't see him. He [Clay Lupe] said, "You can't see him but
he's in there." He pointed and said, "He's in there and he might shoot."

So those mens surrounded him. They were going around and
around that brush place on their horses. My brother said they could
hear him. Then they shot another bullet—not down at him but close, so
the bullet hit the brush. That's when he jumped out, my brother said.
He jumped out and stood up. He came out right there. He was standing
there with his hands up over his head. They got a cotton rope about
that long [3–4 feet] and tied his hands together.

Then they made him walk down to my stepfather's log cabin, where
Joe was supposed to get the sugar and the coffee. They took him down
there. There's not much in the house but Joe took the sugar and all the
other stuff outside. Then they put that man in there. They locked him
up. He wouldn't talk. They tried to talk to him but he wouldn't talk.

Then some of the mens with horses went to the closest house towards Pleasant Valley. It's a ranch. They went to tell that rancher, and
when they got there a policeman was visiting him. So they told him
about it. They told him they had that man in Oak Creek. And the policeman said, "Maybe he's the one we been looking for. Bring him over
here. Bring him this way. I can't go over there 'cause it's on the reservation. I got no authority on the reservation."

It was in the evening when they caught that man and put him in
my stepfather's house. He was in there overnight. And while he was in
there, I guess he rolled up a blanket—it must have been in his pack—
and stuck it under the corn box. It's a big box full of nothing but corn,
and that man went and stuck his blanket *way back* underneath it.

When those mens were talking to the policeman up there at that
ranch, he asked them about that blanket. He said, "Does that man have
a blanket? It's got a design and some sort of name on it. He stole it."
One of the mens said, "No, he don't have a blanket. Maybe he hid it
somewhere, up there at Chediskai or someplace." Then the policeman
said, "Does he have a pistol? It's got a horn handle. He stole that one,
too."

So when those mens got back to Oak Creek one of them said,
"Bring that man over here." They got him out of the house and brought
him over there. He told them that he used to have a horn handle pistol and a blanket. They asked him, "Where did you put those things?"
He won't say nothing. So the mens went back to where they found him
first, where he was hiding in that thick brush. They looked around in
there. They found his gun [his rifle] and the pistol. "You could hardly
even see them," my brother said. "He didn't try to dig a hole. He just
kept pushing them under the leaves of those oak trees." They showed
that man the pistol. Then they asked him about the blanket. "What
did you do with that blanket?" they said. He won't answer them. So
they took him back to my stepfather's house. They put him inside and
locked him in there again.

And that's when Edith Hanna's mother made a big pile of tortillas
and a big pan of gravy with meat. She took those in there for him to eat
and she took in a big pot of coffee and a cup. Then she closed the door
again and went out. That man ate the *whole thing*! I guess he was just
starving! He ate the whole thing! After that, he started talking. Maybe

he was just scared the people wouldn't be friendly, but after they fed him I guess he felt better. They wanted to know, they said, "What did you do with the blanket?" He said, "Maybe it's up the river. I don't know where I put it. I put some stuff way up the river someplace close to Payson." So they still didn't know about the blanket.

Then they brought a horse for him. They took him out of the house. "Get ready to go," they told him. Then Joe went back in there. He got one of my mother's poking sticks [used to stoke cooking fires] and started feeling with it under that cornbox. He was feeling around, feeling around, feeling around. Finally, he found it! He pulled that blanket out!

That outlaw was outside getting ready to go. He was sitting down, putting his shoes on. They brought that blanket and threw it down in front of him. They said he started crying. I guess he thought they *never* would find it. Then they told him to get on the horse. Four mens took him back up there to that ranch. They said that six policemens were waiting for them there. They searched that outlaw man. They took another pistol out of his boot—my brother said it was real little—and they found a knife on him, too. He told those policemens, "These Indians are just like watchdogs! They're *worse* than watchdogs! They smell things they can't even see! I never thought *nobody* would find that blanket!" They said that man stole some money, those guns, that blanket, and two knives. I heard he went to prison somewhere in Kansas.

After those mens delivered that man, when they came back to Oak Creek, my brother Joe went over there to where they found the horn handle pistol and the gun. He took an ax in there and chopped some of the brush down and started digging around. He found the other knife. He kept that knife for a long, long time.

Cattle Drives to Holbrook

My stepfather worked with the Oak Creek cowboys. He worked with them when they took the cattles to Holbrook to sell.[3] He was the horse wrangler. I went with him and my mother to Holbrook three times—'29, '30, and '31. I helped him keep the horses together. I think I was the only woman that did that. I wore a blue jean skirt and a visor-looking thing. I wasn't getting paid, I was just helping my stepfather. I liked it.

Most of the time I liked it, but sometimes the cattles just went too slow. They went *real slow*!

There's about twenty or thirty cowboys all together, I think, a big bunch. They had two wagons. My mother drove one of them. She drove the one that's carrying all the pots and pans and groceries. The cowboys had to bring their own bedrolls and those were on the other wagon. Some of them brought their own packhorses. Nobody led them. They just ran with the other horses, with their packs on. In those times, all the cattles used to have horns, big horns some of them. And some of those cattles were *wild*!

In the spring, the cowboys from each district rounded up the cattles and branded them. They put your brand on the hip—my mother's brand was F-Five-Bar [F5 with a bar underneath]—and there's another brand to show which district they're from. *O* is Oak Creek, *C* is Cibecue, *G* is Grasshopper, like that. And there's an arrow, a broken arrow, over the letter. Those mens really did watch which cattles belonged to which district. They did that 'cause some people might lose one and then try to grab one that belonged to somebody else from another district. That's why those cowboys watched real good. In those days, they did their jobs right.

They started driving the cattles when it cools off, around in September. Before they started, they put them in different grades. The ones for sale they put in one place—those are the ones that were going to Holbrook. The others they just turned back

They used to start from Oak Creek and bring the Oak Creek cattles up to Grasshopper. Those cowboys at Grasshopper were ready and put them together with the Grasshopper cattles. Then they started going to Cibecue. The Cibecue cattles were ready to go, and they put those together with Oak Creek and Grasshopper. The next day, they took all of them over that mountain there, Cibecue Mountain, and right there at the end of that trail there used to be a pasture. They put all the cattles in there. They put them in there for two or three days to graze. That's what they used to do.

Then, when they thought the cattles were ready to go again, they started towards Carrizo. They went in that canyon [Corduroy Canyon] and went 'til they got up on top. When they got on top, they stopped again. From there they went along the edge of that cliff all the way to

Western Apache cowboys herding cattle, probably near Hagan's Hill, Fort Apache Indian Reservation, about 1925. Large numbers of Apache cattle were driven overland to the railhead at Holbrook, Arizona, where they were sold at auction.

Forestdale. That's the hardest part, the hardest thing to do, 'cause it's so slow. You just go so *slow*! What I did was get a coffee can and put rocks in there. And I started shaking that can to make the cattles go a little faster. Those cowboys wanted to know what I did. "I just put rocks in it," I said. Pretty soon, everybody's shaking their coffee cans. Anyway, they stopped again at Forestdale. They camped right where the houses start now. There was water there for the cattles to drink.

The next day, they got as far as Show Low. They stopped where that river is [Silver Creek] and gave the cattles a drink right there. Then they went up to where that roping ground [rodeo arena] used to be and put them in a pasture there. They let them rest.

From there, the next day or two days later, they kept going north toward Shumway.[4] One time—it was on a flat just past Shumway—all the cattles took off. There was an old truck—I guess it dumps trash or something—and it was parked on that flat right in front of the cattle. Well, the truck wasn't on when we got close to it, and I guess that man thought, "I can go before the cattles come too far down." So he turned the motor on and it made *lots* of noise! It sounds like it's gonna fall apart. That scared all the cattles and they started running. It took a long time to get them all back together. They got them back, though. Those boys that worked on cattles then really knew what to do.

When we camped at night, we didn't stay close to the cowboys. We camped about a mile back 'cause we had to watch the horses. If you stayed close to the cowboys it's no good 'cause the horses got scared and started running and it's hard to round them up in the morning. And there was always a mean horse that led the other ones off. My stepfather was supposed to keep them together but he couldn't do it all by himself. That's why I was helping him.

I stayed with the horses all day, and then, before it got dark, I went back to the wagon. I just tied my horse to the wagon and sat with my mother. My stepfather had a big rag and he tied it to a tree. He said, "If you see that rag in a tree, camp there." So that's what we did. He knew where to camp and we stayed there. We built a fire. Then my mother went out and gathered wood and put it in the wagon. Then we made our food for the next day. We made enough for the whole day, but lots of times we didn't eat 'til the next evening. We made traveling bread, *báń ditáné* [thick tortilla], and sometimes we had chili in cans and we had coffee. And sometimes, when that old man [Charley Marley] came back to the wagon, he brought the food the cowboys ate.

John Williams was cook for the cowboys. He was my mother's cousin. He was married to Marcus Gatewood's mother. She was a widow and he married her. At night, in the evening, he dug a hole in the ground. He put a lot of hardwood in there, oak, and made a fire. It's burning while he was cooking supper, and then, after supper, he put a big pot of beans in that hole. He put enough water in the pot to last for a long time 'cause he's not gonna look at it 'til morning. He put the beans in there and salt and some of that big old long salt pork they used to have. He made it to taste good. Then he tied the lid down real hard with bailing wire. Then he put a piece of tin over it. Then he built a fire on top of that tin and left it there all night long. The next morning he had his pot of beans already ready for breakfast.

He made bread, too—big biscuits. In the morning, when the mens got ready to go, they came over and cut one side open and filled it with beans. Then they wrapped it in a piece of paper and put it in their pocket. On the way they ate it. Sometimes those biscuits were real hard. So somebody told him [John Williams], "You make those biscuits so the cowboys can sit on their horses all day." He said, "What do you mean?" The other one said, "They're so heavy and so hard they hold the cowboys down in their saddles." John Williams got mad. He said, "Cook for yourself then. I'm not gonna give you none of my biscuits again." He cooked a lot of meat, too. They killed a beef whenever they had to—they killed those mavericks [unbranded cattle]—and then he roasted the meat. He just built a fire and threw it on the grill that they carry in the wagon. That's the quickest thing for lunch, that and more of those biscuits.

At night, the cowboys sat around and talked. They told stories. John Williams always carried Bull Durham tobacco cans. He had a box full of them. He brought it along and passed the can around and the cowboys rolled their own cigarettes. But we didn't go over there. Like I told you, we stayed at the wagon and watched the horses.

If a cow gave birth to a calf, they brought it to the wagon. We picked it up and put it in there. And when the cowboys camped again, we turned the babies loose so their mothers could find them and feed them. One time, we had two babies that nobody [none of the cows] wanted. We kept them at the wagon and fed them. My mother mixed flour and water and canned milk. She fed them with a bottle, it's like a Coke bottle. She just held the baby's head up and stuck the bottle in its mouth and it started drinking. She kept on doing that. Both of those baby calves lived. We took them with us to Holbrook. That's where the cowboys told my mother, they said, "We don't know who they belong to. You raised them. You're the mother, so you can keep your babies." She took them back to Oak Creek. They branded them F-Five-Bar. They grew up good.

Holbrook was just a small town. All those houses that are there now didn't used to be there. Holbrook was just one street and the corrals close to the railroad tracks. The cattles had to cross that river [Little Colorado River] but when the water was high they can't get through. Even when the water was low—if it's been raining and the sand is wet— they sink way down in it. Two or three cows broke their legs that way. So the cowboys had to gather all the cattles and take them to the bridge and make them go across. It took a long time to get them across that bridge. They didn't like it!

They sold the cattles at the railroad tracks. There used to be corrals there. A train stopped there and they took all the hay off. They put it in the corrals for the cattles to eat. They fed them. After two days, they put them in different grades. They put the different grades in different corrals, and then they auctioned them off—they're sold. And then, wherever they're going, they put them on the train. Those cattles started hollering and hollering. It makes you feel bad when they do that. And then, after a while, when they all got on the train, they started going away. You could hear them hollering a long ways off.

When we got over there to Holbrook, we used to help the white cowboys. They brought their own cattle to sell, but theirs were fatter than ours 'cause we had to bring ours a long ways. They always got hungry and thirsty. They lost lots of weight. And then again, in those days, they didn't pay much. For some of those cows, those skinny ones, they only paid twenty dollars, maybe twenty-five. It's not very much.

The cowboys got paid right there at Holbrook. They went into town and bought clothes and stuff for their families. The next day, early in the morning, they started back home. We went home in the wagon. We traveled only in the morning—only 'til it gets real hot—and then we rested and waited 'til it cools off. Then we started going again and kept on going 'til we camped somewhere. We went home on the same trail, the same way we came.

In those days, the Indians were not allowed to drink in bars. But those people from Holbrook bought it for them and sold it to them. You could see their cars lined up on the road and on the horse trail. Some of those liquor men rode horses and went up ahead, waiting for the cowboys to come. They had it in their saddlebags, and when they seen the cowboys coming they sold it to them. So that's how they got their drinks. Going home they started whooping and hollering. They were *happy*!

One time—it was that time the cowboys gave those two baby calves to my mother—we were getting ready to go home. My stepfather came back to the wagon with a big bottle stuck in his pocket. He was acting funny. I told my mother, I said, "You know, it looks like he's been drinking." She said, "How do you know?" I said, "'Cause I seen it. He's got a bottle in his back pants, in his pocket." So she asked him, she said, "Do you see one of my calves?" He turned around. He said, "Yes, I think so." He was walking off to get a better look 'cause he's only got one eye. She followed him. She got ahold of his bottle. "What's this? Is it something good to drink?" She was holding it. "You're not supposed to know about that," he said. "Well," she said, "I know about it now."

So we went back to Oak Creek. Then we went home to Chediskai. My stepfather bought lots of stuff for my mother and the family in Holbrook. I think the only thing he bought for himself was that bottle of whiskey. That's how he was, though. He was always looking after my mother and us.

Part Three

"Leaving Home Was Hard"

(1945–1975)

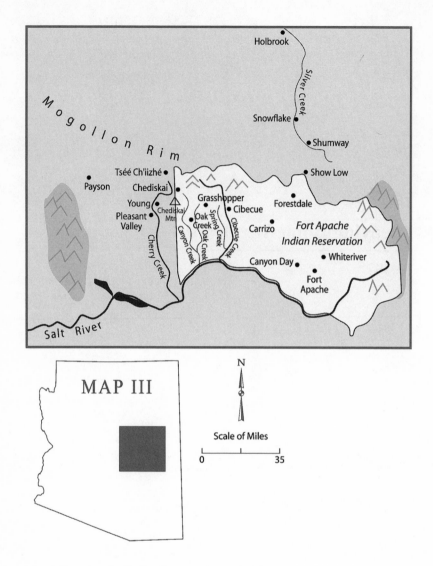

Map 3. Fort Apache Indian Reservation and vicinity.

Chapter Eleven

My mother and my stepfather needed money, so I started working. There's
hardly any jobs at Cibecue at that time [the mid-1940s], so I had to leave home.
Leaving home was hard. My son, Reuben, was four years old. He stayed at
Chediskai with his grandmother. She wanted him to stay with her, so I couldn't
say no. I was gone from home for a long, long time—more than twenty years.

So I was traveling again! I had all kinds of jobs. I worked at Fort Apache for
a while, and then I worked at Show Low, and then I worked in Phoenix. I was
a housekeeper down there for Mr. and Mrs. Lincoln. Then I went to Spokane
with their daughter, Barbara Miller, and looked after her kids. Her husband
was in the air force. I met my husband up there in Spokane—he was in the
air force, too—but we didn't get married 'til later. We had two children, John
and Ora. Bill [William Watt, Eva Watt's husband] was stationed at Williams
Air Force Base in Phoenix. We lived with the kids in Chandler.

Then Bill was sent to Morocco. Me and the kids stayed in Oklahoma with
his father while he was gone. He was gone for three years. He came back. Then
he was stationed at Hamilton Air Force Base in California, so that's where we
went. In '64 he started having trouble with his legs. He didn't know 'til later that
he had cancer. He got discharged from the air force in '65 and that's when we
came back to Cibecue. Finally, after so many years, I was home again. Finally,
I got back home.

"My Grandson Is Safe with Us"—All Kinds of Jobs—"Here Come the Black People!"
—The Horse Shoe Café—Housekeeping in Phoenix—Baby-sitting in Spokane—

Marriage and a Family in Chandler—Three Years in Oklahoma—Hamilton Air Force Base

"My Grandson Is Safe with Us"

I left home in 1944 or '45, somewhere in there. That big war [World War II] was still going on. When that big war started, they picked out four mens from Cibecue to go right away. I think it was Marcus Gatewood, Harley Taylor, Edward Cromwell, and Edward Patterson. Before those four went off, they had a ceremony for them. They took them far away, way out in the country, 'cause it's dangerous for ladies and kids to hear the songs. Those songs make you *mean*, not afraid of *nothing*, and they don't want that for nobody else. John Lupe and David Dale sang for those four mens. They all went off to the war. They all came back—not a scratch.

Anyway, I left home to find a job. Reuben [Reuben Kessay, Eva Watt's son] was still small. He was about four years old. Leaving home was hard. I started working. I had all kinds of jobs. I sent most of the money I made back home to my mother. In those days, money was scarce.

Reuben stayed with his grandmother at Chediskai. I guess he liked it down there. And then again, my mother and my stepfather really wanted him to stay with them. My mother told me, she said, "My grandson is safe with us. We can look after him good all the time." She told me, "You don't know where you're gonna go. You don't know what you're gonna do. You might have to go far away to find a job." She said, "It's better if my grandson stays with us here. That way he's gonna be all right." I couldn't say no, so Reuben stayed with them. My mother said that he always helped them a lot. She said, "My grandson is small yet but already he acts like a man."

All Kinds of Jobs

I had all kinds of jobs. I worked at the hospital in Whiteriver first. I cleaned the rooms for the patients, and I changed their sheets and their gowns. I had a cousin that worked there—Margaret Tessay, Calvert Tessay's older sister—and she's the one that got me that job.

Eva Tulene Case holding her son Reuben Kessay, near McNary, Fort Apache
Indian Reservation, 1941 or 1942.

Then I started working with Miss McKnight. She was a field matron for the BIA [Bureau of Indian Affairs]. I lived with her in Whiteriver. It was the first house on this side of the Catholic church. I stayed
in the back.

We traveled all over the reservation, all over to different districts.
Sometimes we went to Cibecue in case those people needed some-

thing, and we helped them out. Lots of times they didn't have no groceries, so we put them on a list for ration foods and they went and got them. And sometimes we went out when the apples and corn were getting ripe, and we gathered those and canned them for the people. Beans and stuff, we canned those, too.

We had a government car, and that's how we got around. One time, we got stuck over there by Grasshopper. We went to Oak Creek and gave those people some groceries. Coming back, it started raining. It rained all the way to Grasshopper. We got stuck right there by the stockman's house. Nobody was there. The stockman and the cowboys were gone.

We tried everything. I finally found some old tins that blowed off the roof of the house. I dragged them over to the car. We had tools in there, a shovel and an ax. We dug a hole under one of the wheels. Then we put logs in there and put some dirt on top. Then I put the tins on top of that. Then I said to that lady, "Start it. If you start going, don't wait for me. Just keep going to the top of the hill over there. I'll walk over there pretty soon." So she did. She started it. "Don't stop," I said. "Don't stop 'til you get to the top of the hill." She started going. The car climbed out of the mud. She almost stopped, but she kept on going to the top of the hill. That's where she stopped. Then she hollered, "I'm OK. We're OK now." From there on there's lots of gravel on the road, not much mud.

We were going back to Cibecue, and where the old airstrip used to be there's a place on the road that always got lots of mud. Two cars were stuck in there. That lady said, "What are we gonna do?" I told her, I said, "Drive off the road and go around." She said, "What if we get stuck?" I said, "The mud is just on the road. There's gravel over there on the side." So she did that. We didn't get stuck.

After that, I worked in the boarding school at Fort Apache [Theodore Roosevelt Indian School]. I worked in the laundry with Mr. McNabbit. He used to run the laundry, him and his wife. Then, after Fred Banashley's wife got sick, I was assistant cook at the school. I worked with a little Hopi lady over there. Her name was Nora Riley. I had relatives at East Fork, so I lived with them.

"Here Come the Black People!"

Then I started working above Hagan Hill in the woods towards Carrizo. It was way out there. They were cutting down pine trees. There used to be a sawmill down below, and that's where they made the boards. My brother Augustine and his wife were living in the woods, and Charley Stago and his wife were up there, too. The mens cut down the trees and cut off all the branches. Then the ladies had to chop them up and pile them up and burn them.

And you know how it is when you burn pine wood, it leaves a lot of *black*! Well, I guess we all turned black from the smoke—clothes, skin, everything—and we didn't even think about it. Those people that worked at the sawmill used to tease us when we went down there. "Here come the black people! The black people are coming out of the forest!" Sometimes they said, "The black people are really piling their money up!" The reason they said that is 'cause we didn't go nowhere. They brought our groceries to us, so we stayed up there in the woods and worked on Saturday and Sunday. They paid us extra for that. I liked working up there 'cause there's no boss—nobody tells you what to do—and it's way out in the country.

The Horse Shoe Café

After that, I went to work in Show Low. I worked at the Horse Shoe Café. I worked there for Melvin Whipple. He was my boss. Me and my cousin Bessie Lupe were cooks. Mrs. Finney was a waitress. Her husband was the sheriff, Jim Finney. He was a quiet man. He got along good with everybody. He knew my mother from somewhere. "How's your mother doing?" he used to say. "I hope she's doing OK." Apache people used to come in there when they came to town. Nanny, Augustine's wife, always wanted to go there first.

I had the keys [to the café], so I got there early in the morning. I opened the door and turned the lights on and pushed back the curtains. Then I put the coffee on. When Melvin came in, right at six o'clock, the coffee was ready. He got himself a great big cup. "That tastes good, it's just the way I like it." Then he says, "Do you want some breakfast? I'll cook breakfast for you." So he went and got his pork chops. That man ate pork chops every single morning! I asked him, "Why not bacon?" He said, "I don't like bacon, I just like pork chops." So every morning we ate pork chops and eggs.

One time, we were working late 'cause there's a rodeo going on. Lots of people were in there from different towns. They came in there and were all eating. I was still working at eleven [P.M.], close to closing time. We started cleaning everything up. We left four tables out. The rest were all covered up.

And a bunch of Navajos came in, two ladies and some mens. They ate all right, but then they wanted to stay. I was washing dishes 'cause the dishwasher already went home. I washed all the dishes before I left. And those Navajos won't leave! Melvin told them we're not cooking no more—"We're closing up soon," he said—but they kept asking for coffee, more and more coffee. So Mrs. Finney was putting coffee up there for them. I finished what I was doing and cleaned up. Melvin handed me the keys. He said, "You'll be here early in the morning. When you come in, be sure to lock the door behind you and don't open the windows. We don't want nobody busting in here 'cause they're hungry or drunk."

When I went home, those Navajos were still sitting there. I went out the side door and went home. There used to be a big house up on the hill where the Mormon church is now. That house was apartments and we stayed in one of them. We rented that place we lived in. There's four of us in one big room—Pearl Tortice, Wendell Thomas's daughter, Bessie Lupe, and me. All we did is sleep there. We didn't cook or eat there. Anyway, they were already home when I got there. They were going to a sunrise dance that weekend, so they had a lady sewing for them in there. They were trying their dresses on and dancing in there. "Does my dress dance good?" They were saying that.

The window curtains were down, and all of a sudden, outside in the moonlight, I seen somebody with a big hat go by. Then another one went by. I told the girls to stop what they were doing. I said, "Look over to the windows." They did. I said, "Somebody's been looking at you out there." They got real quiet. I told them, "Turn the bright light on." We just sat there. Pretty soon, we heard some giggles out there. Then they went by again, those two hats. Then they tried to open the window.

That big house had four apartments in it. There's a lady living in the apartment across the hallway from us. She was living by herself. We knocked on her door. I said, "Call the police. Tell them there's somebody around this building. They're walking around. We seen their shades [shadows]. They're trying to open the window." She did that. Jim Finney came over right away. He caught those Navajos and put them in jail. They stayed in there for two weeks. He said that they came from somewhere up around Holbrook.

I worked at the Horse Shoe Café for more than two years. Then I lost my job—well, I guess you could say the rain lost it for me. About once a month, I got a big box of groceries and took it to my mother. I did that on my day off. Well, I got down to Cibecue and it started raining. It kept raining and raining. It rained *hard* every day. The road washed out and I couldn't get a ride back to Show Low. When I got back there, Melvin Whipple was gone. Somebody else was running that café. So that was it—no Whipple, no job.

I liked working there. Melvin paid me good money. Show Low was a real small town in those days, just a few buildings. They used to have square dances in the street. People from all over came to those dances. They used to have a real good time.

Housekeeping in Phoenix

When I found out Bessie Lupe wasn't working in the café no more, I went to that apartment where we stayed. She was there. I talked to her. She said, "I'm going back to my old job in Phoenix. I talked to the lady that I worked for before on the phone. She said it's OK for me to come back." Bessie said, "Why don't you come with me? There's lots of jobs for girls down there."[1] I asked her, "Do you think you could find a job for me?" She said, "I'll try. Maybe we can work together." I said, "I'll go with you."

So I went with Bessie down to Phoenix on a bus. And you know what, that *same day* I got a job. Bessie went back to her old job working for Mr. and Mrs. Lincoln. She said to that lady, "This is my cousin and she's looking for work." And that lady said, "Good, you can both work right here."

So that's how I started working for the Lincolns. They were real nice people. We worked cleaning their house. We were housekeepers. It's a big house! Those people had *sixteen rooms*! We were busy all the time. Two of their daughters and one of their sons were living there. The son and one of the daughters had families and they were living there, too. Big house! Big family!

The Lincolns had a ranch over towards Prescott. In the summertime, we used to go up there. Everybody went, all the families. After lunch, those people went to sleep. Then I was free, on my own. There's acorn trees everywhere on that ranch, so I went and picked acorns. I did that every day. I didn't go home 'til evening.

They wanted me to make acorn stew. I said, "Yes, I'll make it, if you find me some meat." They had a lot of metate rocks in their yard. They said they dug them out when they were making their house. I asked that old man [Mr. Lincoln], "Can I use one of those stones?" He said, "Yes, pick out the one you want." So I got a small one and scrubbed it real good. I put it in the sun. After it dried, I started grinding the acorns. They wanted to know how I did it. They *had* to try it themselves. "It looks easy," they said. They tried but they couldn't do it the way I did. "It's not that easy," I said. "It takes time to learn how to do it."

So I made that acorn stew. I put it on the table. That old man tasted it. "That's good! That's *good*!" Then he went inside and got himself a big bowl. He filled it up. Then he covered it with a cloth and took it back inside. "Leave that alone," he told them. "That's *mine*!" Every day he took some out—just enough for himself—and ate it with tortillas. He did that 'til there's no more acorn stew left.

We worked for the Lincolns, me and Bessie Lupe, for a long time. Then Bessie went back to Cibecue. "I'm going home," she said. "I know you can work here by yourself." So that's what I did. Pretty soon after she left, the younger families that were living there moved out to their own houses, so I took care of that sixteen-room house all by myself. But now there's only that old man and his wife and me. We're mostly by ourselves, but sometimes they rented rooms to people that spent the night, especially around state fair time. I stayed in a little house in the back. It had a bedroom and living room. It was nice.

I used to go back to Cibecue—Cibecue and Chediskai—two or three times a year. I stayed with my mother and stepfather. I brought them groceries and gave them money. Reuben was getting tall. They were raising him real good. My mother used to say, "My grandson helps me all the time. He helps that old man, too. If we ask him to do something, he does it right away." I stayed at home for only one week. I worked with my mother—cooking, grinding corn, those kind of things—and that's when she told me what's happened since I been away. Then I went back to Phoenix.

Baby-sitting in Spokane

We were doing fine down there in Phoenix 'til one of the Lincolns' daughters—her name was Barbara Miller—found out that she had to go to Spokane. Her husband was in the air force. He was stationed at Williams Air Force Base in Phoenix. Then he got transferred to the air force base in Spokane. So him and his wife had to get ready to go up there. They had a baby, a girl, only six months old.

That lady [Barbara Miller] wanted me to go with her to Spokane. She wanted me to baby-sit her baby while she was working up there. I told her, "It's not up to me, it's up to your mother." So she asked her mother, "Can Eva go with me to Spokane?" Her mother said, "No, go find your own girl. There's lots of girls looking for a job. Go get one for yourself." Her daughter started crying. "I only want Eva," she said. "She's just like one of the family. I don't trust nobody I don't know. I'm thinking about my baby, in my heart is my baby." Then her father came in. He asked her, "Why are you crying?" She told him. Then he said to his wife, "Now Mom, you should let Eva go with Barbara. Eva likes to see new places and Barbara needs her help. Servicemen always travel a lot, so they might come home in three or four months." Then Mrs. Lincoln told her daughter, "Well, all right. She can go with you this time." Then she said to me, "Eva, don't pack all your clothes. Leave some here for when you come back." I started packing right away. Then I wrote a letter to my mother. I told her I was going to Spokane. I told her I didn't know how long I was gonna be gone.

Barbara and her husband left two days ahead of me from Phoenix. They left the baby with me. Her father and her mother took us to the train station and paid for the train. We had one room all to ourselves. A man brought me breakfast and lunch. That baby was real good. All the way she didn't cry or nothing. We went to Oakland and stopped there for a while. Then we went to Eugene. We stopped there, too. I never did get off the train. Then we went to Spokane. They met us there, Barbara and her husband. His name was Wayne, Wayne Miller. They were really glad to see us! They had a car. We started going north. I was thinking, "Spokane looks like a big town." We went to a Chinese restaurant and ate on the second floor. After that we went west, all the way to their house. We went inside. "This is gonna be your home," they said.

Their house was on a road close to the Columbia River. The house was up high and the river was down below. There's a grocery store close to where we lived. I stayed home with the baby. They [Wayne and Barbara Miller] left to go to work about five or six in the morning. They just got up and went. But I got up anytime I felt like it—you know, when the baby wakes up—and fixed the baby's formula. Then I fixed myself something to eat. And that's it! The house was clean already, so I didn't have to do no cleaning, except sometimes when they brought their friends over there for a party. That's the only time I had to clean.

I used to go to the YWCA. I went there on weekends. I met some Indians there, but they were drinking too much. They lived right close to the river [Columbia River]. They had a little reservation there, I think. I don't know what kinds of Indians live up there.

I had friends from the YWCA, and I had a friend from a Chinese store. Her father had a café on the second floor, way up high, and we used to go up there to eat. One time, it was snowing real hard! I called Barbara. I said, "It's snowing so hard I don't think I can get home." She asked me where I was at. I told her I was with that Chinese girl at her house. She said, "I guess you can stay there for the night, but can I talk to the father of that girl?" She was talking to him for a long time. Then they gave me a place to sleep, and I stayed there with them. After that, they [Barbara and Wayne Miller] knew that Chinese girl was my friend. Her name was Rose. I used to take her home sometimes. We used to go to the movies. She showed me how to cook Chinese food.

Wayne Miller taught me how to play poker. Sometimes I played with his wife and their friends, not for money, just for fun. We went to Vancouver several times 'cause they had friends over there that liked to play poker. I didn't like Vancouver, it's too cold. One time, we went to Coeur D'Alene. There's a gambling house over there. Well, he [Wayne Miller] was losing money. He kept on losing. I think he lost close to

Eva Tulene Case at the home of her employers, Wayne and Barbara Miller, in
Spokane, Washington, 1947 or 1948.

seventy dollars. He told me to play for him. "Maybe you can win my money back," he said. So I started playing poker. I won. I kept on winning. I won all his money back. He was really happy! He told me, he said, "You can have half the money 'cause you're the one that got it back." I said, "The ladies in my family like to gamble, especially my grandmother Rose."

Then Barbara got pregnant again. She quit working before the baby was born. It was born during the night. She called me at home from the hospital. She said, "Can you come over? Just call a taxi and tell him to take you to the air force hospital." So I called the taxi. He came. I got in there with their other baby. He took us to the hospital. I got off and went inside. They took me to Barbara's bed. She said, "Did they show you the baby?" I said, "No, not yet." Then she said, "Well, they're gonna bring it to me pretty soon. It's a girl." And she said, "Now we got two baby girls to look after."

We lived in Spokane for about two years. That's where I met my husband [William Watt]. He was a petroleum man with the air force. He put gas in the planes and helped look after them. Wayne Miller was his boss. He was in Wayne's company. One time, Wayne came home and said, "There's an Indian guy in my company. Would you like to meet him?" I said, "OK." So he brought Bill over to the house. We talked for a while. He told me he's a Cherokee from Oklahoma. He was a nice man. Pretty soon after that, Wayne Miller got transferred. All his company was transferred to Jefferson, Maine. Bill was supposed to go with them but he got permission to go back to Oklahoma. They said he could go back there to visit his family. After that, I didn't see him again for a long time.

I went with the Millers to Maine. We stayed there only about one month, one and a half months. Then that man [Wayne Miller] got transferred to Roswell, New Mexico. He got permission to go home before he went over there, so we headed back to Phoenix. I didn't like that! I don't like to travel too fast—you know, go someplace, then jump right away to someplace else. It's better to stay for a while.

Anyway, we got back to Phoenix. We stayed with Mr. and Mrs. Lincoln. I was wanting to get my old job back, but they already hired a housekeeper, a Mexican girl. Barbara wanted me to go with her to New Mexico and look after her kids. She was begging me to go over there. I told her, "I don't know. Are you gonna stay there for a while?" She said, "Eva, I don't know." And I said, "If you're gonna stay for a while, like for a year, that's all right, I can go with you. If it's just a few months, I can't go." She said, "I don't know." Then I said, "Well, I'm going home to visit my family. If you're still here when I come back, I'll see." So I went back to Cibecue. When I went down to Phoenix again, Mrs. Lincoln said that Barbara and her husband and her kids already went to New Mexico.

Marriage and a Family in Chandler

So I was looking for work again. Nora Bullock and Fanny Bullock were living in Phoenix at that time. Nora was doing housekeeping work. Fanny was baby-sitting a retarded child. I stayed with them for a while. They're sisters from Oak Creek, so I knew them real good.

Fanny introduced me to a lady named Marie. She's a Mission Indian from California. Her home was close to Santa Rosa. She asked me to go home with her for a while, so I did. We went over there on a bus. I stayed with her and her mother. I got tired just laying around doing nothing, so I went to where she was harvesting vegetables and started helping her. After all the vegetables was done, we started picking cotton. I stayed over there for about two months. That lady's mother didn't want me to go. "Stay here with us," she said. I said, "I have a mother, too. I'm going home to find out how she's doing." So I went back to Phoenix. Then I went home. Then I came back to Phoenix again.

Nora [Nora Bullock] worked for a family at Williams Field [Williams Air Force Base]. She helped find me a job over there. I worked for an officer and his wife. Their name was Lane. I looked after their three little girls. I was wanting to live in town with Nora and Fanny, but that man said no. He said, "Stay with us here 'cause we're gonna need you early in the morning. That's when I have to go to work, so I can't go and get you in town. Can you live right here?" I said, "Yes, that's OK."

I had a house all to myself. It's long! They said it used to be part of a hospital. There's a kitchen, bathroom, three bedrooms, and a living room. That was good! Nora and Fanny came over there and stayed with me. They came Friday night. They stayed Saturday all day and half a day on Sunday. Then they went home.

I didn't know it, but Bill [William Watt] got transferred to Williams Air Force Base. He was living right there in Phoenix. That's where I found him again. Well, it's more like he found me. I was shopping with Nora. She said, "Let's go to Walgreens drugstore. I want to show you something in there." So we went in there. We always wanted children's toys 'cause every time we went back to Cibecue we gave out toys to the kids. So we got some. They were in bags for five dollars. Nora got a bag and I got one. Then we came back out and sat in front of the courthouse on Washington Street. There's a water fountain there and a circle of benches all the way around. We were sitting there just watching the people.

And here comes a white guy and an Indian. That Indian man put his hand in the water, that fountain water, and he *sprinkled* it on us! Nora said, "What are you doing? I don't want to get wet! We're just sitting here talking." That man was looking at me. He said, "Don't you remember me?" I said, "No, I don't know anybody in Phoenix that does that." He said, "How about Spokane?" I said, "Oh, is that you, Bill?" And he said, "Yes, you remember my name. How about my other name, do you remember it?" And I said, "Taajo." And he said, "Yes, that's me." *Taajo* means "red bird" in Cherokee.

So that's when I started talking to him. We talked there for a long time. We sat there 'til early in the evening. I told Nora, I said, "We have to go home." He said, "Can we take you home?" I said, "No." See, they had that limousine that belongs to the officers. Bill and that white guy he was with always brought the officers to Westward Ho [a Phoenix hotel] for meetings in that long limousine. I didn't want to get in there. I said, "You could get in trouble if we get in there. They [the officers] might see us."

I guess Bill found out where Nora lived. He came over there and she told him I was working for the Lanes. About two weeks after I met him again, he came to their house. We went to a movie.

We got married in '52. We got married in Florence. We lived in Chandler for eight years. Bill went to work from there at Williams Field, so I was home by myself. I told him I didn't like that. So he said, "Well, let's go get your son [Reuben Kessay] and bring him down here. Then you'll have somebody with you."

So we went back to Chediskai. I thought my stepfather was gonna

Eva and William Watt at Bapchule, Gila River Indian Reservation, Arizona, about 1952.

say no. He told Reuben, "If you go down there, who's gonna look after my horses? Who's gonna ride Blue? Who's gonna take care of him? He's your partner." And Reuben said, "Mama can help me write letters to you. She can write about what I do every day and I can send it to you." Then he said, "I'll go with her. If I don't like it, I'll come back." So we took him back with us. Augustine brought him to Chandler. He went to St. Mary's Catholic School down there. At first he didn't want to go. "There's too many white people," he said. And I said, "That's what you have to do. You have to learn the white people's language." He said, "OK, I'll try." He learned English real good.

Me and Bill had two children. John was born in 1953 and Ora was born in 1955. They were about two years apart. John is "John Langley Watt." He's named after my father, John Langley Tulene. We named Ora Ann after our mothers. "Ora" was Bill's mother's name and "Ann" was my mother's name.

Three Years in Oklahoma

Like I said, we were living in Chandler. Then, in '59, Bill was called to Morocco. He took us to Oklahoma before he left. We stayed with his father in Stillwell. Reuben was going to school at St. Catherine's, that Catholic school in Santa Fe. We picked him up and took him with us to Oklahoma. He didn't want to go. He said, "I want to stay." He said, "I want to go to school." We took him with us. He stayed with us in Oklahoma for about one year. Then he said, "I want to go back to school." So we called over there in Santa Fe to that Catholic school. They said he could come back, so we sent him back on the bus.

Bill sent for us from Morocco. They told us that we had to get lots of shots. We went to a base in Little Rock, Arkansas, somewhere around there, and got all the shots. We were ready to go but then John and Ora got sick. They were having some *bad* kind of stomach flu. We didn't go to Morocco 'cause I wouldn't take the children. We went back to Oklahoma.

I liked living in Oklahoma all right. Most of the people were nice to us over there. I used to write letters to my mother back home, telling her what the kids were doing and stuff like that. Edith Hanna wrote back for her 'cause my mother can't see good enough to write good.

Every year, over there in Oklahoma, they have Strawberry Festival. On every hill there's a strawberry patch, and all over, everywhere, everybody picked. They put the strawberries in quart baskets and sold them. You have to throw gravel or dirt ahead of you when you're picking 'cause there's lots of copperheads. And you have to watch out when you go and get chicken eggs 'cause those copperheads are in there, too. They lie next to the nests all curled up. That's how Bill's uncle got bit. He got bit on the top of his hand. He pulled the skin up and cut it off with his knife. Lots of blood was running out. I think that's what saved him. He almost died.

Bill's father used to have lots of herbs, all kinds of herbs. People came to him almost every day. One lady came to his house and said that the white doctor sent her home. He said he couldn't do nothing for her. She wanted some medicine from Bill's father. They brought her in the house and laid her on the bed. He examined her, asking all kinds of questions, and I guess he found out what to do for her.

That man and Reuben—Reuben was driving—went after the medicine he needed. They brought it back and he fixed it for that sick lady. He made her drink a lot, almost a quart. Then he told her, "This is gonna put you to sleep for about two hours." So we all got out of the house. We sat under some big hickory trees while that lady was sleeping. She slept 'til about two o'clock in the afternoon. Then she got up. She had a cup in her hand. She was banging it against the door. She wanted somebody to come and help her. They seen her and went over there. They brought her to where we were sitting under those trees. Then that man boiled a big bucket of medicine. He poured it in a washtub. He made that lady sit in that hot medicine for a long time. She even got her head washed with it. After she got out, she said that she was feeling stronger.

Then she ate. A lady made soup for her, squirrel soup. She had about fourteen of those squirrels and she chopped them up and boiled them. She strained all the bones out and then she put fresh corn in there. It tastes good! They gave it to that sick lady. She drank it. She wanted some more. She drank about four big bowls of soup. She said, "I never ate like that before." I guess she was feeling better already.

About a week later, that lady came in with a big truck. We were all sitting on the porch. She said, "Where's grandpa?" We said, "He's inside." He came out. She said, "Grandpa, you made me well. I'm all right now. That doctor told me that I was gonna die." She was standing there crying. She said, "Grandpa, you're a good medicine man. Don't give your medicine to white people. Those medicines were given to *you*! Keep them!"

Even white people came to Bill's father for medicine. There's one lady that I guess had arthritis. She had it real bad on her knees. They looked like basketballs, both sides, and her ankles and toes were all swelled up. She couldn't hardly walk. Bill's father boiled a big pot of medicine for that lady. He put all of it in the bathtub inside the house. She had to soak in there. She had a cup and she used that to pour medicine on herself. She stayed inside the house for about an hour. Finally, they got her out. Then that man gave her a big cupful to drink. She drank all that down. He said that would help her from the inside. He told her that after a while her swellings will go away.

About a month later, that lady came back. She was walking *lots* better. She didn't have basketball knees no more and her toes were all straightened out, too. "Thank you," she said. "Thank you, I'm walking again." Bill's father was a *good* medicine man. His name was Charlie Watt.

Bill was in Morocco for three years. He came back in '62, about two years after Reuben went back to school at Fort Apache. Then my husband was sent to Hamilton Air Force Base in California. It's close to San Francisco, close to the ocean. We picked Reuben up in White River, Arizona, and he came to live with us in California. We were following the air force again!

Hamilton Air Force Base

It was hard over there [California] 'cause you can't find a place close to the base to live. Newcomers had to live far away. We lived way up in Petaluma. They had a long list of people ahead of you, so you have to wait your turn. When somebody moved off the base you had a chance. We waited for about six months. Then we moved to Hamilton Air Force Base. Finally, we got on there.

I worked in the officers' club. I took care of the linens—you know,

Eva Tulene Watt with her children John and Ora Watt at the San Francisco Zoo, California, 1963 or 1964.

putting them on the tables and then cleaning up after the meals. Lots of people used to come in there, so I was busy with that. On weekends we took the kids to where they wanted to go. One time, we went to Alcatraz—that prison—on a boat. Me and Bill took the kids over there. They won't let us go inside.

We were doing fine in California, me and the kids. But then, in '65, my husband's legs started bothering him. Sometimes they hurt him real bad. But the doctors couldn't find out what was wrong with him. He went to the air force hospital and they checked him there. He was there for a week. They couldn't find nothing. Then he went to the navy hospital in San Francisco. He was there for a month. Me and the kids used to go over there on weekends and stay with him at the hospital. They still couldn't find out what's wrong with his legs. We didn't find out 'til later that he had cancer.

Chapter Twelve

When I got back home to Cibecue, it was different than when I went away. It was big! Everybody was living at Cibecue so their kids can go to school. Nobody was living at Chediskai, nobody at Oak Creek. My old stomping grounds was empty.

"Finally, I Got Back Home"—Troubles at School for John and Ora Watt—The Death of Rose Lupe—The Death of Charley Marley—The Death of Ann Beatty

"Finally, I Got Back Home"

My husband got discharged from the air force in 1965. He got a medical discharge on account of his legs. So we left California and came back here. Finally, I got back home. We rented a house below Fort Apache for a while and then we moved to Cibecue. That was 1966.

We lived at the old Cibecue school. We lived where the principal used to live. The school's closed—nobody went there 'cause they built another school for the kids—but people were getting in and stealing things from inside the building. They were stealing school equipment—pots and pans and brooms and mop buckets, and I don't know what else they took. We were guarding that place, me and Bill, watching out for people that were taking that stuff away. My mother lived with us there. Before that she was living with my brother Jack and his wife, Edith Hanna. I went over there and asked my brother, "Now that I'm home, if it's OK with you, I can look after our mother." He said OK, so she started living with us.

I liked being home 'cause lots of my relatives were living there in Cibecue. My brother Jack and his family was there, and Dewey and his wife and kids were there, and Joe was there, too. You know, Joe never did get married. My brothers used to tell him, they said, "Why don't you go and get yourself a wife?" He said, "Ah! They're too much trouble." We used to laugh about that. My oldest brother, Eugene, was living down at San Carlos with his wife and kids, and Albert and his family were living in Whiteriver. Augustine and his family was over there, too. Reuben was staying with Augustine. He [Reuben Kessay] was working for the police in Whiteriver. John and Ora were with us. If you put them all together—you know, everybody's kids and grand-kids—it's a big family.

When I got back to Cibecue, lots of the old people were gone. My grandmother Rose was gone, and my stepfather, Charley Marley, he was gone, too. My mother was doing all right. She kept busy all the time. Then old age started stepping on her. She died in 1968. She died at home. All of us were with her.

Bill's legs never did stop bothering him. He could walk—he used to walk up the river [Cibecue Creek] and go fishing—but sometimes he had a real hard time. He went to doctors at the hospital in White-river. They can't find out what was wrong with him. Finally, he went to the veterans' hospital in Phoenix. That's where they found out that he had cancer—bone cancer. He didn't live very long after that. He died in 1987. He was buried in Whiteriver 'cause he told us he didn't want to go back to Oklahoma. I felt real bad after my husband passed away.

Troubles at School for John and Ora Watt

At first, when we were living at Fort Apache, John and Ora went to school at Seven-Mile. When we moved to Cibecue, they went to school there. After they finished eighth grade, they both went to St. Johns.

John didn't stay but one year down there 'cause those Pima boys were real mean to him. They used to try to hurt him 'cause he was Apache. He said that he used to go up on the roof of the dormitory and sleep all night there. He came back down in the morning. Those Pimas don't like Apaches! Ora had trouble, too, but she had other Apache girls with her down there. She said they used to gang up against the Pima girls, so they started to leave them alone.

When my brothers were at St. Johns they had trouble with the Pima boys. There's lots more of them and they used to pick on the Apache boys. They got into fights with them. But then the Apaches got together and went to the main office. They told that Catholic priest what was going on in the dormitory. After that, they said, those Pimas were punished all the time.

When I was going to school at St. Johns, the Pima girls used to be mean to us Apache girls, even in the dining room. See, there's four girls on this side of the table, and four girls on the other side of the table, and two big girls on the ends. We used to eat like a family—you know, with bowls of food on the table—and those two big girls were supposed to serve the smaller kids. Well, they always served the Pima girls first—big helpings!—and what's left over they divided among the Apaches.

One of those big Pima girls was worse than the others. She chopped your fingers. If you put your hands on the table like this [fingers on top, thumb underneath], she got a knife, a table knife, and chopped your fingers. She didn't do that to the Pima girls, just the Apaches. She did that to me one time. My hand was bleeding. The next table was all Apaches and they came running over there. They grabbed me and pulled me away from the table. After that, that Pima girl had to stand out front in the dining room by herself. She stood there at a little square table, and that's where she had to eat. They didn't want her sitting with people anymore. She stayed at that table by herself for three months. That Pima girl was always wanting to fight with Apache girls, especially the little ones. I guess she didn't like them.

See, before our time, the Pimas and Papagos used to fight with the Apaches. The Apaches went down there into their country and brought back captives. My grandpa, William Lupe, did that. He went down there and brought a Pima girl back home. Like I told you, that lady had lots of children for him. I guess the Pimas still talk about those fighting days. They don't forget. Even now, they still talk about it.

The Death of Rose Lupe

My grandmother lived for about ninety years, I think. She passed away at San Carlos in 1946. I guess it was her own fault, too, in a way.

She went to visit a lady. When she got there the lady was gone. There's only little kids there and one big girl. My grandmother asked that girl, "Where did your mother go?" She said, "She went to church. She usually comes back in about an hour." My grandmother said, "Well, I'm going home." I guess she didn't realize it was getting dark. Then that girl told her, "My mother said for you to stay here. She said that when she gets back she can take you home." "No," my grandmother said. "I have to go home." And that big girl said, "It's dangerous! There's lots of boys running around everywhere. They're drinking!"

But my grandmother won't listen. She left. She started walking home. There was a bunch of boys drinking by the railroad tracks— *mean boys!*—and they got her. I never will know why they hurt her over there. They beat her up. Then they poured beer or whiskey all over her, even on her hair. I guess some mens were coming in a car, so those mean boys took off! Two of the mens picked up my grandmother and put her in the car. They took her to the hospital. The doctor examined her there. He started working on her right away.

She got well in the hospital. She came home, but she wasn't active like she was before. She got kind of sick and didn't go nowhere no more. She just stayed home. Her daughter Bessie and my aunt Emma were with her. They looked after her.

I was working in Phoenix when she died. I was working for the Lincolns. I didn't know about it 'til after she was buried. I went back to San Carlos when I found out. My aunt Bessie said, "We knew you were coming. Your grandma was asking for you, so that's why we knew you were coming." When I was small, I used to go everywhere with my grandmother Rose. She always took care of me. I was real sad when she died.

You know, a long time ago, some ladies were just like a doctor. My grandmother Rose was like that. She used to get *all kinds* of herbs. She said, "This is for that, this is for this. This is for your cold, this is for your eyes, this is for your heart." I mean, she had *everything*! She even had a medicine for athlete's foot.

Well, she showed me that medicine, and one time Kenzie Early had it [athlete's foot] real bad. They were having a party at his home [at Cibecue], and I went over there. I asked Ida [Ida Lupe, Kenzie Early's wife], "Where's Kenzie?" She said, "He's sitting outside. He's sitting outside in the sun."

So I went over there and talked to him. He had his legs on a stool and his feet were covered with a rag. I said, "What's wrong with your feet?" He said, "Aww, I got sore feet. I went to a doctor but he said he can't cure it. He said, it's jungle rot or something like that." I told him, I said, "There's a medicine that I think will cure anything on your feet."

I guess I shouldn't have told him that 'cause right away he said, "Where's Ida?" I said, "She's inside the house with the party." He said, "Go tell her I want to see her." So I went and got her out. She came over to where he was sitting. She said, "Oh, Kenzie, you can talk with Eva right here. I'm having the party." He said, "Forget about the party. I want you to take Eva and go with her and get some medicine."

So Ida put Judy [Judy Early Dehose, Ida Early's daughter] in charge of the party, and then we left. Ida said, "Are you sure you know what you're doing?" I said, "I guess I know." She said, "Well, get what you want. I hope it's not too far away." We went over there and I showed her where it [the medicinal plant] was growing. It came out of the ground real easy 'cause it's kind of sandy over there. "Here's another one!" Ida said. "Here's another one!" She kept on going like that.

After we got that medicine we took it down to the river [Cibecue Creek]. We washed it there—we cleaned off the roots real good—and then we brought it back home. Kenzie was still sitting there. He told Ida, he said, "Get Eva what she needs." So Ida got me a big bucket with water in it. She put it on the fire while we pounded on those roots. The water started boiling and I put them in there. I boiled that medicine for about ten minutes. Then I said, "That's it." Then we got a flour sack that's been washed real clean. We put it over a pan and poured the medicine in there. We strained it. Then we sat there 'til it got kind of cool.

I told Kenzie, "You have to put your feet in there." He said, "I think it's still hot." I said, "That's what you need, so slowly put your feet in there." He did. He said it was hot at first. Then he just sat there and talked while his feet were in the water. Then he pulled his feet out. He said, "What am I supposed to do?" I said, "You can use what's left in the pan. Heat it up again and put your feet in there." Then I said, "You can add some more water, if you want to, and boil it again." I said, "It should take about two days or three, then those sores will start drying up." The skin under his feet was just dropping off! It was *raw*! It was bleeding.

He did that for two days, like I told him. Then he found out that the skin under his feet was getting better, getting hard again. Then, about four days later, he came walking to where we were living. He was calling before he got there. "He-e-ey! I'm coming to see you! I'm coming to thank you for what you did! My feet are all good again!"

I learned about that medicine from my grandmother Rose. She was just like a doctor. She cured people all the time. Nowadays, there's hardly any ladies like that.

The Death of Charley Marley

Like I told you, my stepfather had no eye on one side. That happened when he was just a boy. He lost his other eye in Oak Creek. They were living there, him and my mother, a little ways from the cowboys' camp. He was helping the cowboys with their horses. My brothers Jack and Joe were staying there, too.

They had a wickiup there, and right close to it an acorn tree was growing, a little one. But that tree was getting big, so my stepfather went and cut the branches off. My mother told him, she said, "Don't cut the branches off like that. They're just sharp sticks sticking out." She said, "If you're gonna cut one off, cut it close to the tree. Cut the whole thing off and don't leave nothing sticking out." She said, "You and me can't see very good and we might hurt ourselves." But he wouldn't do it. "Oh," he said, "you can hang things on them, your rope or your cane. You can use them to hang up anything." That's what he had in mind.

And one day he went down to the corral. He came home in the evening. He came home feeling high. My mother asked him what he had to drink. He said, "*Tułbáí*, mostly, and some other stuff they made down there"—it was home brew, I guess.[1] My mother said, "You're gonna be running outside all night." So she hung up a quilt on that acorn tree. She tied it so it hung all the way down to the ground. "That's better," she said.

My stepfather came in and went to sleep. Then he got up to go to the bathroom. He went outside several times—I guess he was drinking all day—and close to midnight he got mad. He told my mother, he said, "The only thing I hang onto is all covered up." So he went out and grabbed that quilt and threw it on the ground. Coming back in, he stumbled on something and fell—and one of those branches got him in his eye.

His eye was hanging out. When my brother trained the flashlight on him, it was hanging way down. I guess he felt of it already 'cause his hand was all bloody. My stepfather said, "Cut it off! Cut the whole thing off *now*! If it cools off, it's gonna hurt more!" My brother told him, "We can't do that. We can't do that 'cause you're bleeding bad already. If you lose too much blood, you're gonna die." And my stepfather said, *"They want me to die! That's why they took my eye again! That's all I had!"* He was mad!

They tried to stop the blood. They couldn't do it. He said, "Do like my uncle did. Get a hot iron and stick it in there. It quits bleeding that way. Do that again!" And my brother told him, he said, "But you're old now. You were strong in those days but now you're an old man." So my mother brought him back inside. She did the best she could. She had some gauze, I guess, and she put that on her hand and pushed it [the eyeball] back inside. Then she put a big patch on top of it and tied a kerchief around his head. "That's just to hold it in there," she said.

Some whiteman was there at Oak Creek, a stockman. My brothers and my mother took him [Charley Marley] over there. The stockman told them that he just came in about an hour ago. My brother told him, "We have to take my stepfather to Cibecue. From there he can go to the hospital in Whiteriver." But that man didn't want to do it. He said, "Can you drive? If you want to, you can drive the truck." My brother said, "No, you have to do the driving. We'll go with you and help him get around." So they left. When they got to Cibecue they went to McQuillin's house. McQuillin said, "I'll take him the rest of the way myself." He took him in his truck. He put a mattress in there and made my stepfather lay down on it. He took him to the hospital in Whiteriver.

They operated on his eye and took it out. There's nothing they could do, they said. When my mother went over there to visit him, both his eyes were covered with gauze. "Just tell the doctor to give me *poison*!" he said. He was *mad*! He didn't want to live no more. He said, "That's all I had to live for. *Now I'm no good*! I'm no good this way, I can't see nothing! I don't want to live!" My mother talked to him, talked to him, and finally he settled down. He was in the hospital for about two weeks. The doctor wanted to keep him there but he wanted to go home. He was crying to go home every day.

So they brought him home. He had a big bandage around his head. The doctor told my brothers, "He's got to have a clean bandage put on every day. He's got to wash it [the empty eye socket] and wash his face." So my mother got those herbs and made pain medicine for him. She boiled it and strained it and put it in a jar. Then she put some of it in a little bowl and soaked a rag in there. Then she washed his face and all around the hole. After that, she soaked another rag in clean medicine and put it in there. She left it in there for a little while and then she took it out. Then she put a clean bandage around his head. She kept on doing that.

It got well in no time. All the swelling and the blue went away. After that, my stepfather didn't want the bandage around his face no more. He said that he wanted to get dark glasses. "Why? What do you want dark glasses for?" He said, "Just so they won't see the hole, that's why." So they got him that. He wore those glasses all the time.

So my stepfather was blind, both sides, both eyes. He bothered my mother a lot more after that. If he heard people talking somewhere, he said, "Who's talking over there? Go find out for me." She went over and found out. Then she came back and told him. "Take me over there," he said. "Let me talk with my friends." So my mother had to lead him over there. She took a cushion for him to sit on. Later, after his friends went away, he started calling to her, "Come and get me! Bring me back!" So she had to go and get him.

And then, pretty soon, they started giving him drinks. My mother didn't like that! She told him, she said, "That's no good! You're gonna hurt yourself drinking like that. You're gonna hurt yourself worse than what happened to you before." After that, she won't take him when he heard people talking. He got *mad*! He said, "You don't like me! That's why you don't want me to be with my friends." My mother said, "They're not your friends if they give you those drinks." She told him that. He said, "Well, it makes me feel good. When I drink that stuff it makes me forget everything. I'm all right then." But nobody would take him, so he just stayed home. He just sat there in one place. When my mother gave him something to drink, like water or coffee, he got mad and poured it out on the ground.

After a while, my brothers put up a shade for him. My brother Jack talked to his friends. He said, "Go over there and visit with him. He needs it now more than ever. When he still had one eye, he used to run around among you. But now he can't do that no more, he's just home by himself. Go visit with him over there." So they started doing that when he was at home. But he won't leave my mother alone. "Cook this," he told her. "Do that."

Charley Marley died in 1959. He died about four years after he lost his other eye. He got pneumonia real bad. Some mens came to see him and they took him off somewhere. And late in the afternoon, way late around six or seven, they brought him back. He was just all *cold*! He was just *shivering*! It was snowing, and it looked like he's been rolling around in the mud 'cause his clothes were all muddy and wet. My mother took his clothes off and put some dry clothes on him. Then she put him to bed.

The next day, he won't get up. He was sick for about a week. McQuillin tried to take him to the hospital. He won't go. He [McQuillin] said, "We're going to Chediskai. Do you want to go for a ride?" My stepfather said, "You're not going to Chediskai. I know you're gonna take me to the hospital."

Everybody felt bad after he was gone. I was living in Chandler at the time. They sent me a message and I came back to Cibecue for the funeral. We took my mother down to Chediskai. We took her down there to keep her away from people. We kept her down there about a week. She won't quit crying, though. She was remembering all those times, I guess, those times when they were together, where they been, what they did and all. I told her, "This is no good for you." So we took her back to Cibecue.

Then we told her that we're gonna take her with us back to Chandler. She said, "OK, maybe . . . I don't know nothing about it . . . it might be better that way." I told my brothers that she was going home with us for about a month, maybe more. We took her to Chandler and she stayed with us. She stayed with us for about five months. She liked it. She started feeling better.

She liked to pick cotton, so we took her over there—it's on the other side of Chandler—to pick. Some people from Fort McDowell were there and I guess they recognized her. They told her about Charley Dickens—you know, that man that was my father's friend at Mormon Flat. She said, "Is he still alive?" They said, "Yes, he's living at Fort McDowell. We're gonna tell him that you're over here." So the next day they brought him there. Instead of picking cotton, those two sat under a tree just talking and talking. Charley Dickens's daughter said, "Let them sit there. Leave them alone. They haven't seen each other for a long, long time." So they did that. They sat there talking for a long, long time.

I remember one time when a flood opened the irrigation dam at Chediskai. I was down there visiting my family. Three of my brothers were there to help us fix it. Well, my stepfather got up real early in the morning. He still had his one eye. He said, "I'm gonna go over there and get started." He took the wheelbarrow with the shovels and other stuff in it. He said, "I'm gonna go and get some rocks. Then I'm gonna chop some brush along the river so we can put them in there." He said, "Come along when you get ready."

So he was up there doing that. And for some reason, while he was chopping brush, he looked up in the sky. And you know how jet planes make those white lines all over the sky—well, he seen that. He got scared. He never did see that before. He came *running* back home!

The boys were getting ready to take the wagon over there to the dam. When he got to the wagon, he told the boys, he said, "Go back! Go back to the house! I need to talk to all of you!" Everybody went back. My mother had her bundle ready to go. He made us line up in front of the house. He started praying for all of us. He was *really* praying. The boys didn't understand what it was all about. I thought, "Maybe something happened to him." After he got through praying for us, he went and got some ashes. He was sprinkling ashes on the ground all around us. Then he pointed at me. "You and your mother go back in the house and stay there." "You too," he said to the boys. "Stay around here. Pretty soon, it's gonna get dark."

My mother asked him, "What's this all about? We were gonna fix the dam today, and here you are telling us we have to sit at home. We should get that done while it's still clear yet. If it starts raining again, the high water will open it up more." He said, "Well, we'll see what happens."

Then one of my brothers said the same thing, "What's this all about?" And my stepfather said, "When Jesus is coming back to earth there will be signs in the sky." He said, "When I was over there, I seen white lines in the sky." The boys started giggling and he got mad. He said, "You don't believe nothing! You're always giggling at things I tell you are true." So they told him, "It's jet planes." He said, "What is that?"—and they tried *so hard* to explain it to him. He listened to them. Then he said, "You guys are just newborns. I'm an old man and I learned *so many things* before you." Finally, my mother tried to explain it to him. "OK," he said, "but if something happens, I told you. Let's go then." We all went up there with him and fixed the dam.

The Death of Ann Beatty

My mother got hit by a lightning in 1947. She almost died. Her and my stepfather—he still had his one eye—were staying in Cibecue across from the old school. They came up from Chediskai. I was there when it happened. I was working for the Lincolns at the time, but I was home for a week to visit my family. Boy, it was *awful* when she got hit by that lightning.

Arthur Naklanita was my uncle. He lived right by the Catholic church in Cibecue. When my mother went to the store, she used to go over there and visit him. Well, she came out of Knapp's store and was walking by Arthur's road and it started raining hard. And I guess he seen her through the window of his house. He called her. "Come in! It's raining out there! You're gonna get wet!" So she went inside. There was lots of other people in there, sitting and talking. After a while it quit raining, but it's still cloudy and there was lightning still yet. And my mother said, "I been here too long. I better go home." Arthur told her, "Well, go to the car. It's right there by the back door. I'll take you home across the river [Cibecue Creek]."

So my mother was going out the back door. She was going down the steps and that's when the lightning hit her. She just *fell*! She just lay there on the ground. Instead of taking her home, they took her back inside. They said you could see the burn marks, right here around her eyes, and here around her neck, and down one leg all the way around. Her head was blistered, burned real bad. She can't speak, she can't say nothing. When they talked to her, she just looked at them. They said it looked like she could still see but her eyes were burned real bad.

Some of those people wanted to take her home. But my uncle said, "No, you can't, that could just make her worse." So she stayed there overnight. Right after it happened, somebody went to the store and called my brother Eugene. He was in San Carlos. He came the next day.

And we didn't know what was going on! Nobody came and told us. My mother didn't come home, so the next day my brother Dewey and his wife went looking for her. My stepfather told Dewey, "Maybe somebody gave her a drink." He said, "She can't hold it, it makes her feel weak. It makes her go to sleep right away. Maybe she spent the night sleeping somewhere." So Dewey and his wife went across the river. They went to Knapp's store and then they went to Cooley's store. They asked in there. Old man Cooley said, "She's probably up that way. Maybe she went to Arthur's." So they went looking for her up there. When they got to Arthur's house, somebody told them. "She's inside. She got hit. She's sick." So they went in there.

And Dewey, you know, you couldn't never tell him nothing. He always wanted to do things his way. He said, "That old man [Charley Marley] told us to come and get her, so I have to take her home." But Arthur told him, he said, "No, just leave her here 'til your brother comes. He knows what to do. He's coming pretty soon from San Carlos. He's on his way already." And Dewey said, "That old man wants her home right away, and he wants to know if you guys gave her something to drink." Arthur told him, "Nobody gave her nothing to drink. She didn't drink nothing. She's not drunk." And my brother said, "Maybe she's drunk, that's why she won't talk." And he [Arthur Naklanita] said, "No, it's that thing that hit her. Look at her, she's burned real bad. We're gonna have to wait 'til your brother gets here."

You're not supposed to take a person that got hit by a lightning across a river. You're not supposed to do that. You have to sprinkle yellow powder across the river first and then go across. It's like making a safe trail for the person that got hit. That way, crossing the river won't affect her. But if she goes across without it, it's gonna make her worse. That's what they tried to tell my brother.

But Dewey and his wife wouldn't listen. They dragged my mother out of the house. She could walk—she knows what's going on—but she can't talk to them. They dragged her out and they made her walk across the bridge. They brought her home. When they got there she just went *out*!

Then Eugene came in. I guess he went over to Arthur's house first. He said he sprinkled yellow powder across the river where my mother went across. He said, "I hope that will help her." When he came over there, my mother was still out. Her fingernails were all turning purple. Her mouth was turning purple, too. Eugene started praying for her. He sang for her.

The next day, early in the morning, she came out of it. She said, "I want something to eat." She said that she wanted some corn gravy. My brother Eugene said, "That's the worst thing she can have, corn. Just mix up some flour and water." They gave that to her. She drank it up. She drank some coffee, too. Then, about noontime, she started shaking all over. She was just *shaking*! So Eugene said, "I'm taking her back to San Carlos." He said, "She's got to go to the holy ground."

So he took her back to San Carlos. I guess they done everything for her down there. They sang for her four times. That really helped her out. She came home talking! She could walk! She was walking with two canes. But that seizure, that shaking all over, stayed with her for a long time. It won't go away. It came anytime. Later, when I was back in Cibecue, I used to massage her all the time—her legs, her arms, her neck, her head, everywhere. She stayed good for three or four months. We said, "Maybe we got it now." But then it started again. It got slower and slower, though, and then, finally, it just went away. She didn't have it no more. I said, "You better keep praying like they told you to." She said, "Yes, I do that all the time." You know, it seems like in my mother's mind she never had trouble at all. Trouble came to her but she just ignored it.

My mother died in 1968. She died 'cause her gall bladder got infected, they said. They said it started draining inside. She didn't eat hardly anything for one whole month. She always talked about *ch'ín-k'ózhé* [skunkbush]. "I wish I could taste some of that," she said. "That would be really good. I taste it in my mouth when I'm thinking about it." She talked about *nadah* [agave], too. They used to soak it in water and stir it 'til all the sugar stuff came off. The water got brown, and then they drained it with a cloth or a strainer. Then they put cornbread in there. They broke it up in pieces and stirred it up. That's what my mother was thinking about. I said, "I wish I could make that for you. I want to see you eat again." And she said, "Oh, I ate some of it yesterday." Then she called the name of a person that's already gone [de-

Ann Beatty, resting at home in Cibecue about 1965, as she neared the end of
her life. When she died in 1968, all of her children were with her.

ceased] and said, "She made some and I ate it yesterday." I guess her
mind was already going.

She had a picture of Jesus on the wall above her bed. She went like
this every time she looked at it [she extended her arm and pointed to
the picture with her hand]. "Some day," she said, "he's gonna help me
out. He's gonna help me get up and I guess I'll have to go with him."
She said, "He's gonna hold my hand one day."

That evening, I told everybody what she said. I told Augustine and
all my older brothers. They all came and sat around. We sat up with
her. She wanted lots of blankets behind her back in bed so she could

look at that picture of Jesus. We sat with her for a long time. She went to sleep for a while. Everybody went outside and had something to eat. Then we went inside again. She woke up. She was really smiling. She said, "My children, don't forget each other. Remember, you're all my children." Then she said, "I'm gonna be leaving you very soon. I'm supposed to let you know that I'm going." And she told us, "Don't cry when I'm gone 'cause I'm going to a better home than you have here."

About six o'clock in the morning, she put her head down. After a while, she looked up. Then she put her arm up and pointed to that picture of Jesus with her hand. She did that two times. The third time she put her arm up, she went like this [she slowly closed her hand]. And that was it. Her arm fell *down*! She was gone.

Last Words

My mother was always telling stories. I guess she believed in that.

You know, my mother was still walking to the store right up 'til the end. She said, "I'm going to the store. I want to talk to Boy." That's what she called Boyd Knapp. We told her, "We'll take you in the car." She said, "No, I never had a car when I was young. The only traveling thing I had is my legs." So she walked. We always had somebody go with her. She did all right. She got bananas at the store. She always got bananas and oranges. That's all she had in her sack when she came back from the store.

It seems like every kid that seen her followed her home. She really loved kids. When she got home we made her sit down. She wouldn't go to bed. We told her to lay down and rest 'cause she had a long walk. She said, "No, you're not supposed to sleep in the daytime." She wanted to be with the children. She always told them stories, lots of stories, Apache stories. That's why they followed her home.

That's what my mother used to do with us, you know, tell lots of stories. She told us *all* those things, especially me 'cause I was her daughter and I was with her for a long time. My brothers were mostly in school and then they got married and moved to different places. But I was with my mother a lot of the time—San Carlos, Miami, Apache Trail, Mormon Flat, Chediskai, Cibecue, all those places—and that's when she told me stories about all the things that happened long years ago.

She enjoyed telling stores, and I guess that's why I'm doing it now. She used to tell us, she said, "You children will learn a lot if you listen good to stories." She knew what she was talking about, so we always listened good. She told us, she said, "If you don't listen, you won't learn."

Acknowledgments

From informal start to published finish, this book was in the making for the better part of a decade. During that time, Eva Watt and I were assisted by many people. We are grateful to them all.

Mrs. Watt began her book at the home of her daughter, Ora Seymour, whose warmth and generosity set a gracious tone. This was reinforced by Ora's brother, John Watt, by Ora's two young sons, Cecil and Steven Hendricks, and by one of their friends, George of the Jungle, an inquisitive cat. Mrs. Watt continued her work in the home of her son and daughter-in-law, Reuben and Beverly Kessay, whose respect for peace and quiet helped greatly to get things done. Reuben read a draft of the book, detected a few inconsistencies, and advised us on how to resolve them. The valuable family photographs that add so much to the text were supplied by Reuben and his mother, by Sarah Bush, and by descendants of Jack and Edith Case. *Ahíyi'e.*

Other members of the White Mountain Apache Tribe supported the project with expressions of interest and approval. Prominent among them were Beverly Malone, Cornelia Hoffman, Ann Skidmore, Doreen Gatewood, Lucy Benally, Judy Dehose, Linda Tessay, Bernadette Adley, Ramon Riley, Levi Dehose, Broadus Bones, and Ronnie Lupe. Countenance came as well from Jeanette Cassa, coordinator of the San Carlos Apache Elders Cultural Advisory Council, and from Vincent Randall, former chairman of the Yavapai-Apache Tribe and prominent member of the Western Apache Tribal Coalition. Vincent, who is Eva Watt's nephew, commented at length on her narratives and stressed their importance for Western Apache people. *Ahíyi'e dakówa. Ahíyi'e shik'isn.*

As the project gained momentum, Beverly Malone made certain that Western Apache words and expressions were rendered correctly in print. Charlie O'Hara asked thoughtful questions, Bob Brauchli furnished key historical documents, and Seth Pilsk came to the ethnobotanical rescue. Anthony Cooley, Mike Cooley, the late Clementine Cooley, and Billie Twaits provided rich information about members of their families mentioned in Mrs. Watt's texts. Karl Hoerig and David Bingell shared with us the archives of the White Mountain Apache Culture Center and Museum, and Richard Inman, Bureau of Indian Affairs computer expert, made digital images of photographs we found there. Other forms of assistance, among them humor and plain good will, were given by Scott Rushforth, Michael Graves, Philip Greenfeld, Delmar Boni, David Dinwoodie, Karen Blu, Mariann Skahan, Steven Feld, Patricia Nelson Limerick, Sylvia Rodriguez, Carole Nagengast, Manley Begay, Peter Whiteley, Jack Campbell, Marta Weigle, Morris Foster, Joyce Nevin Mackin, Chris Coder, D. Y. Begay, Bill Douglas, Benson Daitz, and Vine Deloria, Jr. Our thanks to one and all.

We are also indebted to the Office of the Dean, College of Arts and Sciences, and to the Department of Anthropology, both of the University of New Mexico, for financial assistance in preparing the final manuscript. Staff at the following institutions were particularly helpful during the search for and acquisition of illustrative materials: the National Anthropological Archives and the National Museum of the American Indian, the Arizona Historical Society and the Arizona State Museum, the Hayden Library at Arizona State University, the Salt River Project, and the White Mountain Apache Culture Center and Museum.

The manuscript of Eva Watt's book was fashioned by June-el Piper, who brought to the task an arsenal of skills, critical acumen, and considerable forbearance. In collections across the country she searched for early photographs of Western Apache people, made some remarkable finds, and arranged for their use as illustrations here. In these and other ways, her help was indispensable. As the manuscript neared completion, William Longacre brought it to the attention of Christine Szuter, director of the University of Arizona Press, who responded with enthusiasm. Freelance editor Jane Kepp later took charge and made trenchant recommendations for final revisions. A more skillful team of professionals would be difficult to find.

Without the committed backing of John R. Welch, historic preservation officer for the White Mountain Apache Tribe, Eva Watt's work would not have proceeded as smoothly as it did. John's quick mind, his deep respect for the Western Apache past, and his singular ability to foresee potential obstacles and remove them in advance allowed the work to move forward with all deliberate speed. Like Mrs. Watt herself, John never wavered, and it is much to his credit that she considers him a friend.

Gayle Potter-Basso knows better than anyone what this project entailed. What she may not appreciate fully is how much she did to enrich it. As careful reader, gentle critic, and knowledgeable student of Western Apache culture, her thoughts and opinions proved useful at every turn. Perhaps more importantly, she honored the spirit of Eva Watt's achievement by laughing out loud at some of her narratives and wincing visibly at others. If, as has been said, "steadiness does the greatest good," Gayle has no peer.

Finally, Mrs. Watt and I wish to thank our mothers—Ann Beatty Tulene and Etolia Simmons Basso—and to dedicate this book to their memories. Both contributed to it in unforgettable ways. *Ba'isédandzįh.*

Family Genealogy

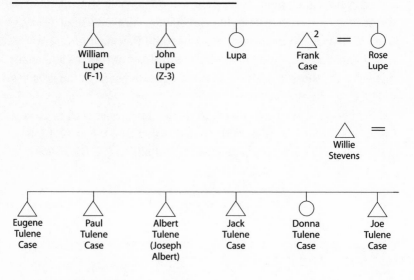

William Lupe (F-1) John Lupe (Z-3) Lupa Frank Case [2] Rose Lupe

Willie Stevens

Eugene Tulene Case Paul Tulene Case Albert Tulene (Joseph Albert) Jack Tulene Case Donna Tulene Case Joe Tulene Case

1 = first marriage
2 = second marriage

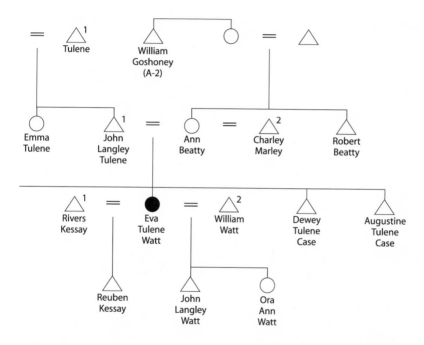

Chronology of Important Events

c. 1860	Tulene born near Camp Verde, Arizona. Rose Lupe born at Oak Creek, Fort Apache Indian Reservation.
c. 1875	Rose Lupe marries Tulene, Fort Apache Indian Reservation. Charley Marley born at San Carlos, San Carlos Apache Indian Reservation. John Langley Tulene born near Young, Arizona.
c. 1880	Ann Beatty born at Cibecue, Fort Apache Indian Reservation.
c. 1895	Ann Beatty taken to U.S. government boarding school at San Carlos; later sent to Carlisle Indian Industrial School in Pennsylvania.
c. 1898	Ann Beatty returns from Pennsylvania, marries John Langley Tulene, Fort Apache Indian Reservation.
c. 1899–1923	Ann Beatty and John Langley Tulene have nine children that survive infancy: Eugene, Paul, Albert, Jack, Donna, Joe, Eva, Dewey, and Augustine.
c. 1905	Tulene shot and killed near Wheatfields, Arizona.
c. 1907	Rose Lupe marries Frank Case, San Carlos Apache Indian Reservation.
1913	Eva Tulene born near Blue House Mountain, Fort Apache Indian Reservation.
1917–1918	Eugene Tulene, Paul Tulene, and Albert Tulene taken to U.S. government boarding school at Rice, San Carlos Apache Indian Reservation. Paul Tulene dies at Rice after handling wood hit by lightning, San Carlos Apache Indian Reservation. Eugene Tulene runs away from boarding school at Rice, begins working at Roosevelt Dam, Arizona. Albert Tulene and Jack Tulene enter St. Johns Indian School and Mission near Laveen, Arizona.

1918–1919   Tulene family moves from Rice to Miami, Arizona; Eva Tu-
               lene hidden from San Carlos police; family survives flu epi-
               demic.
1920–1924   Tulene family lives in labor camps along Apache Trail, later
               at Mormon Flat, Arizona.
               Family name "Tulene" changed to "Case" on revised Apache
               census.
1924   John Langley Tulene dies from pneumonia at his sister's
               home in Globe, Arizona; Ann Beatty and her children return
               to Rice, San Carlos Apache Indian Reservation.
1925–1926   Eva Tulene Case enters St. Johns Indian School and Mission.
               Donna Tulene Case dies from acute tonsillitis at Rice, San
               Carlos Apache Indian Reservation.
               Ann Beatty and her children treated for trachoma at San Car-
               los, San Carlos Apache Indian Reservation.
1926–1927   Ann Beatty and her young son Augustine leave Rice to live
               with her brother's family at Spring Creek, Fort Apache Indian
               Reservation.
               Ann Beatty marries Charley Marley, establishes homes with
               him at Chediskai and Oak Creek, Fort Apache Indian Reser-
               vation.
1929–1938   Ann Beatty suffers recurrence of trachoma, receives treat-
               ment at Fort Apache, Fort Apache Indian Reservation.
               Eva Tulene Case leaves St. Johns Indian School and Mission,
               lives with her family for more than a decade at Chediskai and
               Oak Creek, Fort Apache Indian Reservation.
1940   Eva Tulene Case gives birth to her first child, Reuben Kessay,
               at Whiteriver, Fort Apache Indian Reservation.
1944 or 1945   Eva Tulene Case places Reuben Kessay in the care of Ann
               Beatty, embarks on a series of wage-paying jobs in Arizona
               and beyond.
1946   Rose Lupe dies at San Carlos, San Carlos Apache Indian Res-
               ervation.
1947   Ann Beatty is struck by lightning at Cibecue, Fort Apache
               Indian Reservation.
1948–1949   Eva Tulene Case moves with her employers to Spokane,
               Washington; meets William Watt, a Cherokee aviation fuel
               specialist in the U.S. Air Force.
1952   Eva Tulene Case marries William Watt in Florence, Arizona.
1953   John Langley Watt born in Chandler, Arizona.
1955   Ora Ann Watt born in Chandler, Arizona.
1957 or 1958   Charley Marley dies from exposure to the elements at Cibe-
               cue, Fort Apache Indian Reservation.

1959	William Watt transferred to Morocco; Eva Tulene Watt and her children live with his father for the next three years near Stillwell, Oklahoma.
1962	William Watt returns from Morocco, moves with his family to Hamilton Air Force Base near San Francisco, California.
1965–1966	William Watt retires from U.S. Air Force, moves with his family to Cibecue, Fort Apache Indian Reservation.
1968	Ann Beatty dies from ruptured gall bladder at Cibecue, Fort Apache Indian Reservation.
1987	William Watt dies from cancer at Whiteriver, Fort Apache Indian Reservation; Eva Tulene Watt moves from Cibecue to Cradleboard, Fort Apache Indian Reservation.
1998	Eva Tulene Watt begins recording historical narratives for her book, *Don't Let the Sun Step Over You*," Cradleboard, Fort Apache Indian Reservation.
2002	Eva Tulene Watt moves from Cradleboard to Hon-Dah, Fort Apache Indian Reservation.

Notes

Introduction

1. Encompassing 1.67 million acres in east-central Arizona, the Fort Apache Indian Reservation is home to more than twelve thousand members of the White Mountain Apache Tribe. These Apache people—together with those living on the San Carlos Apache Reservation, the Camp Verde Yavapai-Apache Reservation, and the Payson Tonto Apache Reservation—comprise a larger entity known as the Western Apache. This term is used to distinguish them from other Apache groups and tribes, including the Chiricahua, Mescalero, Jicarilla, Lipan, and Kiowa-Apache. Speakers of Western Apache, a Southern Athapaskan language with several regional dialects, refer to themselves as *ndee* or *nnee* (people; human beings; Apaches). For ethnographic summaries of each of the Apache tribes, see Ortiz 1983. For lengthier treatments of Western Apache language and culture, see Basso 1970, 1990, 1996; Ferg 1987; Goodwin 1938a, 1942; Kaut 1957; and Kessel 1976. A useful dictionary of the Western Apache language has been compiled by Dorothy Bray (1998).

2. Although Western Apache is Eva Watt's primary language, she decided early on to tell her stories in English, for several reasons. It is a sobering mark of modern times, she observed, that many younger Apaches speak their language imperfectly ("They just know some pieces of it") and that growing numbers of Apache children now rely solely on English. Moreover, she stressed, English is the language Apaches are able to read, and this is true of most other groups, including, of course, non-Indians. With a worried eye on the future, Mrs. Watt said, "It's better to make it [her book] in English, 'cause that way, if they want to, more people can try to read it. Like I told you, Apaches are losing their own language, and one of these days English could be just *everywhere*. That's not the way it's supposed to be, but it could happen." She added, "Maybe the ones that read it will know the stories could have been better if I made them in Apache 'cause Apache's my own language. But English is OK. It's not the same, but English is OK."

The manuscript of *Don't Let The Sun Step Over You* was prepared in close collaboration with Mrs. Watt. We selected together the narratives that are included; smoothed out some of their sentences to enhance readability; assigned titles to each of the texts; and arranged them sequentially into parts and chapters. When the manuscript became available in typescript, Mrs. Watt read every page, making as she did a handful of minor changes. In addition, she requested that most of the narratives be read to her out loud. "If they *sound* good," her reasoning went, "reading is gonna be OK." Mrs. Watt selected the photographs that illustrate the book (with occasional pleadings from me) and supplied information for many of the captions. Aside from transcribing the narrative texts, the only major tasks I undertook alone were writing the introduction and the endnotes, which offer supplementary information and suggestions for further reading. Otherwise, I have tried to stay out of the way.

Non-Apache readers may be uncertain as to "what is taking place" in a few of Mrs. Watt's stories, and explanatory notes, authored with Mrs. Watt, have been provided at points where this would seem likely. Such uncertainties serve a valuable purpose by calling attention to probable cultural gaps, that is, to discrepancies in the bodies of knowledge that readers and listeners routinely bring to bear when interpreting narrative texts. One of the strengths of Mrs. Watt's stories is that most of the knowledge required to appreciate them is contained in the stories themselves, a very considerable courtesy that narrows cultural gaps and fosters understanding.

Mrs. Watt requested that I not make use of endnotes to comment at length on the ethnographic contents of her narratives. (Brief remarks along these lines, she felt, would not be inappropriate.) Her request for moderation was neither an expression of mistrust nor a veiled assertion of proprietary rights. Rather, it stemmed from her conviction that what stories are taken to mean is a personal affair and that extensive suggestions for how to interpret them can blunt the imagination. In Mrs. Watt's words, "Too much of that stuff can throw a blanket over your thinking. That's not good. You're supposed to think about a story *yourself*, and lots of times you're not gonna know what's in there right away. So you keep on thinking, and then you know more. It's okay if a story puts out mystery." The idea of stories putting out mystery—and that excessive interpretation may work to reduce it—appealed to me at once, and I promised Mrs. Watt that my interpretive impulses would be kept under close control. "Good," she said laughingly, "that way you won't get a headache."

3. Examples of experience-distant accounts of Western Apache history include Cook 1976; Ogle 1970; Perry 1991, 1993; Spicer 1962: chapter 9; and Worcester 1979. For a rare experience-near account, see the narrative by Clarence Hawkins, a White Mountain Apache, presented in Greenfeld 2001.

4. Readers familiar with standard historical accounts may rightly object that the personal identities of Apache military leaders, such as Geronimo, Victorio, and Mangus, are nothing if not well known. But these illustrious figures

were Chiricahua Apaches, not Western Apaches, a major tribal distinction that Mrs. Watt underscored repeatedly. In works dealing with the Apache wars (c. 1860–86), two Western Apache men, Alchesay and Peaches, are cited as having been prominent scouts for the U.S. Cavalry (e.g., Thrapp 1967). In the scant and uneven literature on the postmilitary period (1886–c. 1930), a number of Western Apache peacetime scouts are also mentioned by name, as are several religious leaders who attracted the worried attention of non-Indian authorities (Goodwin and Kaut 1954; Kessel 1976; Vanderpot and Majewski 1998; Wharfield 1965). An exception to Mrs. Watt's claim that available treatments have "no Apaches in there" is Grenville Goodwin's *The Social Organization of the Western Apache* (1942), in which many of Goodwin's consultants are carefully identified and allowed to speak for themselves on a range of cultural topics. Since then, other anthropologists have written useful historical studies (e.g., Adams and Krutz 1971; Bassett 1994; Buskirk 1986; Kaut 1957; Perry 1991, 1993), but none addresses the fundamental problems that trouble Mrs. Watt— namely, that the everyday lives of Western Apache people have been routinely neglected and that Apache historical accounts are conspicuously absent. A sustained attempt to remedy these deficiencies, *Don't Let the Sun Step Over You* is also intended as a demonstration of their importance.

5. Narratives of the kind included in this book have been described as "oral history," "indigenous history," and "ethnohistory," but these and similar English rubrics, which I discussed with Mrs. Watt at length, are without useful meanings for her. In Mrs. Watt's view, the history of her people is inherently "oral" and invariably "indigenous," so that qualifications of this sort are gratuitous and unnecessary. She believes, in other words, that Apache accounts of the past are "history" pure and simple, and that calling them anything else can appear to diminish their worth. Non-Indian historians, who tend to privilege written accounts over spoken ones based upon memory, will likely disagree with Mrs. Watt's position—and that, she thinks, is unfortunate. "Just 'cause we don't write the history down," she said, "Don't mean it's not true. They [historians] can learn a lot from old papers, but they can learn a lot that's in our stories, too. If they throw our stories away, I think it's too bad for them." Mrs. Watt is not alone in recommending that professional scholars make greater use of material contained in Native American historical narratives. For a general discussion of this and related issues, see Mihesuah 1998. A more focused study, similar in approach and exemplary in many respects, is Rena Martin's history of her maternal and paternal clans as related by members of her Navajo family (Martin 2002).

6. Many of the dates in Mrs. Watt's narratives, as well as others in photograph captions, are only approximate. This is not surprising, Mrs. Watt explained, because Apache people of her parents' and grandparents' generations had little use for calendars and seldom possessed them. "They knew all about the months," Mrs. Watt said, "'cause they had names for them in Apache. But

they never did count them up, or the years neither. Some used to say that's bad luck."

7. Learning family stories, Mrs. Watt observed, is becoming a marginal aspect of Western Apache life. In her opinion, many younger Apaches—busy with work and school, captivated by movies and television, and increasingly caught up in their own social affairs—are uninterested in listening to their elders talk about the past. This lack of curiosity is compounded by the fact that, in growing numbers of households, children and teenagers have difficulty understanding the Western Apache language, which their elders tend to speak more comfortably than English. As a result, older people are less likely to initiate family stories for fear of embarrassing both their audiences and themselves. Another contributing factor, Mrs. Watt believes, is a softening of parental discipline. "Nowadays," she said, "lots of these younger ones just run around and do all kinds of stuff, even late at night. We never used to do that 'cause our parents were *strict*. They made us stay home, and that's where we learned those stories. Nowadays, it seems like to me, when they [younger people] stay home, they're always wanting to do something else. They're not all like that—there's some that really like to listen—but a whole bunch just don't care about it." In view of this assessment, it is regrettable that few Western Apache family stories have been published heretofore. Several dozen appear in Goodwin 1942 (see especially the narratives of Anna Price), and one is given in Greenfeld 2001. An extensive collection of Apache family stories, as yet unpublished, has been assembled by Gayle Potter-Basso.

Chapter One

1. Rose Lupe and her siblings belonged to a band of Western Apaches known as Golkizhń (Spotted Country People), whose ancestors settled on the upper reaches of Oak Creek below the Mogollon Rim. Ten or twelve families continued to farm there until the late 1920s. Most Golkizhń eventually moved to Cibecue, where a number of their descendants continue to reside. Little is known about this small Western Apache band, which makes Mrs. Watt's descriptions of its composition and activities all the more valuable. For a probing study of Western Apache ecological adaptations in the Canyon Creek area, see Graves 1982; in this regard, see also Griffin, Leone, and Basso 1971.

2. In 1876 and 1877, as part of a "consolidation policy" initiated by the U.S. Department of the Interior, more than twelve hundred Chiricahua Apaches were brought to San Carlos, where large numbers of Western Apaches, Yavapais, and Mojaves had already been forcibly gathered. Resentful and suspicious, the Chiricahuas became a continuing source of turmoil, committing depredations against the other tribes at San Carlos and attacking non-Indian settlements off the reservation. These Chiricahuas were the "outlaws" described by Mrs. Watt, and Geronimo, who was among them, may have been the man

who carried off Rose Lupe. It is also possible that her abductor was a Western Apache dubbed the Apache Kid, who embarked on a series of raids—occasionally involving the stealing of Indian women—beginning in 1885. Four years later, while the Apache Kid was en route to a prison in Yuma, he killed two guards and fled into Mexico. He was never seen again. For a detailed history of the Apache wars and the role of the Chiricahuas, see Thrapp 1967. Informative sources on Geronimo include Davis 1929, Debo 1976, and Ball 1980. Most of what is known about the Apache Kid is presented in Thrapp 1964.

3. Before the U.S. Army post at San Carlos was deactivated in 1894, Western Apaches sold large quantities of wild hay and firewood to the garrison stationed there. For many of these people, it was their only source of income. The same was true at Fort Apache, which was deactivated in 1922 and made over into a boarding school for American Indian students. For detailed histories of the implementation of federal policy on the San Carlos and Fort Apache reservations, see Cook 1976 and Ogle 1970.

4. A persistent problem facing authorities at and around San Carlos was the acquisition of whiskey by Apaches from non-Indian bootleggers based in towns adjacent to the reservation. Some idea of the briskness of the whiskey trade—and how difficult it was to stop—can be gained from a report written in 1898 by Albert L. Myer, acting U.S. Indian agent:

There were 8 persons arrested for giving whiskey to Indians during the year—1 Frenchman, 3 negroes, 3 Mexicans, and 1 Chinaman. Two of the cases occurred on the reservation by people freighting whiskey. One case, that of the Frenchman, failed through quibbles of the law. One prisoner escaped from the marshal, after being bound over. One case was lost through faulty indictment, but on my demand the prisoner was held on another charge and is still in custody. Five cases were convicted and sentenced. With two exceptions the cases were all brought to trial by the efforts of authorities on the reservation. It is hoped these convictions may prove a lesson, and the character of the people who engage in such traffic renders it doubtful. (Myer 1898:120)

Mrs. Watt was told by her mother, Ann Beatty, that "in those times—1900, around in there—anybody could get moonshine real easy. She said the Mexicans was worst 'cause they know how to go around at night. They went to a place, and if you went there at night, you could get it. Sometimes, they took it right on the reservation. Very few of the Indians had money, so they used to trade for that moonshine. My mother said they used to trade all kinds of stuff, even horses."

5. Mrs. Watt knows little about the Catholic priest who instructed Rose Lupe and her companions in the vicinity of Christmas, a mining camp near the Dripping Springs Mountains about twenty miles from Globe. The first circuit-riding priests arrived in that area in the late 1870s. Mainly from Belgium and

France, they often served without pay, depending for their livelihood on the generosity of people they met along the way. The traveling priests spent much of their time in mining camps, so it may have been by accident that one of them met Rose Lupe resting beside the road. Accidental or not, as Mrs. Watt shows later in this book, the meeting had lasting consequences for members of her family. For more information about the early Catholic priests in this region of Arizona, see Bigando 1989.

6. In 1871, General George Crook, commander of the Department of Arizona, recruited seventy-five Western Apaches as scouts for the U.S. Army. For the next fifteen years these men pursued bands of Chiricahua Apaches throughout much of Arizona Territory and finally into Mexico. By 1900, a few Apache scouts were patrolling the international border, which was frequently crossed by Mexican thieves and smugglers. Mrs. Watt's statement that Frank Case was shot by Mexicans "coming into the United States bringing all kinds of stuff" strongly suggests that he was one of these scouts. For historical treatments of the Western Apache scouts and their military activities, see Thrapp 1964 and 1967, Vanderpot and Majewski 1998, and Wharfield 1965.

7. In the early decades of the twentieth century, tuberculosis was rampant on Indian reservations throughout the United States. In both pulmonary and glandular forms, it was the leading cause of death among adults and children alike. On reservations in Arizona, the Indian death rate from tuberculosis between 1916 and 1925 was more than seventeen times the rate for the country as a whole (Meriam et al. 1928:201). Mrs. Watt, who entered adolescence during this period, commented on the impact of the disease on Western Apache people. "That TB just went everywhere, all over, there's nothing they could do about it. Every family lost somebody, it seems like to me, some families more than one. I remember people crying." For a lucid discussion of the tuberculosis problem among American Indian peoples at this time, see Meriam et al. 1928:189–208.

8. Beginning around 1875, male heads of Western Apache families were assigned identification markers, or "tag-bands," whose purpose was to facilitate record keeping by reservation administrators. Consisting of a letter and a number (e.g., Z-1), tag-bands were passed down with appropriate modifications to the sons of these men (e.g., Z-3), who later used them as brands for their horses and cattle. In some social contexts, Mrs. Watt recalled, a tag-band might be substituted for its bearer's personal name.

9. During the eighteenth and nineteenth centuries, Western Apache raiding parties plundered Pima settlements, returning home with livestock, grain, and occasional female captives. This practice waned as the U.S. military expanded its presence in Arizona Territory, but raids continued until the 1870s. It is possible, Mrs. Watt speculated, that William Lupe's second wife was the last Pima woman captured by Western Apaches; she was certainly the last to live in the Oak Creek–Cibecue region. For a historical treatment of hostilities

between the Pimas and Western Apaches, see Spicer 1962. Apache accounts of actual raids and war expeditions appear in Basso 1971.

10. Western Apache society was structured by an intricate kinship system based upon membership in matrilineal clans. The principles used by Apaches to classify kin differed from those employed by Anglo-Americans, and this is reflected in Mrs. Watt's atypical usage of certain English kin terms. For example, she applies "grandfather" or "grandpa" to her father's mother's brothers, which is consistent with the Apache classification of persons in this position as *shindalé*, a category including all male siblings of one's paternal grandmother. Other mappings of English kin terms onto Apache genealogical categories appear in Mrs. Watt's texts. For an extended treatment of Western Apache social organization, including kinship terminology and clan relationships, see Goodwin 1942; overviews of these topics appear in Kaut 1957 and Basso 1970.

11. It was a basic feature of Western Apache social life that "the unfortunate were carried along by the fortunate, the unskilled by the skilled, and the lazy by the industrious" (Goodwin 1942:123). John Lupe's concern for hungry boys at his fields below Medicine provides a clear case in point.

12. A boarding school opened on the Fort Apache Indian Reservation in 1898, a decade after the first one was established at San Carlos. Both were run in much the same manner, but the school at Fort Apache initially drew its pupils from a more restricted area centered on communities in the eastern part of the reservation. As the school gained new facilities, the scope of its reach expanded, and by 1910 Apache police rode west from Fort Apache to hunt down children at Cibecue and Oak Creek, more than thirty miles away—a healthy distance on horseback and, for the youngsters, a grim eternity. For a history of educational facilities on the Fort Apache reservation, see Cook 1976.

13. Western Apache curing ceremonies varied in form and complexity, but all were alike in seeking the causes of illnesses and prescribing forms of treatment. This was accomplished by metaphysical powers, animate and prescient, whose aid was enlisted by medicine men with appropriate chants and prayers. Medicine men specialized in treating types of illnesses known to respond to the powers with whom they collaborated, and the objects used in ceremonies, together with techniques for handling and manipulating them, also were determined by the particular powers involved. As this account shows, medicine men presided over swift and effective cures (other successful efforts are described elsewhere in the book), although how they were able to do it might never be known by those they restored to health. For an outline of major features of Western Apache ceremonial forms, see Goodwin 1938a and 1938b and Goodwin and Kluckhohn 1943. Powers and some of their uses are discussed in Basso 1969 and 1970.

14. Cattail pollen, or "yellow powder," was a ubiquitous element in all Western Apache prayers and ceremonies.

15. The store at Grasshopper opened for business around 1905. Mrs. Watt

believes the store closed down during the mid-1920s, an opinion shared by other Apaches from Cibecue. The original building, a modest structure built with pieces of sandstone, still stands in fair condition.

16. Western Apache medicine men attained their privileged status by acquiring knowledge of one or more metaphysical powers who then became available for use in human affairs. As Mrs. Watt's account reveals, attaining such knowledge was demanding and sometimes dangerous, but the effort was well rewarded and the results could be dramatic. The power known to William Goshoney—Lightning—was the most potent power of all, and Goshoney's stature as a medicine man was fully commensurate with it.

17. In the late 1920s, Johnny Lee, who was then in his teens, became the proprietor of Lee Mercantile, a trading post in Whiteriver that had been founded by his uncle. Lee ran the trading post until 1985, when it had to be destroyed to make way for road construction. Mrs. Watt recalled that Johnny Lee was well liked by Apache people and that his respect for local medicine men such as William Goshoney was genuine and sincere. As an example of this respect, she cited Lee's efforts to help Goshoney end the drought.

18. It sometimes happened, Mrs. Watt explained, that Western Apache medicine men demanded excessive payment from persons in need of their services, a form of exploitation widely considered unfair. In the scene recounted here, William Goshoney made it clear that he had no such designs.

19. The success of any Western Apache ceremony depended in part on the conviction of all involved that the ceremony's objectives would be effectively achieved. Persons who doubted this, like those detected by William Goshoney, were urged to reconsider or ordered to leave the premises.

20. Usually made out of cowhide or horsehide, the soles of Western Apache moccasins might get stiff or lose their shape after a thorough soaking. This is what William Goshoney had in mind when he told the dancers, "You people are wearing moccasin shoes, I know, and it's hard to get them wet."

21. The first formal schooling of Western Apache children began on July 1, 1881, when J. C. Tiffany, U.S. Indian agent at San Carlos, convened a class in his private quarters; he soon dismissed the class due to intense summer heat (Tiffany 1881:8). A boarding school for boys opened at San Carlos in 1887, and one year later a larger facility with accommodations for girls—a two-story building made out of stone—commenced operation. This was the school that Ann Beatty attended.

22. In 1874, John P. Clum, U.S. Indian agent at San Carlos, selected four Western Apache men to police the reservation. They were soon providing "very effective assistance in maintaining order" (Clum 1874:216). One year later, the number of Apache policemen was increased to eight and then to twenty-five, each receiving a wage of fifteen dollars a month. "The duties of this force," Clum wrote, "are to patrol the Indian camps, to quell disturbances, to arrest offenders, to report any sign of mutiny or disorder, and to scout the

reservation and arrest Indians who are absent from the reservation without a pass" (Clum 1875:297). By 1880, the San Carlos police had acquired additional duties. These included identifying persons engaged in plural marriages (polygamy was forbidden on the reservation), curbing the manufacture and consumption of *tiswin* (an alcoholic beverage made with corn), and curtailing the activities of native religious leaders (Apache medicine men were regarded as the epitome of "savagery" and thus as a major obstacle to the advancement of "civilization"). Later, when boarding schools were established at San Carlos, mounted Apache police hunted down school-age children and forced them to enroll. Ann Beatty was a victim of this practice, as were three of her sons. I asked Mrs. Watt why the police of San Carlos treated their fellow Apaches in such harsh and coercive ways. "They did it for the money," she said. "They did it to feed their families." For more on John Clum and the San Carlos Apache police, see Clum 1936 and Hagan 1966.

23. I have found no government records of the student revolt in which Ann Beatty took part, suggesting that this disturbance may never have been reported to the Office of Indian Affairs. Such tactics were not uncommon. On Indian reservations throughout the country, ugly incidents were routinely downplayed—or covered up completely—lest culpable parties be judged unfit by their superiors in Washington, D.C. (Meriam et al. 1928). As in the case of San Carlos, reservation authorities dealt swiftly with awkward problems and then carried on, usually much as before, as if the problems had been fixed. Ann Beatty knew better. For joining in the girls' rebellion, she was put on a train and shipped to Pennsylvania. For a partial history of government schools on the San Carlos and Fort Apache reservations, see Cook 1976; Parmee 1968 describes the impact of some of these schools on Western Apache children.

24. The Carlisle Indian Industrial School, which operated from 1879 to 1918, was the first off-reservation school established by the U.S. government for the exclusive use of Indian children. Located near Harrisburg in southern Pennsylvania, Carlisle provided a model for Indian education that was widely adopted elsewhere. Boys attending the school were trained in farming and manual skills, girls learned cooking and sewing, and the use of native languages was strictly prohibited. As stated by Carlisle's first director, a former army officer named Richard Pratt, the mission of the school was to "kill the Indian and save the man" (Hoxie 1996:101). In the case of Ann Beatty, this fortunately did not happen. Thoughtful discussions of Carlisle Indian School and its impact on students are presented in Adams 1995 and Coleman 1993.

25. Many Western Apache people of Robert Beatty's generation grew up without English names. Stories of how these names were later conferred, usually by non-Indians unable to speak Apache, have long been a source of humor.

26. On March 23, 1904, when a government day school opened at Cibecue, Western Apache children reacted with fear and alarm. As reported by Olof G. Olson, the school's teacher,

The children took to the chaparral with a yell at my approach, so it was the 12th of April before we managed to open the school with 10 pupils. By much and persistent persuasion 34 children were enrolled with the parents' consent by the last of May. Then they balked and nine girls were drafted [i.e., taken from their homes and brought to the school by police]. Even without the inducement of a noonday meal, the attendance for June was 41.3. (Olson 1904:135)

Temporarily closed in 1905, the Cibecue school reopened two years later. When drafting of pupils resumed, some Apache people took pains to hide their children (they also denied their children's existence), despite the threat of fines and spending time in jail. Attendance at the school later become voluntary, but Mrs. Watt, who went there before that happened, was not afforded a choice. She disliked the experience intensely. Perhaps this is why she spoke of the school only once, and twice deflected requests to speak of it again.

27. This attack was the Skeleton Cave Massacre of 1872, in which seventy-six Yavapais were killed by a column of the U.S. Fifth Cavalry at a site some twenty-five miles north of Superior. As historians Rein Vanderpot and Teresita Majewski (1998:6) have written, "the Skeleton Cave Massacre broke forever the resistance of the Indians of western Apacheria." In this connection, see also Thrapp 1967.

Chapter Two

1. In the early 1870s, Western Apache families living near San Carlos began to draw government rations of beef, flour, and corn. Rations of food continued at San Carlos until 1902, when they were replaced by distributions of "annuity goods" consisting mainly of clothing, textiles, and basic household items. As Mrs. Watt explained, these distributions were major events because "the families never did have very much, and they needed all that stuff they got to make it through the winter. That's the reason they went down there, to get clothes and material and shoes, and then be ready for wintertime." Mrs. Watt's description of Apaches receiving annuity goods at the army post at San Carlos is, to my knowledge, the only one of its kind.

2. In 1897, the San Carlos and Fort Apache reservations, which had been a single entity, became two separate agencies sharing a common boundary defined by portions of the Salt and Black Rivers. It has been suggested that this administrative division had an immediate impact on traditional patterns of Western Apache life (e.g., Ogle 1970), but Mrs. Watt maintained that much remained the same.

They made those rivers a line but nobody paid no attention to it. People used to go back and forth, back and forth, whenever they felt like it. Even when I was still small, we used to go from Cibecue to San Carlos—like when they were giving out rations down there—and then we came back home. People used to do that all the time. Finally, they quit doing that, going back and forth like that. Now they say they're from San Carlos reservation or Fort Apache reservation, but long years ago they didn't say that. They said, "I'm Apache and both [reservations] is all our land." Lots didn't know those rivers was a line, so they didn't even think about it. It never was that way before, so they didn't even think about it. The ones that knew about it said, "I don't believe in no lines."

When Mrs. Watt went with her grandmother to collect annuity goods at San Carlos, it was probably one of the last times that Apaches from the Cibecue region traveled south for this purpose. "That was around 1920," Mrs. Watt commented. "I guess it was kind of the end, but I don't know. I think some people from Oak Creek went down there again, but not very many. It was getting less, and then nobody did it no more."

3. San Carlos Lake, known also as San Carlos Reservoir, was created by Coolidge Dam, a government-sponsored project on the Gila River that was dedicated in 1928. Bitterly opposed by local Western Apaches, the reservoir submerged dozens of their dwellings and fields, a burial ground, and all the original structures at Fort San Carlos. For a brief account of these and related events, see Perry 1993:147–51.

4. On February 12, 1885, Congress granted a right-of-way through the San Carlos Apache Reservation to the Gila Valley, Globe and Northern Railway, authorizing a survey to identify possible routes. Construction of the railroad was hampered by long delays, but by 1896 track had been completed from a point below Mount Thomas to the reservation line. Two years later, on December 1, 1898, the first train chugged past the agency at San Carlos and pulled into Globe amid joyous celebration (Woody and Schwartz 1977). Sedgewick Rice, the acting Indian agent at San Carlos, wrote that "the road will prove to be one of considerable advantage to the Indians by furnishing a market for their produce, giving employment to many of their number, and producing other good results in the matter of civilization, etc." (1898:130–31).

For many years, Mrs. Watt acknowledged, the railroad provided jobs for Western Apache men, including her father and oldest brother. She emphasized, however, that "the best thing about that train was [Apache] people could travel real easy—and fast! They never could do that before. They went wherever it went, even to Bowie and Douglas. Mainly, though, they went from San Carlos to Bylas, or Bylas to San Carlos, to visit their relatives and do what they needed to do. They had lots of fun riding that train."

5. The boarding school at Rice, which opened in 1900, was the main educational institution on the San Carlos Reservation for more than thirty years. Its overriding purpose was to prepare Apache children for assimilation into Anglo-American society by teaching them manual skills and "civilized" forms

of behavior, including how to speak English. Mrs. Watt assured me that going to school at Rice was a crushing experience in all respects, but none was
more harmful than the poor food given to students and the meagerness of their
meals. Her opinion on this matter is supported by the following passage from
The Problem of Indian Administration, a detailed indictment of U.S. Indian policy published in 1928:

> At Rice School, to cite an extreme example, the average amount spent for
> food [per student] was nine cents a day. The dietary was examined at first
> hand for three successive days, and it was obvious that the children were
> not receiving an adequate amount of food even of the very limited variety
> supplied. Malnutrition was evident. They were indolent and when they
> had a chance to play, they merely sat on the ground, showing no exuber-
> ance of healthy youth. (Meriam et al. 1928:327)

Mrs. Watt's accounts of her brothers' treatment at Rice are among the most telling yet registered on the topic of student abuse in Native American boarding
schools. Revealing works on these schools and their affects upon Indian children include Adams 1995, Coleman 1993, Child 1998, Prucha 1979, and Trennert 1988.

6. Founded in 1897 by Father Severin Westhorf, O.F.M., St. Johns Indian
School and Mission became a full-fledged boarding school in 1901. Located on
the Gila River Indian Reservation a few miles south of Laveen, the school developed into the "hub of the Catholic educational system in that area" (Hagan
1959:128). Students at St. Johns led a rigidly structured life, and some who
found it unbearable attempted to run away. Others, like Mrs. Watt, responded
more favorably and learned from the experience. Mrs. Watt noted that several
Western Apaches who attended St. Johns later became distinguished tribal
leaders, none of them more so, she said, than Ronnie Lupe, former chairman
of the White Mountain Apache Tribe. At ceremonies held in 1976, when the
school at St. Johns officially closed, Mr. Lupe delivered the final address. For
enlightening discussions of Indian schools in central and southern Arizona, see
Hagan 1959 and Trennert 1988.

7. Roasted hearts of century plant (*Agave palmeri*), which Mrs. Watt calls
"cooked mescal," were a prized Western Apache food. After the hearts were
roasted, they were pounded into cakes and allowed to dry in the sun. The cakes
were later cut into smaller pieces to be eaten, stored away, or exchanged for
other goods. Buskirk 1986 and Ferg 1987 provide additional information about
this important food and how it was prepared.

8. In the scene recounted here, Joseph Hoffman was in intense communi-
cation with the metaphysical power whose songs and prayers he was learning.
That Hoffman refused to eat or sleep until his instruction had ended—and that
he practiced the thirty-two songs until he knew them perfectly—illustrates his
desire not to offend the power in even the slightest way.

9. When requesting the services of a medicine man, it was necessary to present him with gifts as partial payment. The nature of these gifts was prescribed by the metaphysical power with whom the medicine man collaborated, and Joseph Hoffman's injunction—"I can't accept nothing that's been alive"— was in reference to such a prescription. For more on the life of Joseph Hoffman, see Basso 1971.

10. The "silver balls" described by Mrs. Watt were globules of mercury, which was widely used by miners as an amalgam for processing pulverized rock containing traces of gold and silver ore.

11. In the late 1870s, a few Western Apaches were working for wages at mining camps and ranches away from the San Carlos reservation. Their numbers increased as economic conditions worsened at San Carlos, and by the mid-1910s upwards of two hundred Apache men were employed at copper mines near Globe and Miami. The mine workers lived on the outskirts of these towns in "squatter camps" that offered few amenities. One of these camps—possibly the one where Mrs. Watt stayed with her family near Miami—has been described as follows:

> Most of the Apaches' homes are wickiups built with a frame of saplings so bowed that the home has the appearance of a rounded dome or old-fashioned beehive. This framework is covered thickly with brush or mats, which are sometimes covered in turn with canvas, sacking, and pieces of tin. Some of the younger and more progressive Indians have put up houses built of a single thickness of board, rarely painted and papered on the inside, and never painted on the outside. . . . Nearly all the homes, whether of board or of brush, are without floors. . . . The Indian families in these camps rarely own a bed, a chair, a table, or any other furniture or household goods such as is found in White homes, excepting perhaps a sewing machine or occasionally a cook stove. Sometimes a few pots, pans, or dishes supplement the pottery and baskets of native make used for cooking, eating, and occasionally tin cans are shaped into eating or cooking utensils. (Meriam et al. 1928:628–83)

Mrs. Watt smiled when I read this passage to her. "That could have been us," she said, "that really could have been us. I guess we were poor in those days— some would say that—but I was still small and didn't even think about it. My father was working and we had plenty to eat. I don't think anybody used to say they was poor 'cause they knew about others that really *was* poor, ones that had hardly nothing." For more on the growth of off-reservation Western Apache wage labor, see Adams and Krutz 1971, Perry 1993, and Cook 1976.

12. The Western Apache puberty ceremony, or "sunrise dance," welcomes a girl to adulthood by casting her in the role of a female mythological figure whom she is encouraged to emulate. Formerly a modest affair, the puberty ceremony has developed into a major social event that requires ex-

tensive planning, support from dozens of people, and large amounts of money. Like other Apache women her age, Mrs. Watt regards these developments as excessive and inappropriate. "It never was that way," she recalled. "That dance used to be small [with] just a few people there. It used to be they exchanged just some cornbreads, that's all. Now it's like a competition [to determine] who can give away the most stuff. That don't look good. That's not the way it's supposed to be." For an ethnographic account of the girls' puberty ceremony, see Basso 1966.

13. Mrs. Watt observed that while the flu pandemic may have peaked in 1919 or 1920, it continued to affect Apache people for several years thereafter. "That flu kept on coming around, coming around. It won't go away for a long time. We were on Apache Trail, so we didn't hear lots about what's going on at Cibecue and Oak Creek and other places on the reservation. But people kept getting sick with that flu, and I heard that some of them died." An informative study of the flu pandemic of 1918–19 has been made by Alfred Crosby (1989).

Chapter Three

1. Dedicated in 1911, Theodore Roosevelt Dam was one of the first projects sponsored by the U.S. Reclamation Service. Impounding more than a million acre-feet of water in Roosevelt Lake, the dam provided flood control and water storage for the Salt River valley as well as limited hydroelectric power. Between 1923 and 1930, three more dams—Mormon Flat, Horse Mesa, and Stewart Mountain—were raised downstream on the Salt River. The Apache Trail, a precipitous road that snaked through the Tonto Basin from Roosevelt to Apache Junction, connected these sites and was used mainly for transporting freight. Scores of Western Apaches built the Apache Trail between 1902 and 1906, and others labored to widen it between 1919 and 1923. Mrs. Watt's family followed the road as it was being improved, winding up at Mormon Flat where her father and one of her brothers worked on Mormon Flat Dam.

For Mrs. Watt, life on the Apache Trail was an eye-opening experience that she remembers with satisfaction. "I seen all kinds of things I never seen before, like those horses with big feet and long hair on them. I don't know, but it could be that I'm the last one still living that went on Apache Trail all the way from Roosevelt to Mormon Flat. Apaches made that road, and that's the reason it's got our name on it. Hardly nobody knows how they worked so hard or what they done when they're fixing that road. People should appreciate what they done." Sources on the Salt River Project and construction of Roosevelt Dam include Meredith 1968, Smith 1986, and Zarbin 1984. Palmer 1979 and Rogge et al. 1995 provide insights into the activities of Apaches and other minority groups at the boomtown of Roosevelt. Works about the Apache Trail are virtually nonexistent, which underscores the importance of Mrs. Watt's accounts.

2. In 1878, more than a thousand Chinese laborers were imported to Ari-

zona to lay track for the Southern Pacific Railroad Company. Later that year, when construction was suspended, those unwilling to return to California found jobs at mines and smelters. Driven out of the mines by virulent acts of racism, some Chinese remained in Arizona, opening small businesses or starting modest truck farms. The Chinese colony of Wheatfields operated one of these farms, and judging from Mrs. Watt's recollections, it must have been successful. "Those Chinese at Wheatfields," she said, "grew lots of vegetables, and what they can't eat themselves they used to take to Globe and other places to sell. Those Chinese people worked hard. They was always doing something in their fields. I don't think they ever just sat around." Sources on the Chinese presence in early Arizona are few and far between, and materials about their truck farms appear to be especially scarce. Thomas Sheridan (1995) presents some information on the role played by Chinese in Arizona's labor economy, and Bradford Luckingham (1994) discusses the development of Chinese communities in Phoenix.

3. Men who gambled at hoop and pole called upon metaphysical powers to help them make high scores. It was these powers, not the game itself, that were dangerous to women and children.

4. Mrs. Watt commented that early censuses of the Western Apache population were often inaccurate and occasionally upsetting. "The reason," she observed, "is that the white people didn't understand how we group our families—you know, who's in this family, who's in that family—so they wrote it down wrong in their book. And then again, they just count the Indians they can find, but lots of them could be gone somewhere, 'cause in those days people used to travel all the time . . . and they just throwed some of the names away. That's what happened to us long years ago. My mother tried and tried to get it back—'Tulene'—but they already wrote 'Case' in their book. They told my mother, they said, 'It's already in there, so you can't get it back.'"

Chapter Four

1. When Western Apaches were given English names, they were sometimes those of famous people. Charles Dickens, after whom Charley Dickens was named, was one of them. Others mentioned by Mrs. Watt were Alexander Hume, Oliver Cromwell, Oliver Holmes, and Theodore Roosevelt.

2. Founded in 1872 and 1876, respectively, Safford and Solomon were Mormon agricultural communities. The main crops planted were wheat, oats, barley, and corn, followed in later years by alfalfa and cotton. Irrigated with water drawn from the Gila River, approximately thirty-five thousand acres of farmland were under cultivation by 1940. According to Mrs. Watt, hundreds of Apache people, most of them from San Carlos, took seasonal jobs in the fields of these two communities as late as 1960.

3. When the members of Mrs. Watt's family contracted trachoma, it was,

after tuberculosis, the most prevalent disease among American Indian reservation populations. A microbial inflammation marked by the formation of minute granules on the inner surface of the eyelid, trachoma resulted frequently in partial or total blindness. Advanced cases of the disease were treated in one of two ways: grattage, in which the trachotamus granules were scraped to stimulate the healing process, and tarsectomy, in which affected portions of the tarsal plate of the eyelid were surgically excised. Both procedures were painful, and neither could be counted on to provide a permanent cure. At the trachoma camp at San Carlos, and at the Fort Apache trachoma clinic where Ann Beatty was later a patient, the method used was probably grattage. For a discussion of the effects of trachoma on Indian reservations in the United States, see Meriam et al. 1928.

4. After receiving a vision in 1904, Silas John Edwards, a Western Apache medicine man, founded a religious movement that attracted many followers. Prominently featuring the ritual handling of snakes, the movement caused alarm among reservation authorities, who feared that it might lead to widespread insurrection. (In fact, as Mrs. Watt makes clear, it offered a new set of practices for preventing and curing sickness.) The inventor of a writing system used to inscribe his prayers, Edwards was falsely convicted of murdering his wife and sent to prison in Washington. During his absence, assistants trained in the writing system kept the religion alive. It has not died and continues to be practiced on both the San Carlos and Fort Apache reservations. Kessel 1976 presents an analysis of the social and economic conditions under which Edwards's religion flourished. His unique system of writing is described and illustrated in Basso and Anderson 1980.

Chapter Six

1. D. V. Marley owned a sprawling cattle ranch whose headquarters were located on Cherry Creek, a stream near the western boundary of the Fort Apache Reservation. An accomplished horse wrangler was crucial on such a ranch, and if Charley Marley had lacked the requisite skills, D. V. Marley would not have hired him. That Charley Marley remained on the ranch "for a long time, many years" indicates that his work was consistently satisfactory, which was probably one of the reasons that he and his employer became good friends. For glimpses of D. V. Marley's cattle operation, see Ellison 1981.

2. Of Welsh-Irish descent, Francis Theodore ("Mac") McQuillin was born in Chicago in 1896. After serving in France during World War I he joined the U.S. Indian Service as an agricultural extension agent. With his wife and three young daughters, he arrived at Cibecue in 1927. McQuillin cleared land and planted trees, gave instruction to Apaches in modern farming methods, improved the community's irrigation system, and served at times in the capacity of policeman. He also distributed government "surplus commodities" and generously built coffins when called upon to do so. His wife, the former

Stella May Ford, spent countless hours showing Apache women how to can fruits and vegetables.

Mrs. Watt recalled that the McQuillins were helpful and popular people. "It seems like to me," she said, "that McQuillin got along good with everybody except some of the Cromwells. He helped everybody out, him and his wife. He used to come to Chediskai. He asked my stepfather, 'Charley, do you need something? I'll try and get it for you.' He asked my mother, 'Do you need dry milk?' He used to bring stuff down there for them. One thing McQuillin didn't like was people drinking too much *tulipai* [a fermented corn beverage], and that's why those Cromwells got mad. I don't know what happened. I heard he knocked over three or four of their cans [of tulipai], and they weren't even drinking it yet. They were saving it for a party or something. One of them started fighting with him. After that, those Cromwells didn't like McQuillin. I don't think he ever had trouble with nobody else. Him and his wife—she was a real nice lady—lived in Cibecue for a long, long time. They always had a garden. It's big! They grew lots of vegetables, all different kinds, and they used to give it away to people that came by."

Chapter Seven

1. For a valuable study of Western Apache agricultural methods and techniques, including those used to cultivate corn, see Buskirk 1986.

2. *Túłbáí*, commonly spelled tulipai, is a mild alcoholic beverage made with fermented corn. Considered a food by Western Apache people, it was served at social gatherings and ceremonial events. Consuming large quantities of túłbáí could produce intoxication, but Mrs. Watt reported that this happened only rarely during her years at Chediskai:

> Hardly nobody got drunk on túłbáí back then. They just drank it to keep the hungry away, or when they were sitting around with their friends and visitors. The ones that got drunk, they got drunk on moonshine. That stuff [moonshine] was *bad*! The police used to come around and tell them, "Don't make no more túłbáí, it's against the law." But they kept on making it. They never did stop. And sometimes a police came around and told them, he said, "Well, I know you got it somewhere. Can I drink some?" They went and got it. They gave him some. He drank it. "That's good," he said. "I was hungry but now I'm OK." Then he took off.

3. Western Apache pit roasting was an arduous activity involving both men and women. As many as five hundred ears of corn might be cooked at one time in this manner. Frequently, the roasted ears were stored in underground caches for use in winter and early spring, the time when other foods were likely to be in short supply. A detailed description of the roasting process appears in the unpublished papers of Gayle Potter-Basso. In this regard, see also Buskirk 1986.

4. The first trading post at Cibecue was built in the 1920s by a man named Schuster, the son of a freighter from Holbrook. For reasons unknown, the store closed down after three or four years. In 1932, F. E. Knapp opened the Cibecue Trading Company, a successful business inherited by his son, Boyd Knapp, who ran it until 1965. Corydon Carleton (Don) Cooley, Sr., built a second trading post at Cibecue in 1934, which he named Apache Traders. The only son of Colonel Eliaphet Corydon Cooley, a famous Arizona pioneer and influential advisor to early leaders of the White Mountain Apache Tribe, "Don Senior," as he was known, ran Apache Traders until it was taken over by his son, Richard Carleton (Dick) Cooley, and later by another son, Corydon Carleton (Don) Cooley, Jr. "Don Junior's" son, Corydon Michael (Mike) Cooley, purchased Boyd Knapp's store in 1966 and has run it ever since. It is the last of the original trading posts at Cibecue still in operation.

Chapter Eight

1. Excellent photographs of the kinds of objects made by Western Apache people, including many mentioned in this book, are presented in Ferg 1987.

2. Acorns of emory oak (*Quercus emoryi*) were a basic Apache foodstuff when Mrs. Watt's family was living at Chediskai. Eaten uncooked and in stews, acorns were also exchanged for baskets, cloth, and other kinds of food. "Long years ago," Mrs. Watt commented, "acorns was kind of like money. If you had some left over, you could get different things. My mother used to do that all the time. She even got stuff from the store with acorns."

3. During the years Mrs. Watt lived at Chediskai, Western Apache women rode horses as often as men. According to Mrs. Watt, many of the women were sure and accomplished riders, and her mother was among them. "My mother never did get bucked off—well, maybe once or twice, I don't know. See, the horses wasn't always real tame, and if they see or hear something they don't like, they started *going*! Nobody cared about getting bucked off 'cause those horses were short, so if you got bucked off you don't fall far. My mother was like that, she didn't care. She rode horses all the time, everywhere. When I was staying down there at Chediskai, I did that too."

4. After 1940, when a fish hatchery was established at Williams Creek on the Fort Apache Indian Reservation, slaughtered feral horses were taken there to be processed for fish food. Initially sporadic, this effort at stock reduction later became widespread, mainly because the wild horses, which numbered in the thousands, were overgrazing extensive tracts of grassland.

Chapter Nine

1. Mrs. Watt is referring here to the featureless face-coverings of Western Apache *gáán* masks. For photographs of some of these masks, see Ferg 1987.

2. Mrs. Watt pointed out that Bikee' Delichí'é was a rarity among Western Apache herbalists, one who learned from singing which plants to use as medicine for her patients. The great majority of herbalists, including Rose Lupe and Ann Beatty, made such decisions using silent or spoken prayers. That Bikee' Delichí'é did otherwise suggests that she, like Western Apache medicine men, had knowledge of a metaphysical power who assisted in her work.

3. The Western Apache gáán ceremony, also known as the "crown dance," was the most elaborately staged of all Apache rituals. Dramatic and compelling, it was frequently performed to combat mental illness. For additional information about the ceremony, see Goodwin 1938a and 1938b and Goodwin and Kluckhohn 1943.

4. The ceremony witnessed at Oak Creek by Eva Watt's mother and stepfather was associated with a religious movement known as *dahghodigá* (They will be raised upward), which flourished on the San Carlos and Fort Apache reservations between 1903 and 1907. The movement was started by a medicine man from Cibecue who proclaimed that his followers would be lifted into the sky while a massive flood or earthquake cleansed the earth of evil; they would then be lowered down and embark on a better life than any they had known before. As Mrs. Watt's account suggests, this prophecy failed to come true. Descriptions and interpretations of the dahghodigá movement are presented in Goodwin and Kaut 1954 and in Kessel 1976.

Chapter Ten

1. Sequestered near the borders of the Fort Apache and San Carlos reservations, moonshiners like Whiteman With Shortened Arm sometimes combined a legitimate business, such as mining asbestos, with the illegal sale of whiskey to Western Apache people. Mrs. Watt recalled that other moonshiners plied their clandestine trade on both sides of the Salt and Black Rivers, and at points near the present towns of Pinetop and McNary.

2. The Civilian Conservation Corps (CCC) was established in 1933 as a New Deal program to combat unemployment during the Great Depression. Unemployed men were enlisted to work on conservation and resource development projects such as flood control and protection of forests and wildlife. On the Fort Apache and San Carlos reservations, where unemployment rates were extremely high, CCC Apache crews built roads, fences, irrigation channels, and a number of large earthen stock tanks. The Civilian Conservation Corps was abolished in 1942.

3. Cattle were introduced onto the Fort Apache and San Carlos reservations during the 1870s and 1880s. Both reservations were later divided into a number of grazing districts managed by non-Indian stockmen. These districts evolved into cattle associations—the Oak Creek, Grasshopper, and Cibecue associations were among them—which were operated exclusively by local

Apache cattle owners. During the 1950s and '60s, the Fort Apache and San Carlos herds of purebred Herefords were considered among the best in the American Southwest. McGuire 1980 presents an in-depth account of the beginnings and early growth of the cattle industry on the Fort Apache Indian Reservation. For a study of the cattle economy on the San Carlos Apache Reservation, see Getty 1963.

4. Founded by Mormon settlers in the late 1870s, Show Low, Shumway, and Snowflake were small ranching communities when Mrs. Watt trailed cattle from Oak Creek with her stepfather and mother. Holbrook, their destination, was a railhead from which cattlemen in the surrounding area shipped thousands of head of livestock. For a lengthy study of the largest ranch in the area, the Hashknife, see Carlock 1994.

Chapter Eleven

1. Mrs. Watt emphasized that she would not have gone to Phoenix, nor would she have stayed there, unless other Apache women were living in the city. Without their support and companionship, she said, working far from home in unfamiliar surroundings would have been more difficult.

> Us [Apache] ladies kind of stuck together. It's hard down there at first 'cause you're just all alone. I didn't know nobody except for my cousin Bessie. One time, I told her, "I'm thinking to go home." She said, "You been here only a few days. If you stay, you'll get used to it." I said, "OK, I'll try." I stayed. After a while, we got to know some of the ladies [that were] down there already, and where they lived, and how to get together with them when they have their days off, like Saturday and Sunday. We used to go places together, like for shopping, and we talked our own language, Apache. We bought stuff to take back home. "I'm gonna give this to my mother. I'm gonna give that to my sister." I guess we was always thinking about our relatives. We got used to it down there, though. After a while, you know [what] to expect. At first, Phoenix was a big city to me, a big one. But it's small—not like today—and it's easy to go around from place to place. Us Apache ladies hardly went nowhere alone unless it's with the families we was working for.

Chapter Twelve

1. Western Apache "home brew" was made with brewer's yeast, malt syrup, sugar, and water. Mrs. Watt reported that it was sometimes "spiced up" with pinches of smokeless tobacco and spoonfuls of cough syrup. "That stuff was just awful!" she said. "It's *terrible*! I don't know how people used to drink it!"

Glossary of Apache Terms and Expressions

báń ditané. Thick tortilla
béshnagháí. Car; literally, metal wagon
béshnałtsoos. Identification tag; literally, metal paper
Bichı̨h Nteelé. Wide Nose; a proper name
Bikee' Déłichí'é. Pink Foot; a proper name
Bisząhą. Clay Riverbank People; a clan
ch'a baané. Bat; literally, big ears
ch'idii. Gossip
chigolshahá. Devil's claw (*Proboscida parviflora*); literally, sharp at the tip
Ch'ígoná'áí nitis dahsol'ees hela'. Don't let the sun step over you.
chíh. Hematite
ch'iłdiiyé. Walnut (*Juglans major*); literally, one pounds it
ch'il nteelé. Shrub live oak (*Quercus turbinella*); literally, wide bush
ch'ínk'ózhé. Skunkbush (*Rhus trilobata*); literally, sour berries
Dahgodighá. They will be raised upward; the name of a religious movement
Dahnagolk'id. Terraced Hills; a place-name
dijı̨́ı̨́zhi. Roasted corn; literally, it shrinks
diltałé. Alligator juniper (*Juniperus deppeana*) berries; literally, it opens up
dinos. Manzanita (*Arctostaphylos pungens*) berries
Dǫ' Bi Gową. Flies' Home; a place-name
Dził Cho. Chediskai Mountain; literally, Big Mountain; a place-name
Dził Nabaa. Hazy Mountain; a place-name
gáán. Crown dancers
Gáán Libayé. Dull-color crown dancer
Gochǫ́' Ha'itin. Bad Where The Road Goes Up; a place-name
gogíshé. Beargrass (*Nolina microcarpa*); literally, sharp one
Golkizhń. Spotted Country People; a Western Apache band name
gonatáhá. Stick game; literally, you try to find it
gozhǫǫ sįh. Goodness songs
hádndín. Cattail (*Typha domingensis*) pollen

Ha'ią́ha. Chiricahua or Mescalero Apache; literally, People of the East

hosh nteelé. Prickly pear (*Opuntia engelmanni*); literally, wide cactus

i'dii ch'il. Yerba santa (*Erio dictyon augustifolium*); literally, thunder bush

igáyé. Broadleaf yucca (*Yucca baccata*)

igáyé ts'ǫ́sé. Narrowleaf yucca (*Yucca augustifolium*)

ik'ah. Grease; fat

ikaz. Century plant (*Agave palmeri*) stalk

ínłgaashn. Witch

isdzaní binii'. Literally, woman's face; plant species not named by tribal request

it'ą̄ą̄. Generic term for several plant species with thick green leaves; commonly translated "wild spinach"

izee. Plant medicine; medicine made with plants

izee łibaahí. Desert lavender (*Hyptis emoryi*); literally, dull-color plant medicine

izee sidogí. Literally, it heats you up plant medicine; plant species not named by tribal request

jeeh. Piñon (*Pinus edulis*) pitch

kǫ' dahosh. Thistle (*Cirsium arizonicum*); literally, fire thorn

kǫ' diyiní. Fire medicine man

łóg łikizhí. Trout; literally, spotted fish

Má' bitsee'. Fox Tail; a proper name

ma' nteelé bidáá'. Black-eyed pea; literally, badger's eye

nadą́' cho. Literally, big corn (*Zea mays*)

nadą́' dotł'izhí. Literally, blue corn (*Zea mays*)

nadą́' łigai. Literally, white corn (*Zea mays*)

nadą́' łitsogí. Literally, yellow corn (*Zea mays*)

nadah. Century plant (*Agave palmeri*); term also designates the heart of this plant

Nadah Cho Si'áń. A Big Agave Heart Sits; a place-name

Nadah Nch'íí'. Bitter Agave; a place-name

Nádots'osíń. Slender Peak Standing Up People; a clan

na'ishǫ' bibésh. A type of arrowhead used in ceremonies

na'iyee' sįh. Strength songs

na'izhǫǫsh. Hoop and pole game

nałbiil. Car

nalwod go'áíleh. It makes him strong; a ceremony

Ndaa Bigan Nagodé. Whiteman With Shortened Arm; a proper name

Ndee ndaaye'. Enemies are coming.

Nest'áń Yoliłé. Harvest carrier; translated by Eva Watt as "She Brings Home Fruits And Vegetables"; a proper name

shik'isn. My sister

shindalé. My grandfather

Sįh doo yinaldíh dah. He Can't Remember His Song; a place-name

táts'aa. Burden basket

T'iiskaadń. Cottonwoods Standing People; a clan

T'iis Sikaad. Cottonwoods Standing; a place-name

Tséch'ishjiné. Rock Protruding Out Darkly People; a Western Apache clan

Tséé Bika' Naaditin. Trail Goes Across On Top Of Rocks; a place-name

Tsééch'iizhé. Sandstone; literally, Flaking Rock; a place-name

Tsééda'i. Edge Of The Cliff; a proper name

Tséétęh Na'áá. Rock Standing In The Water; a place-name

Tsééyaa Goltsogí. Yellow Below The Rocks; a place-name

túłbáí. Tulipai; literally, dull-color water; a mild alcoholic beverage

Túłgayé Dotł'izhí. Blue Donkey; a proper name

túnch'íí'. Whiskey; literally, bitter water; also a proper name

Tú Ńlįį'. Water Flowing; a place-name

tús. Water jug

References Cited

Adams, David
1995   *Education for Extinction: American Indians and the Boarding School Experience, 1873–1928.* Lawrence: University Press of Kansas.

Adams, William, and Gordon Krutz
1971   The Development of San Carlos Apache Wage Labor to 1954. In *Apachean Ethnology and Culture History*, Keith Basso and Morris Opler, eds., pp. 115–129. Tucson: University of Arizona Press.

Ball, Eve
1980   *Indeh: An Apache Odyssey.* Provo, Utah: Brigham Young University Press.

Bassett, Everett
1994   "We Took Care of Each Other Like Families Were Meant To": Gender, Social Organization, and Wage Labor among the Apache at Roosevelt. In *Those of Little Note: Gender, Race and Class in Historical Archeology*, Elizabeth Scott, ed., pp. 55–79. Tucson: University of Arizona Press.

Basso, Keith
1966   *The Gift of Changing Woman.* Bulletin of the Bureau of American Ethnology no. 196. Washington, D.C.: Smithsonian Institution.
1969   *Western Apache Witchcraft.* Anthropological Papers of the University of Arizona 15. Tucson: University of Arizona Press.
1970   *The Cibecue Apache.* New York: Holt, Rinehart and Winston.
1971   *Western Apache Raiding and Warfare: From the Notes of Grenville Goodwin.* Tucson: University of Arizona Press.
1996   *Wisdom Sits in Places: Landscape and Language among the Western Apache.* Albuquerque: University of New Mexico Press.

Basso, Keith, ed.
1990   *Western Apache Language and Culture: Essays in Linguistic Anthropology.* Tucson: University of Arizona Press.

Basso, Keith, and Ned Anderson
1980   A Western Apache Writing System. In *Western Apache Language and*

Culture: Essays in Linguistic Anthropology, Keith Basso, ed., pp. 25–52. Tucson: University of Arizona Press.

Bigando, Bob
1988   *Holy Angels Church: The Catholic Church in Globe, Arizona (1876–1976)*. Globe: Charles B. Bigando, Jr.

Bray, Dorothy, ed.
1998   *Western Apache–English Dictionary: A Community-Generated Bilingual Dictionary*. Tempe, Arizona: Bilingual Press/Editorial Bilingüe.

Buskirk, Winfred
1986   *The Western Apache: Living with the Land before 1930*. Norman: University of Oklahoma Press.

Carlock, Robert
1994   *The Hashknife: The Early Days of the Aztec Land and Cattle Company, Limited*. Tucson: Westernlore Press.

Child, Brenda
1998   *Boarding School Seasons: American Indian Families, 1900–1940*. Lincoln: University of Nebraska Press.

Clum, John
1874   *Annual Report of the Commissioner of Indian Affairs to the Secretary of the Interior*. Washington, D.C.: U.S. Government Printing Office.
1875   *Annual Report of the Commissioner of Indian Affairs to the Secretary of the Interior*. Washington, D.C.: U.S. Government Printing Office.

Clum, Woodworth
1936   *Apache Agent: The Story of John P. Clum*. New York: Houghton Mifflin.

Coleman, Michael
1993   *American Indian Children at School, 1850–1930*. Jackson: University of Mississippi Press.

Cook, Charles
1976   A History of San Carlos and Fort Apache Indian Reservations. Defendant's Exhibit C-1, *San Carlos et al. v. United States*. Docket Number 22-H. Washington, D.C.: Indian Claims Commission.

Crosby, Alfred
1989   *America's Forgotten Pandemic: The Influenza of 1918*. Cambridge: Cambridge University Press.

Davis, Britton
1929   *The Truth about Geronimo*. New Haven: Yale University Press.

Debo, Angie
1976   *Geronimo: The Man, His Time, His Place*. Norman: University of Oklahoma Press.

Ellison, Glenn
1981   *Cowboys under the Mogollon Rim*. Tucson: University of Arizona Press.

Ferg, Alan, ed.
1987   *Western Apache Material Culture: The Goodwin and Guenther Collections*. Tucson: University of Arizona Press.

Geertz, Clifford
1976   "From the Native's Point of View": On the Nature of Anthropological Understanding. In *Meaning in Anthropology*, Keith H. Basso and Henry A. Selby, eds., pp. 221–237. Albuquerque: University of New Mexico Press.

Getty, Harry
1963   *The San Carlos Indian Cattle Industry*. Anthropological Papers of the University of Arizona 7. Tucson: University of Arizona Press.

Goodwin, Grenville
1938a   *Myths and Tales of the White Mountain Apache*. Philadelphia: American Folklore Society.
1938b   White Mountain Apache Religion. *American Anthropologist* 40:24–37.
1942   *The Social Organization of the Western Apache*. Chicago: University of Chicago Press.

Goodwin, Grenville, and Charles Kaut
1954   A Native Religious Movement among the White Mountain and Cibecue Apache. *Southwestern Journal of Anthropology* 10:385–404.

Goodwin, Grenville, and Clyde Kluckhohn
1943   A Comparison of Navajo and White Mountain Apache Ceremonial Forms and Categories. *Southwestern Journal of Anthropology* 1:498–506.

Graves, Michael
1982   Western Apache Adaptation to the Mountains. In *Cholla Project Archaeology: The Q Ranch Region*, vol. 3, J. Jefferson Reid, ed., pp. 193–213. Archaeological Series no. 161. Tucson: Arizona State Museum.

Greenfeld, Philip
2001   Escape from Albuquerque: An Apache Memorate. *American Indian Culture and Research Journal* 25(3):47–71.

Griffon, Bion, M. Leone, and K. Basso
1971   Western Apache Ecology: From Horticulture to Agriculture. In *Apachean Culture History and Ethnology*, Keith Basso and Morris Opler, eds., pp. 69–72. Tucson: University of Arizona Press.

Hagan, Maxine
1959   An Educational History of the Pima and Papago Peoples from the Mid-Seventeenth Century to the Mid-Twentieth Century. Ph.D. dissertation, Department of Education, University of Missouri, Columbia.

Hagan, William
1966   *Indian Police and Judges: Experiments in Acculturation and Control*. New Haven: Yale University Press.

Hoxie, Frederick, ed.
1996   *Encyclopedia of North American Indians: Native American History, Culture, and Life from PaleoIndians to the Present*. Boston: Houghton Mifflin.

Kaut, Charles
1957   *The Western Apache Clan System: Its Origins and Development.* Publica-
         tions in Anthropology no. 9. Albuquerque: University of New Mexico
         Press.
Kessel, William
1976   White Mountain Apache Religious Cult Movements: A Study in Ethno-
         history. Ph.D. dissertation, Department of Anthropology, University
         of Arizona.
Limerick, Patricia
2000   Believing in the American West. In *Something in the Soil: Legacies and
         Reckonings in the New West,* by Patricia Limerick, pp. 308–318. New
         York: W. W. Norton.
Luckingham, Bradford
1994   *Minorities in Phoenix: A Profile of Mexican American, Chinese Ameri-
         can, and African American Communities, 1860–1992.* Tucson: Univer-
         sity of Arizona Press.
Martin, Rena
2002   Two Navajo Clan Traditions: Our Mothers, Our Fathers, Our Connec-
         tions. M.A. thesis, Department of American Studies, University of
         New Mexico.
McGuire, Thomas
1980   *Mixed-bloods, Apaches, and Cattle Barons: Documents for a History of the
         Livestock Economy on the White Mountain Apache Reservation.* Archeo-
         logical Series no. 142. Tucson: Arizona State Museum, University of
         Arizona.
Meredith, H. L.
1968   Reclamation of the Salt River Valley, 1902–1917. *Journal of the West*
         7:76–83.
Meriam, Lewis, et al.
1928   *The Problem of Indian Administration.* Institute for Government Re-
         search, Studies in Administration. Baltimore: Johns Hopkins Univer-
         sity Press.
Mihesuah, Devon
1998   *Natives and Academics: Researching and Writing about American Indi-
         ans.* Lincoln: University of Nebraska Press.
Myer, Albert
1898   *Annual Report of the Commissioner of Indian Affairs to the Secretary of
         the Interior.* Washington, D.C.: U.S. Government Printing Office.
Ogle, R.
1970   *Federal Control of the Western Apache, 1848–1886.* Albuquerque: Uni-
         versity of New Mexico Press.
Olson, Olof
1904   *Annual Report of the Commissioner of Indian Affairs to the Secretary of
         the Interior.* Washington, D.C.: U.S. Government Printing Office.

Ortiz, Alfonzo, ed.
1983   *Handbook of North American Indians*, vol. 10, *Southwest*. Washington, D.C.: Smithsonian Institution.

Palmer, Ralph
1979   *Doctor on Horseback*. Mesa, Arizona: Mesa Historical and Archeological Society.

Parmee, Edward
1968   *Formal Education and Culture Change: A Modern Apache Indian Community and Government Education Programs*. Tucson: University of Arizona Press.

Perry, Richard
1991   *Western Apache Heritage: People of the Mountain Corridor*. Austin: University of Texas Press.

1993   *Apache Reservation: Indigenous Peoples and the American State*. Austin: University of Texas Press.

Prucha, Francis
1979   *The Churches and the Indian Schools, 1888–1912*. Lincoln: University of Nebraska Press.

Rice, Sedgewick
1898   *Annual Report of the Commissioner of Indian Affairs to the Secretary of the Interior*. Washington, D.C.: U.S. Government Printing Office.

Rogge, A. E., et al.
1995   *Raising Arizona's Dams: Daily Life, Danger, and Discrimination in the Dam Construction Camps of Central Arizona, 1890s–1940s*. Tucson: University of Arizona Press.

Sheridan, Thomas
1995   *Arizona: A History*. Tucson: University of Arizona Press.

Smith, Karen
1986   *The Magnificent Experiment: Building the Salt River Reclamation Project, 1890–1917*. Tucson: University of Arizona Press.

Spicer, Edward
1962   Western Apaches. In *Cycles of Conquest: The Impact of Spain, Mexico, and the United States on the Indians of the Southwest, 1533–1960*, by Edward Spicer, pp. 229–261. Tucson: University of Arizona Press.

Thrapp, Dan
1964   *Al Sieber: Chief of Scouts*. Norman: University of Oklahoma Press.
1967   *The Conquest of Apacheria*. Norman: University of Oklahoma Press.

Tiffany, J. C.
1881   *Annual Report of the Commissioner of Indian Affairs to the Secretary of the Interior*. Washington, D.C.: U.S. Government Printing Office.

Trennert, Robert
1988   *The Phoenix Indian School: Forced Assimilation in Arizona, 1891–1935*. Norman: University of Oklahoma Press.

Vanderpot, Rein, and Teresita Majewski
1998   *The Forgotten Soldiers: Historical and Archaeological Investigations at Fort Huachuca, Arizona.* SRI Technical Series no. 71. Tucson: Statistical Research.

Wharfield, Harold
1965   *With Scouts and Cavalry at Fort Apache.* Tucson: Arizona Historical Society.

Woody, Clara, and Milton Schwartz
1977   *Globe, Arizona: Early Times in a Little World of Copper and Cattle.* Tucson: Arizona Historical Society.

Worcester, Donald
1979   *The Apaches: Eagles of the Southwest.* Norman: University of Oklahoma Press.

Zarbin, Earl
1984   *Roosevelt Dam: A History to 1911.* Phoenix: Salt River Project.

Photograph Credits

Arizona Historical Society, Tucson

Members of William Lupe's family: neg. 28895 (detail)
John Lupe (Z-3): neg. 22780, Ellison Collection
Western Apache women carrying firewood: neg. 58631, Gladys Woods Collection
Western Apache women gambling: neg. 30409 (detail)
D. V. Marley: neg. 53909, J. W. Ellison Collection

Arizona State Museum

Joseph Hoffman: photograph by Grenville Goodwin

Arizona State University Libraries

Western Apaches riding the train: neg. CP SPC 187:4.51, Uplegger Collection
Western Apaches seeking rations: neg. CP SPC 187:4.55, Uplegger Collection
Western Apache homes on shore of Roosevelt Lake: neg. CP SPC 44:75 27136, Russell Todd Collection
Fish Creek Canyon: neg. CP SPC 44:75 27110, Russell Todd Collection
Apache Trail descending to Mormon Flat: neg. CP SPC 44:75 27096, Russell Todd Collection
Silas John Edwards with assistants: neg. CP SPC 290.1, Odd Halseth Collection

Bush, Sadie

Rose Lupe with her daughter-in-law

Case, Jack

Western Apache laborers (Eugene Case)
Students at St. Johns Indian School

Gáán dancers at St. Johns Indian School
Western Apache students departing for vacation
Ann Beatty and Charley Marley's wickiup
Ann Beatty with unidentified children
Blue, Charley Marley's donkey, ridden by Jack Tulene Case
Eva Tulene Case, about 1930
Joe Tulene Case

National Anthropological Archives, Smithsonian Institution

Woman bringing grass to sell at Fort San Carlos: photograph by D. A. Markey, Inv. 02083600, Colonel E. A. Mearns Collection
Western Apaches delivering grass: photograph by A. Miller, neg. 74-11686
William Lupe (F-1): photograph by Walter Hough, neg. 43,733A
John Lupe's home at Oak Creek: photograph by Walter Hough, neg. 43,733
Government boarding school at San Carlos: Inv. 02009200
Western Apaches waiting to collect rations: photograph by C. S. Fly, neg. 43,005F
Western Apache homes near Fort San Carlos: photograph by C. S. Fly, neg. 43,004A
Western Apache woman uprooting an agave plant: photograph by Edward S. Curtis, neg. 76-4665
Homes of Western Apache mine workers: photograph Neil M. Judd, Inv. 02079800

National Museum of the American Indian

Government boarding school at Rice: photograph by Frank C. Churchill, neg. N26419
Western Apache girls with superintendent, Rice: photograph by Frank C. Churchill, neg. N26421
Western Apache girls at Rice Indian school: photograph by Frank C. Churchill, neg. N26418
Western Apache homes on Cibecue Creek: photograph by Edward H. Davis, neg. N34925

Nohwike' Bagowa, White Mountain Apache Culture Center and Museum

William Goshoney (A-2)
Temporary Western Apache home near Roosevelt Dam
Western Apache woman grinding corn
William Taylee (C-1)

Western Apache family at home near Cibecue
David Dale, Western Apache medicine man
Western Apache cowboys herding cattle

Salt River Project Research Archives

Roosevelt Dam: neg. R-487
Western Apache laborers on the Apache Trail: photograph by Walter J. Lubkin,
    IN-11 (detail)
Western Apache laborers working with mules: photograph by Walter J. Lubkin,
    IN-09 (detail)
Western Apache laborers using mule-drawn sleds: photograph by Walter J.
    Lubkin, RD-56
Mormon Flat Dam: 8034/10
Entrance to the salt cave: photograph by Walter J. Lubkin, WJL 287

Watt, Eva

John Tulene and Ann Beatty with son Dewey
Eva Tulene Case and her son Reuben Kessay
Eva Tulene Case, 1947 or 1948
Eva and William Watt, about 1952
Eva Tulene Watt with her children John and Ora Watt
Ann Beatty at home in Cibecue

Index

acorns, 175; gambling for, 111; making stew with, 258; picking, 41, 159, 187, 189, 229; using as currency, 318n. 2
alcohol, 11, 102–3, 178–79, 224–25, 229–30, 234–36, 246–47, 274, 276, 278, 305n. 4, 319n. 1. *See also* Túłbáí
Apache Trail, 77, 79–81, 88–93, 98, 314n. 1
asbestos mine, 40, 223–24
athlete's foot, 274

Bat (Ch'a baané), 42–43
bears, 93, 156–58, 196. *See also* Tommy
Beatty, Ann, xix, xx, 100, 154, 284; birthplace of, 32; death of, 281–85; goes to Carlisle Indian school, 35–36, 87; as herbalist, 45, 73–75, 92, 200–201, 206–8; making baskets, 64, 118, 175, 208; marries Charley Marley, 140; marries John Langley Tulene, 39; as midwife, 203–6; moves family to trachoma camp, 116–18; as proficient English speaker, 87; raising pet animals, 193–96
Beatty, James, 36–37, 217–18

Beatty, Robert, 24, 36–38, 40, 173, 218
Beatty, Victor, 28, 36–37, 202
Bichįh Nteelé (Wide Nose), 184, 193–95, 218–19
Bikee' Déłichí'é (Pink Foot), an herbalist and singer, 208, 319n. 2
Blue House Mountain, 11, 17, 23–24, 217
boarding schools: Carlisle Indian Industrial School, 35–36, 309n. 24; children's work at, 54–55, 137–38; Fort Apache, 254, 307n. 12; hunger at, 33, 54, 312n. 5; punishment at, 33–35, 54–55, 131–32, 143, 312n. 5; Rice, 54–56, 311n. 5; San Carlos, 32–35, 308n. 21, 309n. 22; use of Apache language at, 36, 54, 131. *See also* St. Johns Indian School and Mission
Bullock, Francis: wife of, 207
Bullock, Nora and Fanny, 263
Button, George, 75, 208

Camp Verde: home of Tulene, 10
Case, Augustine, 39–40, 98, 118–19, 145, 255
Case, Dewey Tulene, 37, 40, 53, 57, 81–82, 100, 217–18, 282

Case, Donna Tulene, xix, 39, 59, 73–74; death of, xx, 40, 107, 123–26
Case, Eugene Tulene, 39, 50, 53, 107, 283; helping Silas John Edwards, 119–23; working at Roosevelt Dam, 58, 77, 80
Case, Frank, 14–15, 42, 64
Case, Jack Tulene, 39, 79, 233–34; on Blue, 190; at St. Johns school, 59, 130–31
Case, Joseph Tulene, 37, 40, 59, 79, 131, 216, 218–19, 233; helps capture an outlaw, 236–41
Case, Paul Tulene, 39, 50; death of, xx, 59
cattle drives, xx, 241–47, 320n. 4
ceremonies, xix, xxii, 307n. 13; boys', 201–3; curing, 25, 28–29, 208–13, 215–16; gáán, 210–13; holy ground, 120–23, 283; sunrise, 71–72
Chediskai: farms at, 149, 153, 164
Chediskai Mountain. See Dził Cho
Cherry Creek: cattle ranch at, 88, 151
chickenpox, 136–37
chigolshahá (devil's claw), 23
chíh (hematite), 48
childbirth, 203–6
ch'iłdiiyé (walnut), 31
childrearing, xxi, 39, 41–43, 153, 304n. 7
children's work: carrying water, collecting firewood, gathering plants/roots/nuts, and grinding corn, 71, 92, 123, 159
Chinese farmers near Wheatfields, 82–84, 315n. 2
ch'ínk'ózhé (skunkbush), 72, 175, 201, 283
Christmas parties, 181–83
Cibecue day school, 37–38, 159, 271, 309n. 26

Civilian Conservation Corps (CCC), 231, 319n. 2
Clum, John, 308n. 22
colds, 200–201
Cooley, Lucinda, 159–60
corn (nadá' cho): roasting, 61–62, 167, 317n. 3; varieties of, 23

Dahgodighá (They Will Be Raised Upward), 319n. 4
Dahnagolk'id (Terraced Hills), 84–86, 107
Dale, David: as medicine man, 209–11, 252
Davis, Paul, 187
Dazen family, 165, 225
Declay, Lee, 174
Dehose, Gussie, 36
Dehose, Judy (Early), 275
Dickens, Charlie, 99, 108, 110, 279–80
dijíízhi (roasted corn), 116, 175. See also corn
diltałé (alligator juniper berries), 175
dinos (manzanita berries), 63, 91, 175
Dǫ' Bi Gową (Flies' Home), 158, 188
"Don't let the sun step over you!" (Ch'ígona'áí nitis dahsol'ees hela'), xxii, 203; phrase explained, 41–42
Dził Cho: Chediskai Mountain (Big Mountain), 156, 169, 184
Dził Nabaa (Hazy Mountain), 163

eagles, 162–63
Early, Kenzie, 132, 208, 274–76
Early, Scott: as medicine man, 208–9
Early, Zema, 132
Edwards, Silas John, 107, 119–23, 316n. 4
English language, xx–xxi, 12, 35, 76, 87, 131, 222, 225, 266; use of, for

Don't Let The Sun Step Over You, 301n. 2

farming, 16–19, 23, 101, 166–69, 317n. 1
Fish Creek, 94–97, 105
food and foodstuffs, 13, 16, 31, 49, 91–92, 101, 104, 153–55, 168–70
food storage, 153, 168, 174–76
Fort Apache, 7, 305n. 3
Fort San Carlos, 6, 46–48, 52, 305n. 3, 311n. 3
funerary and burial customs, 113–15

gáán (crown dancers), 205, 210–13, 319n. 3
gambling, xix, xxii, 81, 84–86, 93–94, 99, 108, 111, 233–34, 260, 262
Geertz, Clifford, xv
Gochǫ' Ha'itin (Bad Where The Road Goes Up), 93, 108
gogíshé (beargrass), 175
Golkizhń (Spotted Country People), 304n. 1
gonatáhá (stick game), 232–34
Goodwin, Grenville, 302n. 4, 304n. 7
Goshoney, William (A-2), 39, 59; death of, 220–21; as medicine man, 26–31, 308n. 16
gossip, 175
gozhǫǫ sįh (goodness songs), 202
Grasshopper: (white) cowboys at, 176, 188
grinding stones (metates), 158–60

hádndín (cattail pollen), 25, 119–23, 307n. 14
Ha'iáha (Chiricahua/Mescalero Apache), 14
Hanna, Edith, 161, 165, 205, 224–25, 266
Hanna, Engel, 160, 165, 224–25; wife of, 167, 224–25, 240

Hanna, Lee, 165
Hawkins, Clarence, 302n. 3
herding cattle, 62, 88, 243. *See also* cattle drives
heroes, xxvi
history: Apache view of, xv, xvi, xxiv, xxvi, 303n. 5; conventional (experience-distant) view of, xv–xviii, xxvi, 302n. 3
Hoffman, Joseph, 8–9, 46, 62–63, 74, 312n. 8, 313n. 9
Hoffman, Terry, 129
Holbrook, 243, 245–46
hosh nteelé (prickly pear), 91
humor/teasing, xxi, 14, 88, 96, 103, 151, 171, 187, 196, 219

i'dii ch'il (yerba santa), 63
igáyé (broadleaf yucca), 23, 71, 97, 175, 185, 186, 212–13
igáyé ts'ǫsé (narrowleaf yucca), 28
ikaz (century plant stalks), 97
Indian agents, xvii, 305n. 4, 308nn. 21–22, 311n. 4
Indian policemen, xvii, 33, 50–51, 56–58, 68–71, 117, 123–24, 307n. 12, 308n. 22
Indian scouts, 14, 302n. 4, 306n. 6
influenza: pandemic of 1918–19, 45, 67, 72–75, 314n. 13
intermarriage: with Mescaleros, 14; with Mexicans, 21, 38; with Pimas, 16, 18, 273
Iron Mine: Jack Tulene Case's home at, 161, 196
isdzaní binii' (a specific medicinal plant), 92
it'ąą (wild spinach), 128
izee libahí (desert lavender), 45, 72–75, 207
izee sidogí (a specific medicinal plant), 206–8

javelinas, 230–32
Johnson, Carter, 173
Johnson, James, 165, 174–75, 224,
  235

Kessay, Reuben, xxiii, 106, 253, 264;
  lives with his grandparents, xxii,
  251–52, 258–59
kinship terminology: explained,
  307n. 10
ko̧' dahosh (thistle), 92

Lavender, Rufus, 180–81
Lee, Johnny, 29–31, 221, 308n. 17
lightning strikes, xxii, 26, 172–73,
  308n. 15; effects of, xx, 28, 56–58,
  62–63, 281–83
Limerick, Patricia, xxvi
Lonely Mountain, 213, 217
Looking Out For Enemies (a medicine man), 214–18
Lupa (Rose Lupe's sister), 16, 21, 23
Lupe, Bessie, 14, 108, 111, 218, 255–
  58, 274
Lupe, Clay, 239
Lupe, Ida, 274–75
Lupe, John (Z-3), 10–11, 16–17, 19,
  24, 40, 49, 210, 215–16, 252
Lupe, Rose, xix, 3, 39–40, 42;
  becomes Catholic, 11–12, 127;
  captured by outlaw, 4–10; death
  of, 273–76; gambling by, 81, 111;
  as herbalist, 5, 12–13, 57, 92, 274;
  hides Eva from police ("child
  catcher"), 68–71; making baskets,
  12–13
Lupe, Rufus, 174
Lupe, William (F-1), 10, 16–17, 164,
  173, 210, 273; daughters of, 18

Ma' bitsee' (Fox Tail), 214
Machuse, Ned, 165
Marley, Charley, xx, 140–41, 229–
  30; butchering deer, 170; death

of, 276–81; as medicine man, 218–
  20; working with horses, 150–53,
  184–86, 188, 241–47, 316n. 1
Marley, D. V., 151–52, 155, 229–30,
  316n. 1
Martin, Rena, 303n. 5
Martinez, Paul, 187
Martinez, Pearl, 142, 165
McQuillen, Francis T. (Mac), 153,
  174, 179–80, 195, 198–99, 277, 279,
  316n. 2
medicine men, xxi–xxii, 17, 23,
  25–31, 62–64, 74, 119–23, 208–
  21, 267–68, 307n. 13, 308n. 16,
  309n. 22, 313n. 9
medicine woman, 208
mescal. See nadah
Mexicans: fights with, 14; intermarriage with, 16; trade with, xix, 11,
  46, 62, 305n. 4
Mihesuah, Devon, 303n. 5
mining. See wage labor
mobility: family, in early reservation period, xvi, xviii, xix, xxii, 3,
  39–41, 209
Mormon Flat, 77, 97–103; weekend
  family gatherings at, 104–5
Mormon Flat Dam, 97–99, 314n. 1
mother-in-law avoidance, 63–64
motorized vehicles, 86–87, 179–80,
  188–89, 254
mountain lions, 161–62
murder, xxii, 225–27
Myer, Albert, 305n. 4

nadah (century plant), 91, 168, 283,
  312n. 7; roasting, 59–62
Nadah Cho Si'áń (A Big Agave Heart
  Sits), 32–33, 59–62
Nadah Nch'íí' (Bitter Mescal), 212
Na'isho̧' bibésh (Lizard's knife), 25
na'iyee' si̧h (strength songs), 202
na'izho̧osh (hoop and pole game),
  84, 94, 99, 107, 315n. 3

Naklanita, Arthur, 180, 215, 281–82
nalwod go'aíleh (boys' puberty
  ceremony), 202
Navajos, 256–57
Ndaa Bigan Nagodé (Whiteman
  With Shortened Arm), 223–24
Nest'áń Yolíłé (She Brings Home
  Fruits And Vegetables), 43–44,
  84–86

Oak Creek: cowboys from, 153; Lupe
  family home at, 4, 17, 18–20
Olson, Olof, 309n. 26
Ortiz, Alfonzo, 301n. 1
outlaws, 4–10, 236–241, 304n. 2

Patterson, Peter. See Túnch'íí'
personal names: acquisition of, 10,
  32, 37, 43–44, 106, 129, 151–52,
  309n. 25, 315n. 1; loss of, 106,
  315n. 4; tag-bands explained,
  306n. 8
Pimas, 16, 272–73, 306n. 9
plows/plowing, 20, 24, 101
pneumonia, 279
Price, Anna, 304n. 7
priests, Catholic, 11–12, 48, 70, 73–
  74, 104–5, 119, 124, 128–29, 144,
  305n. 5. See also St. Johns Indian
  School and Mission

railroad. See travel; wage labor
rations, xvi, xix; at Cibecue, 180; at
  San Carlos, 14, 45–49, 310n. 1
resistance: by Apaches in response
  to U.S. authority, xvii–xviii
Rice, Sedgewick, 311n. 4
Roosevelt Dam, 78–80, 314n. 1

St. Johns Indian School and Mission,
  xx, 58–59, 75, 127–45, 272–73,
  312n. 6
Salt Banks, 41, 171–74
Show Low, 255–57

Sįh Doo Yinaldíh Dah (He Can't
  Remember His Song), 46
snakes, 93, 219–20; chasing Ann
  Beatty and Rose Lupe, 87–88; at
  Fish Creek, 94–97, 105; use of, in
  ceremonies, 120–22
Snowflake, 228–29
Spring Creek: home of Robert
  Beatty at, 36
Stago, Charley, 165, 255
Stago family, 225–28
Stevens, Henry, 135
Stevens, Jimmy, 138
Stevens, Sam, and wife, 141–42
Stevens, Virginia and Sadie, 128,
  142
Stevens, Willie, 38–39, 57, 106, 111–
  12, 142
stores and trading posts: in Apache
  Junction, 109; Cooley's store in
  Cibecue, 176–77, 282, 318n. 4; in
  Grasshopper, 25, 176, 307n. 15;
  Knapp's store in Cibecue, 176–
  78, 222, 281–82, 318n. 4; in Mesa,
  101–2; in Rice, 118; in Sandstone,
  222; in Snowflake, 228–29; in
  Whiteriver, 29, 308n. 17; in Young,
  227
storytelling, xviii, xxiv–xxv, 15,
  41–43, 289–90, 304n. 7
string games, 78
Sunrise Dance, 71–72, 313n. 12

Taylee, William, 164–65
Tessay, Calvert, 252
Tessay, Margaret, 252
theft, 227–28
Tiffany, J. C., 308n. 21
T'iis Sikaad (Cottonwoods Standing), 237, 239
Tommy (a pet bear), 107, 184, 196–
  99
trachoma, xx, 107, 116–18, 144–45,
  315n. 3

trade: with Mexicans, xix, 11, 46, 62,
305n. 4
travel: on foot, 37, 44, 59–60, 214,
289; on railroad, 21–22, 59
Tséé Bika' Naaditin (Trail Goes
Across On Top Of Rocks), 17
Tsééch'iizhé (Flaking Rock), xx,
222–25, 234
Tsééda'i (Edge Of The Cliff), 151
Tséétęh Na'áá (Rocks Standing In
The Water), 14, 16, 17
Tsééyaa Goltsogí (Yellow Below The
Rocks), 150
tuberculosis, 15–16, 36–37, 306n. 7
túłbáí (tulipai), 167, 182, 215, 236,
276, 317n. 2
Tulene, xix; birthplace of, 10, 39;
death of, xix, 10–11, 39
Tulene, Albert (aka Joseph Albert),
38–39, 50, 58–59, 79, 106, 171
Tulene, Emma, 15, 38–39, 110–12,
274
Tulene, John Langley, xix, 39–40,
64–65, 100; death of, xx, 107–15;
working on Apache Trail, 79–
81, 88–92; working in mines, 45,
65–68
Túłgayé Dotł'izhí (Blue Donkey),
170, 184, 189–93, 230
Túnch'íí' (Whiskey, aka Peter Patterson), 37
Tú Ńłįį' (Water Flowing), 39

wage labor, xvi, xix, xxii, xxiii, 6–
7, 41, 77, 80, 88, 251–52, 313n. 11;
building CCC fences, 231; building dams/roads, 58, 77, 79–80,
88–90, 97–98; harvesting corn in
Solomon, 116; herding/driving

cattle, 88, 246; logging, 255; in
mines, 45, 65–68, 110; picking cotton in Safford, 115; on railroad, 21,
51, 107, 119, 311n. 4
Watt, Eva Tulene, 234, 253, 261, 265,
269; attends St. Johns school, 124–
25, 127–45; birthplace, 23; first
sees a car (Model T), 86–87; marries William Watt, xxiii, 264–66;
moves to Phoenix, xxiii, 257–59;
moves to Spokane, xxiii, 259–63;
raised with boys, xxi, 40, 51, 162,
186; raises a bear, 184, 196–99;
shoots a deer, 169–71; works in
Show Low, xxiii, 255–57
Watt, John Langley, 266, 269, 272–73
Watt, William, 262, 264–70
Watt (Seymour), Ora Ann, 266, 269,
272–73
Western Apache: definition of,
301n. 1
Wheatfields: Apache ceremonial
grounds at, 84; Chinese farms at,
82–84
Whiteriver: home of Goshoney, 26
Wickiups: building of, 24, 97,
313n. 11
wild dogs, 105–6
wild horses: taming of, 38, 55, 187
wild turkeys, 167–68
women's work, xxi, 12–13, 49–50,
72, 82–83, 93, 97; cooking, 13, 49,
72, 91, 160–61; drying meat, 8;
grinding corn, 71, 159; harvesting,
16, 43, 49, 61; making baskets, 12–
13, 64, 86, 118, 175, 208; selling
grass/firewood, 6–7, 38, 65, 69, 80,
87, 305n. 3

About the Author

Eva Tulene Watt, a member of the White Mountain Apache Tribe, lives with members of her family on the Fort Apache Indian Reservation in central Arizona. A recognized authority on Western Apache culture and history, she has served as consultant to the Tribe's Cultural Advisory Committee, Historic Preservation Office, and Culture Center and Museum. In 2003 she received an award as an Arizona Indian Living Treasure. This is her first book.

Keith H. Basso, who assisted Mrs. Watt, is University Regents Professor of Anthropology at the University of New Mexico, where he teaches alternate semesters. His most recent book, *Wisdom Sits In Places: Language and Landscape among the Western Apache*, was awarded the Western States Book Award for Creative Non-Fiction, and the J. I. Staley Prize by the School of American Research.